RETIRE RICHER WITH TIAA-CREF

APPLICABLE TO ALL 403(b) AND 401(k)
RETIREMENT PLANS

ROBERT M. SOLDOFSKY, Ph.D.

Murray Professor of Finance
Emeritus, The University of Iowa

Published by Useful Press
Iowa City, IA

Editor: Mary L. Snyder, Ph.D.
Managing Editor and Publisher: Bradley M. Loomer, Ph.D.

First Printing July, 1996.
Printed in the United States of America

Library of Congress Catalog Card Number: 96-60593
ISBN 0-9651682-0-4

Soldofsky, Robert M.

Retire richer with TIAA-CREF

Applicable to all 403(b) and 401(k) retirement plans.

    311p.

1. Pensions - college teachers - United States.

2. Nonprofit pension plans, 403 (b).

3. Corporate pension plans, 401(k).

4. Annuities

5. Retirement income

6. Investments, basics.

ACKNOWLEDGMENTS

Very important help in the preparation of this book is enthusiastically acknowledged. Direct and indirect assistance was received from within the University of Iowa and from other sources through the nation. Within Iowa City, Richard Saunders, Manager of Staff Benefits and his group, collected the basic information needed for the new employees', allocation-decisions survey. Dr. George Lopos, Associate Dean, Continuing Education, provided administrative support for the TIAA-CREF seminars. Questions raised at these sessions taught me what participants at various stages of their careers wanted to know, what they did not understand, and important things they should have wanted to know but of which they were not aware. I had the opportunity to practice various responses to questions until I found those that worked best. Within the College of Business Administration Linda Knowling prepared the charts, and Joyce Ruplinger, Irma Herring and others in Instructional Support Services prepared innumerable drafts of the text. Jim Grifhorst, Computer Services, prepared the statistical analysis for me. I thank Dean Gary Fethke, College of Business Administration, for providing administrative support for this project, which took more than two years.

Outside the University of Iowa, Professor Joe Belth, University of Indiana stressed to me the importance of fixed-period annuities. The personnel at the TIAA-CREF's Chicago office have provided annual updates to TIAA-CREF benefits matrix, and suggested other important topics that needed to be stressed. Ms. Tricia M. Konu, Russell Data Services, provided a history of the Russell Equity Indexes, information about their construction, and some proprietary information needed for some tables. Mr. Elliott Shurgin, Chairman, S&P 500 Index Committee, Standard & Poor's Corporation, provided some of the early history of the S&P 500 Index.

Absolutely vital help and cooperation was made available through the Public Relations Office of TIAA-CREF itself. Their personnel were very patient in answering my questions and explaining the answers until I understood them. The answers to a goodly number of my questions came from special, small research projects conducted within many different part of TIAA-CREF. On other occasions I had the opportunity of talking with responsible officers in various divisions of the organization to discuss technical problems in such matters as accounting, investment reporting, and survey research techniques.

Above and beyond all of these matters, the love and support of Micki, my wife of almost 50 years, has been, is, and will continue to be an inspiration to me.

Any errors of omission or commission in this book are my own responsibility.

PREFACE

RETIRE RICHER WITH YOUR TIAA-CREF: A GUIDE TO THE USE OF 403(b) AND 401(k) PENSION PLANS

"Retire Richer" is much more than an eye-catching title; it is the major objective this book holds out for you, its reader. Retire Richer has two distinct aspects, both of which are important to you. The first is to help you achieve a greater cash flow during your retirement than you otherwise would have had. A goal is to achieve not only a higher retirement income, but also to provide a cash-flow stream that keeps you up with or ahead of long-run inflation.

While writing this book I kept in mind its likely audiences and their various levels of need. My insight into the characteristics of the audiences and levels of their needs are based upon long experience in these matters. I became a member of the University of Iowa's Funded Retirement and Insurance Committee in 1960 and remained on it until I was fully retired in 1990. I campaigned to be appointed to the Committee because it was dealing with my own eventual retirement income and because I wanted to participate as a good citizen in the University community. Also, I had acquired detailed knowledge of pensions and other fringe benefits while working for the Wage Stabilization Board during the Korean War.

The largest audience will probably consist of people who are within about five years or less of retirement because they are becoming increasingly concerned with their likely, prospective retirement income. Another prospectively large audience consists of those who are between 40 and 60 years of age and who—for one reason or another—become interested in learning more about the allocation of their monthly investments among stocks, bonds and other securities. Some specific event such as reading an article about retirement planning, hearing a television or radio program on this subject, the retirement of a colleague, the receipt of an inheritance, or the addition of a new investment option may trigger the purchase of a book of this type. Generally, concern with retirement increases as a function of age. A third likely audience consists of people who have just entered the TIAA-CREF system or a 401(k) plan, and who have their interest aroused enough to learn about the meaning and importance of their investment allocation options.

I wholeheartedly compliment those who read this book because it is very likely to result in a financially more secure retirement. A few people may have chosen an asset allocation within the recommended range. My statement of that optimum range will serve to reinforce their judgment. Even those people who have made such excellent choices are most unlikely to know about the wide range of options for the selection of the amounts and timing of their retirement benefits. I have yet to counsel an individual who did not benefit substantially from our discussion of his or her options. Those attending my seminars have gained information and insights that help them design their asset allocations and select their benefits options when they retire.

The audiences for this book also have different intensities of concern, differences in knowledge of the investment basics, and differences in training in reading statistical and mathematical information. I recall several people whose faces lit up when they saw the risk profiles of their investment alternatives expressed in terms of means and standard deviations for the first time. In effect they said, "Eureka! Now I have a key to understanding investment information." My insights into these different groups comes from responses during seminars and during individual counseling.

This book is written at different levels and with differences in the extent of detail designed to suit the needs of the various sets of readers. Some impatient readers are only looking for "correct" answers to their questions from someone whom they believe they can trust. A second broad group wants to know the mechanics of how and why TIAA and CREF work, and the differences between them in clear terms. They are concerned with the differences among the investment options and their importance for their eventual retirement benefits. A third group wants to know how TIAA and CREF operate to provide them with an excellent return on their investments. They also want to understand how and why investments in general work to provide such returns, and the extent of the risks involved in each option.

This third group is asking about the investment basics and relevant investment institutions. Chapters 8 and 9 are specifically addressed to such people who want to learn and/or review investment basics and the related background topics so that they can evaluate TIAA-CREF's investment policies, the policies of other pension funds, and their own separate investment portfolios. These two chapters provide a deep and broad permanent reference for security investors. They are vital for 403(b) and 401(k) investors, and for anyone else who is planning for his or her retirement income.

Topics are selected for their importance to you. Many people are curious but uninformed about how insurance companies invest their money in order to provide a secure return that they can count on for the next fifty years or more. Chapter 4 discusses the income, assets, and safety of TIAA, in particular; it provides insights into the investment policies of life insurance companies, in general. The material is not difficult to understand, but may be tedious. However, if the largest part of your wealth--$100,000s—is invested in an insurance-based retirement plan, you may be motivated to read through the information. Chapter 5 discusses the returns, risks, and safety provided by the various stock, bond and money market funds managed by CREF.

HOW TO USE THIS BOOK

Suggestions about how to use this book may well be helpful to readers. The three-level Table of Contents names the major and minor topics discussed in each chapter. Chapter 1 provides the introductory definitions, and the broad and narrow frameworks within which investment allocation planning should be done irrespective of age. I believe these frameworks should be understood by everyone whether they are plan participants in TIAA-CREF or in one of its competitors. These frameworks are equally important for 401(k) plan participants. Most financial plans and planners do not discuss the role of social security and real estate in overall retirement planning. These two topics are introduced in Chapter 2, but many readers may only wish to scan them or use them for later reference. Chapter 3 discusses ways of estimating retirement benefits and the recommended investment allocation goals. This chapter compares the methods by which returns are computed by TIAA and CREF. The differences between these two systems are essential to your understanding of the investment risk from TIAA's traditional, insurance-company operations and CREF's common-stock oriented operations. Attitudes toward risk are important. Specific techniques by which those attitudes are measured are introduced in order to provide a common language on the basis of which these attitudes can be discussed.

Chapters 4 and 5, which discuss TIAA and CREF respectively, can be better understood within the frameworks and definitions provided earlier. You may be one of the readers who does not want to become immersed in as much detail as is provided about TIAA's and CREF's investment practices, their sources of income, and their safety. They are provided, however, if you wish to read them or refer to them. Chapter 6 discusses the investment-allocation decisions of new employees. It points out the typical mistakes new participants in TIAA-CREF make in their allocations when age and prudent investment principles are considered. Too many people, in my opinion and in the opinion of acknowledged authorities in the field of financial planning, do not understand investment basics and the nature of return and risk on securities. Higher returns increase in importance relative to risk, cyclical fluctuations, and liquidity in the long-term investments that will be used to provide you with most of your retirement income. Chapter 6 goes on to compare the 100-year performance record of stocks and bonds. In effect, this record compares what TIAA and CREF and 401(k) plans might have done had they been in existence that long. Finally, Chapter 6 sets out the advantages and disadvantages of TIAA and the available CREF accounts. Chapter 7 points out three ways that both 403(b) and 401(k) plans can be utilized to enhance retirement benefits other than through the use of the recommended allocation.

Chapter 8 discusses the six most fundamental ideas and concepts that you must understand in order to become an informed investor and a competent critic of investment advice and investment advisors. Among these six concepts, the relationship among bond prices, interest rates, and the remaining term maturity on a marketable bond are the most complex. Nevertheless, understanding these relationships will pay great rewards to those who struggle to understand the problem of bond maturities, return, risk and timing. The final section will help you understand how to measure the objective return and risk functions of securities, and how to measure your attitude toward risk in ways that can be compared directly with the objective measurements of return.

Chapter 9 presents investment background that most people would like to have, but that is not readily available. The history and meaning of the major stock-price indexes are told. A knowledge of these indexes—and especially the Standard & Poor's 500 Index and the Russell 3000 Index—is valuable because the CREF-Equities performance can be evaluated by comparing it with that of these two very broad, stock-price indexes. The history of rising (bull) and falling (bear) stock prices since 1914 is provided. The hoped-for impact of this information is to bring into focus this long, stock-market background so that you will be much less likely to panic during the next market decline and be less likely to be elated with the next market rise.

During your retirement you are likely to live through four, five or more stock-market cycles. The level of the stock market at the moment you retire and at the moment after you retire are not the keys to your continuing income during your 20-30 years of retirement. Tax-exempt securities are an important means of increasing your returns from fixed-income investments both before and after you retire.

Chapter 10 discusses in depth TIAA's procedures in calculating your returns. These methods are used by most insurance companies. Chapter 11, Retirement Annuities, sets forth in clear language, illustrations, and tables the available retirement settlement options. The extent to which each option has been used is given together with the differences in the benefits based upon the option selected. People who understand the implications of the typical single- and joint-life annuities may select fixed-period annuities. The latter are not discussed in TIAA-CREF publications, but may be an important alternative for you. If you have special needs or more than enough cash flows at retirement, ways of postponing receiving part of that income for some years while your investment continues to build up tax-deferred are discussed.

Chapter 12 may be one of the most important in the book for you. It reviews the actual performance of TIAA and CREF retirement annuities, and compares their performance with the cost of living. The results startle many who attend my seminars and others who have individual counseling. The lessons of the past are clear. Finally, a technique is demonstrated which will enable you to compare your working cash flow with your immediate post-retirement cash flow. Not until that is done, should you sign the final settlement-option papers.

An elaborate index is included to help you locate topics of interest. Many topics are closely related, but are presented in different contexts and relationships other than the one of concern to you. My objective is to make this book highly useful for your financial planning.

OBITER DICTA

In the very dynamic fields of investment, pension planning, and annuities, new and important developments are always forthcoming. The reader is urged to seek information about changes that may have occurred between the time this book was written and the time he or she makes important decisions related to the financial aspects of their retirement plan.

My hope and mission are to help you, the reader, achieve a more financially successful retirement. May you <u>Retire Richer</u> in terms of both the amount of your investments and your continuing cash flow. To date my own planning has been very successful, and I know many others who are living very well a decade or more after their retirement. Those whose planning provided for little or no hedge against inflation will continue to have their standard of living deteriorate.

RETIRE RICHER WITH TIAA-CREF

TABLE OF CONTENTS

CHAPTER 3
TIAA-CREF MONTHLY INVESTMENT ALLOCATIONS:
NARROW FRAMEWORK

CHAPTER 4
TIAA: INCOME, ASSETS AND SAFETY

CHAPTER 5
CREF AND COMMON STOCKS

CHAPTER 6
TIAA-CREF RETURNS AND NEW EMPLOYEES' ALLOCATION DECISIONS

CHAPTER 7
ENHANCING YOUR TIAA-CREF RETIREMENT BENEFITS

CHAPTER 8
INVESTMENT BASICS

CHAPTER 9
INVESTMENT BACKGROUND

CHAPTER 10
TIAA AND CREF: PROCEDURES AND COMPETITORS

TABLE OF TABLES

TABLE OF FIGURES

CHAPTER 1

ASSET-ALLOCATION GOALS FOR RETIREMENT PLANNING

INTRODUCTION

- What should your asset allocation goals be for retirement planning purpose?

- What assets should be included in your wealth or asset portfolio for retirement planning purposes?

- Why should these assets be included?

The asset-allocation goals that I recommend are shown in Table 1.1. For present purposes an asset is a thing of value that may be sold or a source of future income. It need not be a physical thing such as a house; it may be an intangible thing such as your Teachers Insurance and Annuity Association (TIAA) contract.

The asset-allocation goals for each group of the assets are shown as reasonable ranges. These ranges are not inviolable; the upper and lower limits should be viewed as strong warning signals that the individual should not exceed them without very strong reasons. If he does, he (she) may place the amount and stability his eventual retirement income at considerably higher risk as he nears retirement. As will become clear, the dollar amounts on which these percentages are based are themselves somewhat fuzzy around the edges. For example, the market value of your home will only be a good estimate until the very moment it is sold. The accumulation value of your social security account, which will be the basis of your benefits, is only a well-informed estimate. The value of your College Retirement Equities Fund (CREF) account changes every day the stock markets are open and with each of your investments into that account. Nevertheless, on the basis of a few essential assumptions your TIAA-CREF Annual Report does provide income estimates on the basis of projected accumulation values. The percentage of your assets in one group may well influence the reasonable percentage of assets in held in one or more of the other groups, as will become clear.

The question of how much income you should reasonably seek and expect for your retirement is addressed at length in many sections of this book.

DEFINITIONS OF ASSETS

The next few paragraphs provide simple definitions and illustrations of the five asset classes shown in Table 1.1. The comments on the operational meanings and methods of evaluating these assets may be new to some readers.

"**Cash.**" Cash refers to more than the cash in your pocket. It includes your checking accounts, savings accounts, certificates of deposits, U.S. government securities such as Series E, U.S. Treasury bonds that are due to mature in about a year or less and similar items. These items are your emergency sources of funds for one of those minor or major emergencies that affect each of us sooner or later. The total amount of cash held in such accounts is often set at about one year's, after-tax, net income. (The impact on your income and cash position may be softened if your personal emergency is a temporary disability covered by your employer's disability insurance plan.)

The purpose of this cash accumulation is not income; the cash is held as a prudent precaution against those larger or smaller emergencies that have a financial aspect. Most people participating in a TIAA-CREF plan have the capacity to borrow from a bank or other lending institution, but at a rate of interest that is daunting—if not absolutely prohibitive.

Fixed-Income Securities. Debts or obligations that pay a fixed sums of money at a fixed date(s) are called bonds or notes. (Notes are arbitrarily considered to have maturities of five years of less and bonds have maturities of more than five years.) These obligations specify a fixed interest rate such as 6 percent per year. Hence, a $1,000 bond will pay interest of $60 per year. Securities of these types, which may be traded or transferred among owners, are called fixed-income securities. TIAA invests its assets, which includes your money, almost entirely in fixed-income securities. TIAA contracts are called fixed-income contracts because a fixed payment rate is set annually on the amount you have accumulated or converted to a source of regular income after retirement. A participant's TIAA accumulation is a part of his fixed-income securities by conventional language. For most TIAA participants the TIAA accumulation is the bulk of their fixed-income assets.

Home Ownership. Home ownership is a very important wealth category for most people. A considerable proportion of one's income a allocated to the purchase of a home over a considerable period of years—or even several decades. That asset, your home, becomes a very important source of income for you in the sense that if the home were not owned, you would be paying out a substantial amount regularly for comparable shelter. Put another way, you could have set aside a large sum of money by saving regularly and at retirement you could use the interest on that money to pay your monthly rent. The implied assumption is that the money was invested in bonds or other fixed-income securities.

Social Security. A brief statement explaining why the social security benefits expressed as an asset at the time one starts drawing upon those benefits is essential to understanding the wealth allocation goals. Social security benefits are very often referred to as Old Age and Survivors Insurance (OASI) benefits. The accumulations built up over a lifetime of covered work are the basis of the payments to be received in retirement. (A more detailed explanation is provided in the second part of Chapter 2.)

The accumulation necessary to provide the likely initial year OASI benefits can be estimated in a way somewhat similar to that used in the reasoning about housing above. One just asks the question, "How large of an accumulation or nest egg would you have to have in order to provide an income equal to that very likely to be paid by social security?

If you are likely to get $1,000 per month or $12,000 per year, the approximate amount needed to produce that much interest income is $200,000 when the interest rate is assumed to be six percent. (This amount, $200,000, when multiplied by the six percent interest rate assumed, provides $12,000 per year for as long as the interest rate remains unchanged.) On the one hand this approximation is a little high because it assumes the amount will be paid forever, when in actuality, the life expectancy of a person retiring at age 65 is about 20 years. On the other hand, the estimate is considerably low because it makes no allowance for rising benefits that are geared to cost-of-living increases. Nevertheless, this estimate is an essential part of the goal structure need for long-run retirement planning. Without it you would have a distorted image of your wealth and your relative sources of fixed-income, almost fixed income, and variable income.

Equities. Equity represents the ownership of an asset. The ownership of a corporate business is represented by shares of stock, which are called common or capital stock. (Other classes of stock may exist in some corporations, but are not discussed in order to keep the presentation relatively simple while not omitting any topic of importance for this book.) The net value of a corporation's, assets, which is called its Net Worth, is the book value of what it owns minus the dollar value of what it owes. The Net Worth divided by the number of shares issued and outstanding gives the book value of a share of stock. Except for a rare chance, the book value of a share and its market value will not be the same. When the market prices of several thousand corporations' stocks are reviewed, that exercise will show that the market prices will range from something below their respective book values to several times their respective book values. A market price as much as ten times book value is not unusual for stocks of companies widely acknowledged to have a remarkable potential for growth and price appreciation.

DEBT AND EQUITY COMPARED
Understanding the implications of equity and debt, which are frequently referred to as just stock and bonds, is essential for your planning to invest in corporate securities directly, through mutual funds or through pension funds. If a corporation has bonds and other debt instruments outstanding and cannot pay the interest on that debt when it is due, it is bankrupt. The same is true of not paying—defaulting—on a debt itself when it becomes payable. Nothing so dramatic happens when a corporation that has been paying dividends stops declaring and paying them. The market price of its stock is most likely to fall somewhat, but its business activities continue. From the owner's viewpoint stocks in general have much more financial risk than corporate bonds and other corporate debt instruments such as mortgage obligations. Hence, one would expect stocks in general to provide higher returns than bonds over a period of years in order to compensate the holder for the added risk.

Various ways in which returns on stocks and bonds are defined and different ways of measuring risk will be presented. The essentials of these measurements of return and risk are not difficult for the reader who does not already understand them.   Understanding and utilizing these concepts is important if you are concerned enough with your financial future including your eventual pension benefits to make the modest effort involved.

BROAD AND NARROW WEALTH ALLOCATION FRAMEWORKS
The goals for personal financial planning may be set in a comprehensive or broad framework, or in a narrow framework. The broad framework, as I conceive it, includes all items that will provide income during your retirement period. In Table 1.1, Broad Wealth Allocation Goals, five asset groups which will be the sources of your retirement income are shown. Other sources may exist such as some continuing income from part-time employment, a spouse's earnings, income from an inheritance, and royalties from past or continuing writings. These items, which may exist in a relatively few cases, can be converted into asset values by the simple technique of capitalizing income discussed later. An additional asset class might be set up for such an asset, but most likely it could be included as a part of one of the five named. The meaning, logic and function of each of these asset groups is discussed briefly in

this chapter and each is discussed at more length later. Most of this book is concerned with pension benefits that will flow from assets accumulated through plans such as TIAA, which invests in fixed-income securities, and CREF, which invests primarily in equity securities.

The discussion of your retirement benefits from social security, implicit income from home ownership, and from cash held to tide you over personal emergencies are brief. The purpose of your cash accumulation is not primarily as a source of retirement income, but it will provide a modest amount of income when invested the virtually riskless money market and very short maturity securities.

The narrow framework of wealth-allocation goals consists of only three categories: stocks, bonds and cash. I have reviewed literally dozens of personal finance books and find that they use only these three items. Some will include real estate and many will introduce social security benefits, but these items are not placed in a comprehensive, planning framework.

Illustrations of these narrow-framework allocation goals will be given at the end of this chapter. Comments will be made about the likely reasons for the popularity of such goals and their specific allocation recommendations.

IMPORTANCE OF THE WEALTH ALLOCATION GOALS
This goal structure provides a beacon toward which you may steer your course from the time you enter your pension program until your retire and start drawing upon your accumulations. If you leave your pension plan and must do all of this saving for yourself, the same general goal structure will be very helpful.

The income provided by the asset groups will not be in the same proportion as they are in the wealth portfolio because each group will provide a different rate of return. Also each asset group will perform a somewhat different function during retirement. In the case of home ownership, the services provided are an alternative for the direct outlay for shelter.

OASI benefits, as discussed in somewhat more detail in Chapter 2, are provided from the individual's and employer's contributions to the individual's social security account during his working lifetime. Your social security accumulation will provide a minimally adequate income based on earnings up to the contributions ceiling, which is $57,600 as this section is being written. When I entered into the social security program that ceiling was $3,000. Home ownership provides shelter and creature comfort at the level you have been able to provide during your working years. Cash, as noted, will continue to provide funds to be used during those emergencies that are at least as likely to occur during retirement as before. The TIAA contractual benefits will provide for a relatively stable, assured income at least within a five-to-ten year perspective. The great and widely acknowledge problem with TIAA benefits and interest income from bonds and the like is that they provide no offset against inflation. The complex interaction between TIAA benefits and the inflation rate is introduced later.

The function CREF-Equities and other of stocks is to provide rising income over time that will offset or even exceed the rise in the cost of living that will surely be experienced during your retirement. Each of us very likely knows several people in their 70s, 80s and even 90s whose income apparently becomes less adequate for their needs and accustomed way of living as they continue to age.

No doubt stocks will appear to be risky—perhaps very risky—to most TIAA-CREF participants who focus primarily on risk as seen over a period of a year or so, but the view of risk from the perspective of decades is different. Unless you formulate and stay with a plan, you may retire with inadequate protection from inflation.

THE GOALS AS SEEN FROM A YOUNGER PERSPECTIVE

When a person is in his 20s, 30s, and even into his 40s, estimating what the retirement wealth allocation will be based upon the then current position is virtually impossible.

What can be done and how should you guide your decisions toward the retirement allocation goals?

As long as you work for an employer that is covered by the social security program, you have no decisions to make for this category. As quickly as you reasonably can you should try to put away cash for that proverbial "rainy day." If you have to use that emergency fund, you should seek to rebuild it to a level equal to six-months to one-year's after-tax income. If both husband and wife are gainfully employed, this suggested level may be modified toward six months. Some few people are lucky enough to have available financial resources from their parents or other family members in the event of emergencies. Until the cash goal as described is achieved, building up wealth aside from your pension plan in the form of bonds and stock ownership is not suggested.

The purchase of a home if you intend to live in the same area for at least four-to-five years and can meet the down payment, is usually a good idea. As you make your monthly, level mortgage payments you will slowly at first build up an equity in your home. That equity will increase as you make improvements in the house and grounds. The market price is likely to increase with even slow inflation. As long as you can meet the mortgage payments on your approved loan you are very likely to be building your home ownership allocation toward the 15-to-25 percent recommended as the goal. Chapter 2 discusses this decision and the underlying reasons for your home-ownership allocation.

You will have some discretion within your TIAA-CREF program about the amount contributed (invested) toward your fixed income and equities goals. Experience shows that most younger people do not allocate enough to CREF. Shifting funds from TIAA to CREF later is possible as will be explained, but is not the preferred strategy.

GOALS AS SEEN FROM A MIDDLE-AGE PERSPECTIVE

By the time you are in your 50s your income-earning capacity is very likely established and your financial assets at that time in life can be totaled. Estimates of your growing wealth for the next 15-to-20 years are useful even though the outcomes are far different from these as early estimates. Social security benefits can be very roughly estimated and you can prepare a workable view of what your home and other real estate may turn out to be worth. As distasteful as the subject may be, you may have already received your inheritance or have a fair estimate of what it is like to be.

Based upon your TIAA-CREF allocation and the returns achieved on each of these asset groups you can calculate your position relative to your long-run goals. In these middle years adjustments to your TIAA-CREF and other programs can be made to facilitate the achievement of the recommended allocation goals as you approach closer and closer to retirement.

MEANINGS OF TIAA-CREF ALLOCATIONS

Two meanings of your TIAA-CREF allocations must be keep in view for clarity of though even though these distinctions are not made in what you read or hear.

As a TIAA-CREF participant you receive quarterly and annual reports that show your accumulations in each of the funds in which you have made monthly investments. These accumulations are just the sum of your regular investments plus interest earned in the case of TIAA and your regular investments plus dividends and the change in the price of a unit of the fund in the case of CREF-Equities. In the simplest case the percentage of the total accumulations held in TIAA and CREF-Equities will differ from the percentage allocated to each account in your regular monthly investment even though you have allocated 50 percent to each account since you became a participant. An example will make these points clear. The example assumes that you have been a participant for a number of years.

| | MONTHLY INVESTMENT | | ACCUMULATIONS | |
	AMOUNT	%	AMOUNT	%
TIAA	$ 500	50.0	$ 65,000	42.8
CREF-EQUITIES	$ 500	50.0	$ 87,000	57.2
TOTAL	$ 1,000	100.0	$ 152,000	100.0

Reason that the two allocation percentages differ in even this simple example is differences in the returns achieved by each of the funds. The wealth allocation goals are usually stated in terms of the accumulation targets—not in terms of monthly investments.

If you have changed your monthly allocation at some time or, perhaps, several times, the differences between your current monthly allocation percentage and the accumulation allocation percentage may be quite large. The longer you have been the in TIAA-CREF system also the larger the difference between the two allocation percentages is likely to be.

NARROW WEALTH ALLOCATION GOALS

Wealth-allocation goals are published with considerable frequency in magazines such as Money, investment advisory letters such as Standard & Poor's Outlook, and financial newspapers such as the Wall Street Journal. A few samples of these asset-allocation goals are illuminating. One mutual fund's investment advisory letter recommended the following:

TYPE OF FUND	ALLOCATION
Equity Funds	30 %
International	
Equity Funds	5
Bond Funds	25
Money-Market Funds	40
Total	100 %

A regular monthly feature of Investment Advisor, a magazine for professional money managers, is the asset-allocation recommendations of 11 individuals and the firms they represent.[1] Their asset-allocation range is given in Table 1.2, Brokerage Firm Recommended Asset Allocations. These brokerage firms' recommendations are limited to stocks, bonds and "cash." They buy, sell and trade securities of these types except Standard & Poor's; they are not in the real estate business. Pension income and long-term, personal financial planning are obviously not considered.

Usually no distinction is made about asset allocations as a function of age, but a Wall Street Journal column, "Your Money Matters," on May 5, 1992 by Georgette Jansen had a brief discussion related to this topic. She wrote,

> These days, someone who retires at age 65 can expect to live an average of 20 more years. Assuming a 5% inflation rate, the cost of living will nearly triple during that time. In other words, in the year 2012, it will take more than $130,000 a year to buy the life style that costs $50,000 a year today.

Ms. Jansen referred to a conversation she had with S. Timothy Kochs, a San Francisco financial planner. He said that most financial planners recommend that retirees keep a substantial part of their assets-- 30 percent or more—in common stocks after they retire. He said, "Even people in their 70s and 80s need some exposure to equities to keep up with inflation."

TIAA-CREF's aged-based recommendations and Soldofsky's are given in Tables 3.1 and 3.2 in Chapter 3.

---

[1] Investment Advisors, May 1995, p. 30.

CONCLUSIONS

Asset-allocation goals must be set and kept in mind as steady guide-posts throughout your working years. The tops and bottoms of the ranges should not be violated without exceedingly good reasons. Most of the violations should be temporary. You should seek to keep your allocations close to or within the guidelines as you go closer to retirement.

The five major asset classes into which your wealth may be classified are defined and illustrated for your convenience. Home ownership and social security are rarely included in discussions of personal wealth and asset allocation, even though their importance is self-evident. Financial planners, who are basically either stock brokers or insurance agents, probably omit these two categories because they are not items that they can sell to you.

The relative allocations given for cash, bonds and stocks in the five asset class formulation are generally consistent with those for these three asset classes as set forth in the narrow asset-allocation goals discussed here and in Chapter 3.

The asset-allocation goals must be considered from younger and middle-age perspectives as you move along toward the universal goal of retirement. The meanings of your monthly investment allocations to TIAA and CREF-Equities should be clearly distinguished from your growing accumulated assets in these two separate funds.

The average, recommended ranges for cash, bonds and stocks are given for comparative purposes together with the ranges suggested by analysts who represent the middle ground.

TABLE 1.1

**BROAD WEALTH ALLOCATIONS GOALS
(REASONABLE RANGES IN PERCENTAGES[a])**

ASSET GROUP	LOW	HIGH
"CASH"	5	15
SOCIAL SECURITY ACCOUNT (OASI)	15	40
HOME OWNERSHIP[b]	15	25
TIAA AND RELATED FIXED-INCOME ITEMS	20	30
CREF-EQUITIES AND OTHER STOCK ITEMS	25	50

[a]Assumes at least 20 years of work under TIAA-CREF or similar pension plan. Retirement at age 62 or older.

[b]And other real estate as appropriate.

TABLE 1.2

ASSET ALLOCATION RECOMMENDATION (%)

PART A - HIGHS AND LOWS

ASSET	HIGH	LOW	AVERAGE
Stocks	65 %	10 %	49.1 %
Bonds	55	17	33.0
Cash	65	0	17.9

PART B[a] - INDIVIDUAL ANALYSIS (FIRMS)

ANALYST (FIRM)	STOCKS	BONDS	CASH
Charles Clough (Merrill Lynch)	55	25	20
Rao Chalasani (Kemper Securities)	55	25	20
Arnold Kaufman (Standard & Poor's)	55	25	20
A. Marshall Acuff (Smith Barney)	50	35	15
Eric Miller (Donaldson Lufkin & Jenrette)	50	35	15
Raymond Worseck (A.G. Edwards & Sons)	40	40	20

[a] Recommendations of 6 of 11 analysts whose views represent the middle ground.
SOURCE: Investment Advisor, May 1995, p. 30.

HOME OWNERSHIP AND OTHER REAL ESTATE, AND SOCIAL SECURITY

INTRODUCTION

- Why should you own real estate in addition to your home to keep your wealth allocation of such assets in the 15% to 25% range?

- What do TIAA-CREF participants do about housing upon retiring?

- How does home ownership and ownership of other real estate provide desirable asset diversification and a hedge against inflation?

- How much replacement income is social security designed to provide?

- How much does retiring before age 65 impact upon your social security and TIAA-CREF benefits?

- How do you estimate the asset value of your social security benefits?

This chapter discusses financial and other aspects of home ownership and social security. The recommended proportion of wealth allocated to each of these assets at retirement was stated in Chapter 1. The rationales behind these recommendations for home ownership and social security are developed in this chapter. The wealth allocation to home ownership and social security benefits are a part of the broad, wealth-allocation framework. Most of the rest of this study concentrates on the narrow, wealth-allocation framework which includes stocks, bonds and cash only. For most TIAA-CREF participants stocks refers to their CREF investments and bonds refers to their TIAA investments. Incidentally, a little more than half of retired TIAA-CREF participants receive some of their benefits from CREF.

HOME OWNERSHIP AND OTHER REAL ESTATE

A home has personal, psychological, sociological, financial, and economic value for the individual and his or her family. For the larger society, home ownership is a source of political stability. Individuals and families feel good about owning their own homes, and home ownership gives one status in his community. It results in concern with, if not actual participation in, community affairs. Home ownership is still a goal of most Americans, and political institutions continue to support and encourage that goal. Home ownership - not merely renting or using a house or apartment - is being stressed. The home owned may be a one-family dwelling, an attached home, a condominium or a "mobile" home.

Home is a place in which you can express and develop your personality. It is a refuge at times from your burdens and the cares of the world. It is a place in which you can rear your family and aim to nurture the most desirable moral and spiritual values for your spouse and your children.

This section is concerned primarily with your home and other real estate as a part of your broad, wealth-allocation plan. It bears directly upon the sources and amount of retirement income. The topics considered are the functions of home ownership; home ownership and income taxes; inflation, home ownership and wealth; asset diversification and wealth;

implicit income from home ownership; and home ownership and lifestyle. Several rules of thumb that are well known to realtors such as the relationship among income, house payments, and the affordable loan size will be discussed.

FUNCTIONS OF HOME OWNERSHIP

Home ownership provides many important economic and financial benefits us and our families. First, it encourages the initial savings necessary to make the down payment on your first home. Second, a home builds savings or equity as the mortgage payments slowly and then with increasing speed pay off the principal of the loan itself. In almost all cases price appreciation will further increase the equity. Improvements in the home itself also tend to increase its market value.

Although the struggle to meet the level, monthly mortgage payments may be intense for some years, few regret that struggle. In fact, the opposite is more likely to be true.

Consider, for example, the case of Andy and Millie, who could never save enough money to make a down payment and meet the other financial commitments that go with home ownership. Other uses of money, time, and energy were always more important to them. Andy and Millie thrived. Income was adequate, they took vacations, their children attended private colleges and went on to earn graduate degrees. But Andy and Millie never owned their own home.

Now they are retired, in fair health, and still living in a rented apartment. Even the part-time job Andy took is barely bringing in enough to meet the rent increases. One day the burden of the job will become too much for them. In a few years they are likely to be pushed to seek a lower rent by either moving to a smaller unit or by moving to a less desirable neighborhood. An alternative is to accept financial help from their children. They will be facing a very difficult choice when that happens.

Some cases are even more tragic. The adult children themselves may not be financially successful. They cannot help their parents even if they want to do so. They may continue to call upon their parents for financial help even after the parents have retired.

The third function of home ownership is management of income taxes; many people later regret not having struggled for home ownership. Utilizing the opportunities available within the existing income tax codes is a part of thoughtful financial planning. Finally, understanding the relationship between the ownership of a home and other property and capital gains taxes is essential.

INCOME TAXES AND HOME OWNERSHIP

Three major influences of income taxes on home ownership and the ownership of other property are considered. First, interest payments on home loans are a deductible expense when calculating annual income taxes using the long or itemized-expense form of the 1040. Most people who own a home find that itemizing expenses results in lower income taxes than using the short form. Although a limit exists on the amount of interest that may be deducted on home loans, that limit of $1,000,000 is so high that it is most unlikely to apply to people who work for colleges, universities, and nonprofit institutions. The interest deduction on home mortgages, which is retained in the tax code to encourage home ownership, is one of the few tax "loopholes" remaining in the law. This feature of the tax code reduces the effective cost of home financing. On the other hand, those who do not own their own homes face a cost differential that makes building up their wealth more difficult.

Second, if and when you sell your home, you are most likely to have a capital gain, that is, in increase in the price over what you paid for it after adjusting that original basis for improvements. For whatever reason you sold your house, you will have 24 months to buy another home of greater or equal value before you have to pay income taxes on that capital gain. During that period you could build a new home, move to a different city and delay purchasing a replacement home until you know where in that area you may prefer to live, or make some other change that you believe is to your advantage. If, however, you purchase a home of lesser value, you will owe capital gains tax on the amount of the adjusted base price of your previous home minus the price of your new home.

Third, the tax code as now written permits a one-time exclusion from income on a capital gain of up to $125,000 on the sale of your main home under clearly defined conditions. This gain is available to you if you are 55 or older on the date of the sale and have owned and lived in this main home for at least three years out of the last five prior to the date of the sale. Furthermore, neither you nor your spouse can have had an excluded capital gain on a home sale since July 26, 1978.

This capital-gain exclusion provision is only available once. Therefore, much deliberation is necessary before utilizing it. However, if it turns out that your exclusion decision was not well done, provisions in the Code provide ways by which you make amends without being outside of the law. Experience with this part of the Code have made the details exceedingly complex. An experienced tax attorney or accountant should be consulted if you ever have to face such a situation.

The $125,000 exclusion from a capital gains tax is no small thing. For example, the investment of $125,000 at 6 percent will provide an annual income of $7,500 less income taxes at your applicable rate. If that amount were invested in tax-free municipal bonds, usable income could be even larger depending upon your federal and state income tax rates.

When the capital gains tax rate is less than the marginal tax rate, that is, the tax rate on your last dollars of income, you may be able to take steps to trade off current income for capital gains.

INFLATION, HOME OWNERSHIP AND WEALTH
From 1970 through 1993, the median prices on existing and new one-family homes rose an average of 6.9 percent and 7.6 percent per year, respectively. In terms of dollars, the median prices of existing homes rose from $23,000 to $106,800 during this 23-year period. The rate of price increases ranged from a low of 2.1 percent in 1982 to a high of 14.4 percent in 1979. Prices rose more than 10 percent per year in six of the seven years from 1974 through 1980. The median price of $32,000 in 1974 almost doubled to $62,200 in 1980. Table 2.1 shows these annual prices and percentage increases for existing median-priced houses.

New home prices rise faster than those of existing homes because of the new materials and new conveniences built into the new homes. How many homes had built-in entertainment and electronic communication centers in 1970? New homes also tend to be larger.

The market values of both improved and unimproved land around growing cities have also tended to rise. Large numbers of people who have held such property for considerable periods of time have made very substantial gains. But in real estate speculation, location and luck are everything.

The average inflation rate for housing will probably not be much different in the coming decades than it has been in the past few decades. A burst of inflation even greater than that experienced from the mid-1970s to the early 1980s is not out of the question. When the United States experiences its next burst of inflation, housing prices are very likely to increase at a faster rate than general inflation. Whether you will gain or lose during the next inflationary episode is problematical. If you own your home and other property, you have a better chance of maintaining your real or inflation-adjusted wealth.

If you have a real estate mortgage, you will be paying off your loan, which is fixed in dollars, with "cheaper" dollars on the one hand. However, if you are employed by a college, university, or nonprofit organization, your salary may not be rising nearly as fast as the inflation rate, and you will feel trapped by the difference between these two growth rates. You may feel the income pinch even more if the interest rate on your loan adjusts with some measure of inflation or interest rates. Almost 25 percent of retired TIAA-CREF participants have home mortgages.

If you are retired and get little or no increase in your income, your financial experience will be even worse. The cost of repairs, maintenance, property taxes, essential household help, and other things will rise and aggravate your situation. Even if your mortgage is paid off, you will experience these increased costs essential to providing shelter, heat, and air conditioning. Services such as trash and garbage collection, which were once provided "free," are almost universally priced separately by most communities. Property taxes and insurance premiums increase. New services may well be developed and have to paid for.

Most adults know that market prices of some parcels of real estate in their communities or in their favorite parts of the country have increased many fold. They are likely to believe that if they pick well, have the funds to finance the purchase, and get some pleasure out of the additional property, they may well have an offset against inflation. At worst, they are unlikely to sustain a dollar loss. Many times such purchases turn out well.

HOME AND OTHER PROPERTY OWNERSHIP AS A PERCENTAGE OF WEALTH

The broad, wealth-allocation goals recommend that about 15-25 percent of one's total wealth be allocated to home ownership and to other real estate ownership as appropriate. Stay within this range. How does that range for home ownership work out following rules of thumb used by realtors and mortgage lenders?

The purchase of a home financed in part by a mortgage loan is not likely to be approved if the monthly payment is more than 25 percent of your income or the income of yourself and your spouse. Of course, rules of thumb are always violated, but the higher the mortgage payment relative to income the less likely the loan is to be made. If the loan is made, the buyer will have more difficulty in meeting the payments. In general, default rates are higher the higher the income-to-payment ratio.

A related rule of thumb is that the price of the house purchased should not be more than about 2 ½ times the buyer's income. If the buyer's income is $50,000 per year, the maximum affordable house is about $125,000. A typical down payment on such a house will be about $25,000 or 20 percent of the purchase price.

Younger TIAA-CREF participants are likely to find initially that the equity in their home is considerably larger than the suggested 25 percent of wealth. By the time they have been in TIAA-CREF for ten or 20 years or more, they can make some approximate calculations of the relationship of home equity to wealth.

Your TIAA and CREF annual reports will state your accumulations in those plans; you may also have accumulated some stocks or bonds, and you know what you have in cash. Total these items and your home equity. Unless you are well over 50, a useful estimate of the implicit value of your social security benefits may not be worth the effort. Excluding the social security asset, your home and other real estate should be roughly 20 to 30 percent of your total wealth.

Your equity will grow more rapidly as you come closer to paying off the mortgage. More and more of each monthly payment will be principal and less and less will be interest on the remaining loan balance. Once the loan is paid off, the equity or market value in your home will increase more slowly. The primary reason for equity growth after the loan is paid off is price appreciation.

About the time the home mortgage is fully paid is a good time to check your real estate using the approach suggested. If your real estate-to-wealth ratio is below about 20 percent, you may wish to consider how to increase it. By the time you are 60, you may be able to make a good estimate of your total wealth. With or without the help of a financial planner, you should try to make a wealth estimate for the year in which you are most likely to retire and prepare your projected wealth allocation. Compare your projected allocation with the recommended ranges. If you are within about 10 years of retirement when you make these estimates, you still have time to adjust your investments to achieve your personal allocation goals. These goals may include more than just retirement income stability. Other goals may include a larger home, a second home, income-earning property (such as a farm), land speculation, or additional property ownership through a REIT or similar arrangement.

Those people who do not want the joys, burdens, or responsibilities of additional property ownership may want to increase the property-ownership percentage in other ways. One such way is through the ownership of an equity Real Estate Investment Trust (REIT). These pools are similar to mutual funds that hold common stock. The term "equity" REIT was used deliberately because some REITs hold all or part of their assets in real estate mortgages.

Another way of holding some real estate participation is through real estate limited partnerships. Though worthwhile financially, the burden of record keeping and the complexities of income tax preparation increase quite remarkably.

HOME OWNERSHIP AND "LIFESTYLE"
About 80 percent of TIAA participants own a home or condominium when they retire. Many faculty members own a second home or an acreage also. The first home a person buys is most unlikely to be the last one in this mobile society. Typically, a second and larger home is

purchased as income increases and as children are born. Faculty members and other participants may change jobs and move two or three times or more during their working lives. Each move may involve the purchase of another home. Sometimes that decision to buy a home in the new location is delayed up to 24 months as the income tax code permits in order to learn about the new community and to search out a location that seems to have the desired and affordable characteristics. The financing restraints and rules of thumb related to the new purchase are learned (relearned) upon each purchase.

What do TIAA-CREF participants do about housing upon retirement? TIAA reports that almost 60 percent of new retirees move shortly after they retire, and almost another 30 percent move at a later date.

These studies do not show why or where they move, but the major reasons are quite clear. Retirees move to warmer climates, and to places that offer desired recreational activities such as boating, skiing, or bird watching. Others move for reasons of health. Some move back to the areas in which they were raised or to the areas where their children live.

Occasionally people sell their homes and move to a lifetime care facility. The reasons for such decisions are complex and personal. Some have neither children nor relatives who would help take care of them as they grow older. In some cases a spouse has died and the surviving spouse cannot face the tasks of maintaining a home. When the lifetime care facility provides many services, more time is available for travel, learning, and social activities.

Even those who dream of roving by boat or recreational vehicle tire of that after some years or no longer have the strength to keep up that vagabond life. They, too, buy another home or condominium, or enter a care facility.

ASSET DIVERSIFICATION AND WEALTH
One purpose of maintaining an adequate-to-higher percentage of your wealth in real estate is to have an offset against inflation. Insofar as the rise in real estate prices equals or exceeds the inflation rate, your real or inflation-adjusted value for that segment of your wealth can be stabilized. And you will have a home to live in! Perhaps your property in addition to your home, will help stabilize and even increase your real wealth. Property beyond your home could be sold or given your heirs when your time comes.

Another aspect is to provide the "right kind" of asset diversification to stabilize your real wealth and reduce portfolio risk. Real estate prices and stock prices tend to move in opposite directions; that is, they are negatively correlated. Especially during periods of higher and rising inflation, the differences in the direction of real estate and stock prices are dramatic. During the nine-year period, 1973-81, a period of high inflation, the returns on CREF-Equities were negative four out of nine years. In 1974, CREF-Equities fell 30.9 percent while the prices on existing homes rose 10.7 percent. From 1982 through 1985, when the inflation rate was generally falling, median home prices increased an average of 3.3 per year and CREF equities increased an average of 20.6 percent per year.

The relative returns among TIAA and the several risk classes of CREF investments are discussed in detail in Chapter 3. Modern portfolio investment theory with its beta coefficients and risk-reduction techniques is described there as well. Only rarely do portfolio theorists include real estate among the assets in their portfolios, but doing so is an essential part of long-run, personal, financial planning. Simple as it sounds, a prudent, broad, wealth-allocation plan is a key element of risk reduction, wealth preservation, and real-income maintenance in retirement.

IMPLICIT INCOME FROM HOME OWNERSHIP

Earlier in this chapter the point was made that if you own your own home you should count as income the amount you would have to pay for equivalent accommodations. You may be able to make an estimate of the rent you would have to pay including utilities and so forth by knowing your community or by making a few judicious inquiries. Realtors use a rule of thumb for such estimates. They believe that rentals are about 1 percent per month or about 12 percent per year of the reasonable market price of a home. If your home is worth about $150,000, you would have to pay about $18,000 a year or $1,500 per month in rent for equivalent housing.

SOCIAL SECURITY

The Social Security Act was passed in 1935 and became effective January 1, 1937. The first payments under the program were not made until 1940. The initial payroll tax for those covered at that time was 1 percent on both the employee and employer on earnings up to $3,000. The social insurance part of the program was never intended to provide all of the income for retired persons; it provides only a minimum amount and percentage as replacement income. The intention was and is that the individual's own savings would provide for the larger part of his or her income in retirement. During the Great Depression, 1929-35, only a very small number of organizations had retirement plans. Private plans started to grow rapidly during World War II, 1942-1946. During that period wage and price controls were in effect to help contain inflation, but unions and others were able to increase benefits through pension plans that provided deferred income. During the Korean War, 1950-1953, wage and price controls were used again and health insurance and pension plans were encouraged.

This section is concerned with such topics as the relationship of your income from your social security benefits to your total post-retirement income, and the impact on that income of retiring at the earliest permitted age or an age beyond 65. Your social security benefits relative to your total retirement benefits will depend also on the level of income earned while working. Your spouse may receive old age and survivors insurance (OASI) based on his or her earnings or upon your earnings. If your earnings were always at or close to the maximum covered by social security, your benefits will be at the highest level paid, but if your earnings were above that moving limit, your benefits will not be any higher than for the person whose earnings were just at the taxable maximum. On the other hand, if your earnings were well below that maximum, the social insurance feature of the law will work in your favor.

The Social Security Act as amended covers several important areas in addition to Old Age Benefits; it provides benefits for widows (widowers), for disabled persons, and for the minor children of deceased, covered individuals. As of 1990, 160 million Americans were insured under social security; of this number, some 26 million or about 16 percent were retired. Benefits paid in 1990 were $248 billion; the largest part of this amount, $157 billion (63.3%), was for retirees. Another $40.7 billion (16.4 percent) went to widows (widowers); $22 billion (8.9%) went to disabled persons, and $14.5 billion (5.2%) went to minor children.

This section is not a "how to" manual on social security. Many such excellent manuals exist. Social security benefits are covered briefly in most personal finance books, but little effort is made to place these benefits in a wider retirement income framework. The Social Security Administration (SSA) itself provides many clearly written booklets on different aspects of its programs. If you want to get an estimate of what social security benefits will be, call 1-800-772-1213 and ask to have a Personal Earnings and Benefits Statement (SSA-7004) prepared. The SSA will prepare such a statement for you as long as you have some covered employment.

Another prudent step is to ask the SSA to send you a statement of your last three years' earnings according to their records. They make recording errors with sufficient frequency so that this request is prudent and should be repeated every three years. If an error has been made in your recorded earnings, it will generally not be corrected if it occurred more than three years, three months and 15 days ago.

For 1995 the maximum OASI benefits payable to an individual are $1,199 per month or $14,388 per year at age 65. The maximum annual benefits for recent prior years are as follows:

1995	$ 14,388
1994	13,888
1993	13,536
1992	13,056
1991	12,264
1990	11,700

These benefits have increased at the average rate of 4.3 percent per year for the years 1990-95, which is almost the same as the cost of living increase for these years.

Of course, if you retired and started receiving benefits in 1994 you received a 1995 cost of living increase of 3.6 percent. If your benefits started in 1991 your cost of living increase in 1992 was 3.7 percent and you received the 1993 cost of living of 3.0 percent on top of your 1992 benefits. The total cost of living adjustment for the 1990 retiree has been 22.9 percent through 1995. Automatic cost-of-living increases on OASI benefits were started in 1975 and have been paid each year except 1983 when they were postponed for financial and political reasons.

BENEFITS LEVEL AND FICA COSTS

The Federal Insurance Contribution Act (FICA) taxes have gone up sharply in recent years as shown in Table 2.2. Since 1980 the total FICA taxes have increased at an average annual rate of 8.6 percent because both the tax base and the tax rate have grown. Until 1992, the hospital insurance (HI) part of the social security tax was seldom stated separately and both old age and hospital insurance rates applied to the same maximum tax base. However, starting in 1992 the HI tax base was raised to $130,200, it was raised to $135,000 in 1993 and removed completely in 1994. The HI tax is 1.45% of the wage base. The purpose of these increases is to provide enough funds to continue to provide for the benefits payments until at least the middle of the twenty- first century according to actuarial calculations.

Replacement income, the income received from OASI for a new retiree in 1994 to replace income not earned was a maximum of 23.5 percent computed by dividing the 1995 maximum payment of $14,388 by the tax base of $61,200. The assumption is that the individual always had earnings at least equal to the rising tax base. As the tax base continues to rise, payments for new retirees will rise also.

OASI BENEFITS AND BROAD, WEALTH ALLOCATION GOALS

The OASI benefits range was shown as 15 to 40 percent in the broad-framework goal, Table 1.1. Several complications must be pointed out. First, to the extent your income is well above the tax base, the OASI benefits will not increase and, therefore, these benefits will be lower as a proportion of replacement income. They may well be as low as 15 percent of total income from all five asset groups considered in the broad framework if your working income level is about twice the rising tax base. Second, the OASI percentage will also be affected by your income from other sources. Third, if your spouse has never worked in a job covered by social security or is not qualified for benefits because he or she has not worked long enough or earned a high enough wage when working, the spouse will receive benefits nevertheless when he or she becomes eligible because of age.

If your spouse—usually the wife—has no social security benefits earned in her own account, and she is the same age as you, she will receive an amount equal to half of your benefits. At age 65, that would amount to $7,194 in 1995 giving the two of you a total of $21,582, which would obviously be a higher percent of your total income at that time. If your spouse has worked and is entitled to OASI on her own account, at age 65 she may take 50 percent of her husband's amount or the amount to which she is entitled on her own account, either of which is higher.

Incidentally, upon the death of the spouse with the higher OASI benefits, the surviving spouse may claim the higher amount.

CAPITALIZED VALUE OF SOCIAL SECURITY BENEFITS

The capitalized value of social security benefits means the amount of money that you would have to invest in order to purchase an annuity policy that would provide an equal income. For example, if your maximum benefits were $13,000 per year, you could purchase a policy for about $218,000 that would provide that income, assuming the guaranteed interest rate was 6.0 percent. In mid-1995 the long-term government bond rate was about 6.5 percent. If the rate of 7.0 percent is assumed, the purchase price is about $185,714. (For a discussion of the meaning and uses of compound interest and its mirror image, see the Magical Compound Interest section in Chapter 8.)

Four qualifications to the above numbers need to be mentioned. First, interest rates can and do change. Long-term U.S. government bond rates have ranged from 5 to 14 percent during the past two decades. A practical way to proceed is to use the present annualized rate and the average long-term government bond rate for the last 10 years when the calculation is made. Second, if benefits for the spouse are to be included, the amount to be capitalized will be greater. In most cases that will be about 50 percent of the benefits of the primarily insured person. Third, this rough-and-ready estimate does not include future cost-of-living increases. Future benefits will be greater, but the calculation made assumed that they would not be increasing. No one can project with much assurance what these increases will be or if public policy will change the amount to be granted relative to the actual cost-of-living increases. One thing is clear: if higher cost-of-living increases were anticipated for the coming year—and perhaps, several years thereafter—the long-term interest rate would rise. The larger expected benefits would increase the capitalized value and a higher interest rate used in the procedure would decrease that value. The two changes would tend to offset one another. Given the uncertainty about both adjustments, this added calculation is not recommended.

Fourth, the capitalized earnings calculation assumes that the earnings stream goes on forever. Clearly, people die; the assumption is contrary to fact. However, if both husband and wife are 65, for example, their joint life expectancy is about 25 years. When the value of a level 25-year annuity is added up year-by-year at the assumed interest (discount) rate of 7 percent, about 82 percent of the value of the perpetual annuity or perpetuity is accounted for. Given the other assumptions made and the purposes of the calculation to begin with, the simple capitalization procedure is quite adequate. If you have a present value of an annuity table or a finance calculator, the more exact calculation can be done quickly.

A brief review of the purposes of the capitalized value of OASI benefits may be useful at this point. The total value of the individual's portfolio cannot be completed and, therefore, the projected allocation among the five asset groups cannot be constructed without it. After an estimate of this OASI item is completed, the extent to which the portfolio will provide some protection against inflation can be judged better. The primary safeguard against a long-run, relative decline in income is common stock. When viewed in this broad, portfolio-allocation framework, you may be surprised at the minimal protection you have against such long-run inflation. Probably the second best safeguard against inflation is real estate ownership, and, third may be social security benefits. However, the extent to which cost-of-living adjustments for OASI payments will be continued is an intensely debated political issue. Fixed-income securities such as TIAA probably offer the least protection against long-run inflation of the five asset classes in the broad portfolio. Your direct estimates of your social security benefits at the likely retirement date and your estimates of implicit income from your home provide two of the components of your initial retirement income. Estimating your OASI benefits presents some problems.

ESTIMATING OASI BENEFITS
Your estimate of what your own social security benefits will be becomes more accurate as you approach retirement age is. Most people do not seek such estimates until they are between 55 and 58. Even then the estimate prepared for you by the SSA will consider only the cumulative amounts actually paid into your account at by date.

If you are 58, for example, and want to know what your benefits are likely to be at age 62, the SSA form, Request for Earnings and Benefit Estimate, asks you to submit an estimate of what you believe your average annual earnings will be until your planned retirement date. With that information, an estimate of your likely OASI benefits will be prepared and mailed to you.

SOCIAL INSURANCE
The social security program has a strong social insurance aspect; that is, an income transfer aspect. A report of the Advisory Council to the SSA discusses income transfers from persons earning at the highest taxable wages to those earning at various lower levels down to the

Federal Minimum Wage rate. In other words, the highest income earning groups receive less than they would be paid on an actuarial basis so that the benefits will be larger for the lower-earning groups. As shown in Table 2.3, Social Insurance Aspects of Social Benefits, a person who earns only 60.1 percent of the average indexed wage will receive 74.2 percent of the maximum benefits; the benefit-wage ratio is 1.235. In order for the payment system to balance, the people earning the maximum indexed wage must receive less than the amount they earned on an actuarial basis in order for the lower-earning individual to receive more than what they would have earned.

RETIREMENT AGE AND OASI BENEFITS

Four topics need to be considered, but none of them will clearly answer the question about when you should retire. The information will help you consider the financial consequences of earlier or later retirement, and changes in public policy that will have an impact on your retirement age and income.

Early Retirement. Retirement at age 62 at reduced social security benefits was authorized in 1956. The benefits percentages are shown in the second column of the following tabulation:

AGE	% OF AGE 65 BENEFITS	PERCENTAGE GAIN BY WAITING ONE MORE YEAR
62	80.0 %	- - %
63	86.6	8.25
64	93.3	7.74
65	100.0	7.18

The rate of increase in benefits by delaying retirement from age 62 to 63 is 8.25 percent figured as follows: the increase by delaying from age 62 to 63 is 6.6 percent of 80.0 percent. Hence, the rate of increase is 6.6 percent divided by 80.0 percent, or 8.25 percent. The other calculations are prepared similarly.

Once you retire your only increases will be the cost-of-living increases. These benefit levels apply to the social security benefits component of your retirement income only.

Your TIAA-CREF benefits will be lower also if you retire earlier. Current information is that benefits will be almost 10 percent per year less for each year you retire before age 65. Hence, your TIAA benefits at age 62 will be lower by just over 30 percent.

Delayed Retirement. Social security benefits will increase 4.5 percent for each year retirement is delayed beyond age 65. If you turned 65 in 1992 and retired in 1993, benefits would be 4.5 percent more than what they otherwise would have been for you in 1993. Likewise, if retirement is delayed until 1994 when you are 67, the benefits will be 9.2 percent more than what they otherwise would have been when you turned 65.

Currently, these benefits for delaying beyond age 65 are scheduled to be 5 percent per year for 1996 and 1997; 5.5 percent for 1998 and 1999, and 6 percent for 2000 and 2001. They are scheduled to rise to 8 percent starting in 2008.

The SSA is not giving anything away by providing these premiums for delayed retirement. On an actuarial basis, the social security system is probably earning over 8 percent for each year retirement is delayed. These added benefits come from three sources: you continue to pay money into your social security account, interest is earned on both your accumulation and the new money, and you are closer to death so that payments will be one year less for each year you delay.

A few years ago payments for delaying retirement beyond age 65 were only 3 percent per year. Publicity about the gains to the system and political pressure induced the SSA to provide the higher premiums for delayed retirements.

The modest increase in social security benefits and a substantial increase in TIAA-CREF benefits induces many people who are in good health and enjoying their work to continue working until age 70.

Raising the Normal Retirement Age. As a part of the 1983 review of the Social Security Act, amendments were passed to gradually increase the age for normal retirement to 67. These shifts are to start in 1999 when the normal retirement age starts to increase by two months each year until it reach 66 in 2005. No further changes are to take place until 2016 when the age again starts to increase by two months per year until it reaches 67 in 2016.

The two major reasons for the change in the retirement age are clear. People are living so much longer that rescheduling is necessary to help keep the payroll taxes from increasing even further than they have to date. Putting the beginning of the change off 16 years from the date of the amendment diminished the political backlash to almost nothing. More recent research estimates that shifting the normal retirement age upward by one year will reduce total benefits by more than $10 billion for each year the plan is in effect. A shift of two years will reduce outlays by $20 billion per year. Given the financial pressures on the federal government, no one should be surprised to learn these upward shifts in the normal retirement age are accelerated. Even a shift to age 68 or beyond sometime in the future would not be surprising.[1]

Second, the declining ratio of employed to retired people under social security is making financing the retirement benefits more burdensome on the employed. The 1960 ratio of workers covered by social security to those receiving benefits was 5.1. By 1990 that ratio

---

[1]See the Kerry-Danforth.

was 3.3 and is projected to decline steadily to about 2.3 by the year 2020. Increasing the retirement age will help reduce that burden on those employed.

Tensions on the Actual Retirement Age. Several forces are working to reduce the actual retirement age. As noted, early retirement programs for social security were started in 1956. Much of the pressure for early retirement with reduced benefits was due to the increasing proportion of women in the work force. Earlier and earlier retirement is a goal of many people. Paid work with its attendant responsibilities and discipline is viewed as being undesirable by larger and larger proportions of the population. The percentage of men in the work force at age 60 continues to decline. As more people retire early, social pressures lead more and more people to seek early retirement. New forms of entertainment and recreation that are being advertised heavily and effectively encourage earlier retirement. During the past decade, more businesses and government organizations have tried to reduce their costs by enticing employees to accept early retirement programs. As work becomes more stressful and the nature of work and the skills required continue to change more rapidly, the frustration factor also tends to encourage earlier retirement.

The question of how to finance a longer retirement both because of retiring at an earlier age and because of the increasing actual length of life is often not considered rationally. The emotional aspects of the decision to retire early appear to be winning.

On the other hand, financial pressures are making earlier retirement more expensive for the whole society. The ratio of working to retired people is declining to the point that the FICA taxes, that is the social security taxes on the employed, have increased rapidly (8.5% per year) over the past 10 years and are likely to continue to do so. Talk of intergenerational tensions, if not "warfare," is increasing. People who have retired are more frequently taking part-time jobs after some years of retirement for the sake of income and not just out of boredom. As inflation and climbing medical costs reduce more and more of our most senior citizens to the poverty level and below, the problem will receive more political attention, but satisfactory solutions will be very difficult—if not impossible.

CONCLUSIONS

The financial aspects of home ownership and social security should be included in your broad financial plan. Of course, home ownership has wide implications for your life-style and for that of the nation, but its personal, financial aspect should not be overlooked. A home is a hedge against inflation and a continuing source of income in retirement.

In establishing your broad asset-allocation goals, the wealth and income aspects of social security should be considered. Both of these aspects can be estimated, but the further you are from the beginning of your retirement, the less accurate they will be. The financial and personal implications of retiring earlier or later than the typical age of 65 merits continuing consideration. On this issue, keeping an open mind until the decision must be faced is the best policy.

TABLE 2.1

PRICES FOR EXISTING ONE-FAMILY HOUSES
AND ANNUAL PERCENTAGE INCREASE
(1970-1993)

Year	% of Yearly Increase	Median Price ($)	Year	% of Yearly Increases	Median Price ($)
1970	-- %	$ 23,000	1982	2.1 %	$ 67,800
1971	4.3	24,800	1983	3.7	70,300
1972	7.7	26,700	1984	3.0	72,400
1973	8.2	28,900	1985	4.3	75,500
1974	10.7	32,000	1986	6.4	80,300
1975	10.3	35,300	1987	6.6	85,600
1976	8.2	38,100	1988	4.3	89,300
1977	12.6	42,900	1989	4.3	93,100
1978	13.5	48,700	1990	2.6	95,500
1979	14.4	55,700	1991	5.0	100,300
1980	11.7	62,200	1992	3.4	103,700
1981	6.8	66,400	1993	3.0	106,800

SOURCE of Selling Price Data: <u>Statistical Abstract of the United States</u>; Washington, DC, Government Printing Office, 1994.

TABLE 2.2

GROWTH IN TAXES FOR SOCIAL SECURITY BENEFITS

Calendar Year	Contribution and Benefit Base	Employee Tax		Tax Increase Over 1950	
		Rate	Amount	Amount	Percentage
1950	$ 3,000	1.50 %	$ 45	$ --	--
1960	4,800	3.00	144	99	220 %
1970	7,800	4.80	374	230	511 %
1980	25,900	6.13	1,588	1214	2698 %
1990	51,300	7.65	3,924	2336	5191 %

TABLE 2.3

SOCIAL INSURANCE ASPECT OF SOCIAL SECURITY BENEFITS: 1991

	Maximum Indexed Taxable Wage	150% of Average Wage	Average Wage	75% of Average Wage	Federal Minimum Wage
Indexed Wage	100%	82.4%	60.1%	45.0%	31.0%
Primary Benefits	100%	92.7%	74.2%	60.9%	48.6%
Benifits-Wage Ratio	1.00	1.125	1.235	1.353	1.568

SOURCE: 1992 GREEN BOOK: Overview of Entitlement Programs. Committee on Wages and Means, U.S. House of Representatives. Washington, D.C., 1992, p. 49.

CHAPTER 3

TIAA-CREF MONTHLY INVESTMENT ALLOCATIONS: NARROW FRAMEWORK

INTRODUCTION

- How can a rough estimate of my TIAA-CREF retirement benefits be prepared?

- How should my monthly TIAA-CREF investments be allocated among the various available funds?

- Why and How are the returns on TIAA and CREF measured differently?

- What have the rates of return been on the available TIAA-CREF funds?

- How are return and objective risk measured in modern investment practice?

- What are these return-risk results as applied to TIAA-CREF?

Your regular, monthly investment allocation among the TIAA-CREF options can make the difference between a financially adequate retirement income and a highly satisfactory one with rising income that may keep pace with or even exceed the inflation rate.

As a TIAA-CREF participant, you must keep your focus on your long-run future. Keeping your eye on your goal which is 20-50 years in the future is remarkably difficult in view of the national and international political and economic problems that our nation has experienced and will continue to experience. Personal, financial, health, job security, and family problems all tend to distract you from a clear and constant view of long-run financial goals.

If you and your spouse are the same age and retire at age 65, your joint life expectancy is just over 25 years. One of you may reasonably expect to live to be 90. If you enter the TIAA-CREF retirement system at age 35, work to 65, and live to 90, you will be in the system for 55 years. As a personal note I entered the system in 1954 at age 34 and have now been in the system for 41 years. Given the present state of health of my wife and myself, 55 years in the program appears highly plausible.

INVESTMENT ALLOCATION GOALS

Both TIAA-CREF and Soldofsky set forth monthly investment allocation goals. The differences between them are discussed. The TIAA-CREF recommendations do not comment on the distribution of the amounts accumulated at the point of retirement. Furthermore, these allocation recommendations are limited to funds within the TIAA-CREF system; they do not consider either other sources of wealth such as stocks, bonds, and real estate; or other retirement cash flows from such items as social security and, possibly, other pensions. Some participants may have pensions they earned in military service, in various government jobs, or ministerial positions. A broader, comprehensive set of assets and the allocation of wealth among them was discussed in Chapter 1.

The second part of this chapter presents the historical return and the risk performance of the eight TIAA-CREF options now available. The return and a measure of risk for the 20 years ending with 1994 are shown for each series or a proxy for it.[1] The risk for each series is measured as the dispersion of the annual yields around its own mean. The discussion goes on to demonstrate the riskiness of each series relative to each of the others. It proceeds by showing the extent to which risk is reduced by owning two or more of the eight funds. Underlying material, which amounts to a primer on the relevant fundamentals of finance and economics, is presented in Chapter VIII.

RETIREMENT BENEFITS ESTIMATES

Even though your annual TIAA-CREF reports provide you with an estimate of your retirement benefits, those numbers incorporate several assumptions which greatly reduce their usefulness. The further away you are from your likely retirement date, the less useful those estimates are. One rule of thumb for people who have been in the system for at least 20 years and hope to retire at age 65, assuming that their regular contribution totals 15 percent of salary, is given below. That contribution may be paid in any combination by them and their employer. This rule of thumb applies to TIAA only.

Hence:

	TIMES	
Number of years of service	2.00 percent	Pension Estimate - %
20	2.00	40%
30	2.00	60%

To estimate the pension benefits in dollars, multiply the pension percentage estimate by your anticipated last five years average salary. If your regular pension contribution is only 10 percent, reduce the 2.00 percent multiplier to 1.33 percent. If your regular contribution is 20 percent of salary, increase the multiplier to 2.67 percent.

For each year you plan to retired before 65, reduce the benefits by about 10 percent per year, and increase them by about the same percentage for each year worked beyond 65. (Note: percent per year signals compound interest.) This rule of thumb has worked out reasonably for the last 25 years, but that does not assure that it will continue to work equally well into the distant future.

The major limitations of the TIAA-CREF assumptions are:

1. The omission of any salary growth rate.

2. A 6% rate earned on investments until retirement and after retirement.

3. In the case of CREF, a 6% rate earned until retirement and a 4 percent assumption for the year of retirement to May 1 only.

4. No CREF assumption is made for years after the first year of retirement.

---

[1]The two newest funds, CREF Equity Index and CREF Growth, were started April 29, 1994.

These points are discussed in more detail in the Annual Benefit Report section of Chapter 12.

MINIMAL RETIREMENT INCOME GOAL

Usually, initial retirement income of 60 to 80 percent of pre-retirement income is deemed to be adequate. What happens in the years after retirement is another question.

The statement of Principles on Academic Retirement Plans of the Association of American Colleges and the American Association of Universities recommends the retirement income be at least two-thirds of pre-retirement income. The Commission on College Retirement has recommended that continuing, real retirement income be in the range of 67-100 percent of pre-retirement income. The crucial difference here is that continuing, real income should remain in the area of 67-100 percent. The Commission on College Retirement recognizes that employers should take steps to keep income up with the increases in the cost of living so that real income does not fall.[2]

Neither of these statements considers the changes in income tax rates before and after retirement, but they are clear that social security benefits should be included in the post-retirement income. These statements do not consider the impact on the "bottom line" or cash-flow income resulting from the end of your regular, personal contributions to your pension plan upon retirement. Payments into social security, health care payments and other regular payments are not considered in estimating pre- and post-retirement cash flows.

Other, wider considerations in calculating post-retirement cash flow and the distribution of income-earning assets over a person's entire wealth are discussed in the Annual Benefit Report section of Chapter 12. The use of deferred-tax, salary option, and the tax-sheltered annuity as two means of increasing retirement benefits are discussed in Chapter 7.

RECOMMENDED INVESTMENT ALLOCATIONS

Tables 3.1 and 3.2 report TIAA-CREF's recommended investment allocation and Soldofsky's recommended allocation, respectively. TIAA-CREF does not give any explicit justification for its investment allocations recommendations. It does present some rank-order and general-risk comments, and summary data about past rates of return on each fund.

The TIAA-CREF Global Equities Fund was started July 1, 1992. When that fund was introduced, TIAA-CREF modified their equity fund recommendations slightly to those shown as follows:

AGES	EQUITIES FUND	GLOBAL EQUITIES FUND
20s and 30s	30% - 40%	20% - 25%
40s and 50s	20% - 25%	10% - 15%
55 to Retirement	20% - 30%	5% - 10%

[2]Hammond, Brett P. and Morgan, Harriet O., Ending of Mandatory Retirement for Tenured Faculty. National Academy Press: Washington, D.C., 1991

In effect, the percentage ranges for equities previously recommended were divided between Equities and Global Equities. The total recommended allocation percentage for all equities remains the same. The recommended percentage for the Global Equities shifts downward in steps which recognize that Global Equities—in TIAA-CREF's opinion—are likely to be somewhat more risky than their CREF-Equities fund.

One of TIAA's publications remarks that a participant's actual allocations are generally inversely related of their recommendations; that is, younger participants are likely to opt for a much higher allocation to TIAA than recommended, and older participants select a higher percentage of equities. TIAA is silent about what is recommended for or what actually exists at the date of retirement.

Many corporate 401(k)s pension plans offer participants a choice among investment vehicles. New York Life Insurance Company had the Gallup organization conduct a poll for them about the investment allocations their participants selected. More than half of the 25-34 year olds placed more than 25 percent of their regular investments in low yielding, money-market funds.[3] That choice is clearly a poor one because of the relatively and absolutely low returns on such funds in 1992. The reason suggested for that allocation was the almost complete lack of investment knowledge and concepts by the respondents.

Ellen Schultz wrote in the Wall Street Journal that where workers had an investment choice, only one-fourth had money in common stocks and only 3.7 percent had more than 50 percent in common stocks.[4] These percentages may be compared with investment allocation samples of TIAA-CREF participants presented in Chapter 6.

Soldofsky's recommendations are similar to TIAA's but differ in six notable ways. First, Soldofsky uses only two age classifications: namely, 11 or more years to retirement, and 10 years until retirement. The transition allocation from the younger age to the older age group as retirement is approached may come at a slow and steady pace, not abruptly as suggested by Table 3.2. The age at which individuals plan to retire differs. Some may plan to retire as early as 57 under early retirement programs, and others plan to work until age 70. Mandatory retirement age of 70 for professors expired on December 31, 1993. Some people may now plan to continue to work much longer. And, of course, plans may change.

Second, Soldofsky provides percentage ranges for the major allocation decision between TIAA and CREF. Individual attitudes toward risk differ widely.[5] Third, for the younger group, a 100 percent allocation to CREF is not unreasonable. The rate-of-return advantage for CREF that is most likely over periods of 10-to-20 years or more is overwhelming. (See Table 8.1 below.) Few people may want to allocate 100 percent CREF Equities (and/or Global Equities).

Fourth, an allocation of up to 50 percent in the Social Choice fund is suggested as a limit, because this fund is a mixture of debt and equity securities; it will have a return between that of the Marketable Bond fund and the Equities fund.

---

[3]Stanger's Investment Advisor, July 1992, p. 12.

[4]Ellen P.E. Schultz, Wall Street Journal, "Passing the Buck," July 7, 1992, p. C1.

[5]Measurement of attitudes toward risk dates from the late nineteenth century.

Fifth, on rare occasions, a much higher percentage in the Money Market fund may be quite reasonable. For example, in Chapter 6, when the guaranteed rate on TIAA is below the rate being earned in the money market, placing funds in the Money Market account is a safe and reasonable thing to do. Other reasonable occasions are also described in Chapter 6.

Finally, a steady allocation of 50 percent to TIAA and 50 percent to CREF-Equities is likely to result in an accumulation which is well over 50 percent in CREF equities when the individual approaches retirement. Assume that $1,000 is invested per year at 6 percent, 9 percent, and 12 percent. The accumulations will be as follows:

Years	6%	9%	12%
20	$ 36,790	$ 51,160	$ 72,050
30	70,060	136,310	241,330

Assume the 6% represents TIAA and the 9% represents CREF-Equities. The sum of the accumulations at the end of 20 and 30 years, and the CREF proportions are as follows:

	20 YEARS	30 YEARS
TOTAL ACCUMULATIONS (6%)	$ 87,950[a]	$ 215,370[b]
CREF ACCUMULATIONS (9%)	51,160	136,310
CREF/TOTAL	58.20%	63.30%

[a]$36,790 plus $51,160.
[b]$70,060 plus $136,310.

You can work out the results for yourself with the 12 percent rate. The reasonableness of these rate of returns can be checked against the actual results shown in Table 6.3 below.

The point of this aside is that the monthly allocation at a steady percentage of the monthly investment (inputs) is most likely to result in accumulations (outputs) that are substantially different from the inputs. Several mid-career adjustments before retiring may be needed. Finally, Soldofsky's guidelines may be used as retirement allocation goals, but they should be considered in the wider context of the individual's total wealth and prospective retirement cash flow.

PERFORMANCE CHARACTERISTICS BY FUND

The investment and performance characteristics of each fund will be considered after an essential aspect of the investment procedure is described. Then the relevant liquidity aspects and rate-of-return aspects will be considered in terms of relative riskiness and correlation characteristics. (See Tables 3.7 and 3.8.) TIAA-CREF characterized each six of its funds briefly in its 1992 publication, The CREF Global Equities Account, as follows:[6]

---

[6]The CREF Global Equities Account, New York; TIAA-CREF, 1992. Pp. 13-15.

FUND	RISK
TIAA (Traditional Annuity)	Very Low
CREF Money Market Account	Very Low
CREF Bond Market Account	Low-to-Moderate
CREF Social Choice Account	Low-to-Moderate
CREF Stock Account	Moderate
CREF Global Equities Account	Moderate

Some three or four additional characteristics for each of these funds were given. TIAA, according to these statements, is for people who want maximum safety, and the Money Market Account is for those who want to keep up with inflation and are not looking for a high, real rate of return. TIAA is for people who have other stocks and bonds and may want to offset higher risk investments with this very low-risk investment vehicle.

The TIAA and Money Market Accounts are for "risk-averse" people, and the latter may be suitable for persons closer to retirement.[7] The Social Choice Account is less volatile than a stock market account. The Bond Market and Equities Accounts are mentioned as being better suited for those who have a longer time to retirement. Nothing is said about the time-to-retirement for the TIAA and the Social Choice Accounts.

Some critical comments are made in this chapter about what is said and not said in TIAA's simple risk, return, and time-horizon summary. Specific risk-and-return information, and comment upon these results, are made in a liquidity-return and time-horizon framework.

A discussion of the very different methods used by TIAA and CREF funds is given next. The different method used by the CREF-Money Market fund is treated separately later. After this essential discussion of how return is reported, the topic of risk is introduced as it is used in modern finance.

RATE-OF-RETURN CALCULATIONS

Your primary concern as a TIAA-CREF participant is the (net) rate of return earned by each of the investment pools, such as CREF-Global Equities, that hold your pension funds. A deeper understanding of each of these funds helps you decide how best to allocate your investments among these funds and to reallocate your accumulations from time to time. The historic investment results, the methods of calculating these results, the types of assets held, and the ways in which losses are reported will be discussed for each fund.

MARKED TO BOOK AND MARKED TO MARKET

The returns on TIAA and the CREF equity and bond funds are calculated by dramatically different methods. Investments in TIAA are marked to book value, as contrasted with CREF equity and bond funds, which are marked to market. Your investments in TIAA are entered on the company's books at the amount that you invest. If $1,000 per month is invested, that investment will show up as $12,000 at the end of the year plus interest which is added monthly. In other words, your investment grows during the accumulation period just as it

---

[7]The meaning of risk-averse is expanded in the last section of this chapter.

would in a bank savings account. Table 3.3 illustrates the TIAA rate-of-return calculation for 1991 using approximate numbers rounded to the nearest million dollars.

The book value of your investment accumulation will continue to grow as long as funds are not withdrawn. The book value does not reflect changes in the market value of these assets. Generally, insurance companies do not report the market value of fixed-income assets such as mortgages. In most cases, no active market exists for such assets.

The rates earned on TIAA's asset portfolio rises and falls slowly as shown in Table 3-4. These rises and falls reflect the demand for funds in the market, changing rates of inflation, portfolio turnover, "sweeteners" on loans made, and charges for bad loans. ("Sweetner's" are described in a subsection of Chapter 4.)

The share prices of CREF-Equities, Marketable Bonds, Social Choice, and Global Equities funds reflect changes in the market prices of the securities held. The prices of these funds are marked to market. The prices of these shares held in your account are changed to reflect the market-price changes as you may observe in your quarterly reports. The illustration presented in Table 3.7 is based upon numbers that are in the recent range of CREF- Equities experience.

In preparing the Total Annual Return (TAR) for CREF-Equities, the beginning-of-the-year price of a unit is subtracted from the end-of-the-year price. The difference is the capital gain (loss). Dividends are folded in as they are received and raise the price of the units held. In the illustration they are added to the capital gain. The sum of the capital gain (loss) and the dividends are divided by the beginning-of-the-year price, and the result is the TAR. Calculated this way, the annual rate of return may be a gain or a loss. The actual results starting with 1979 are shown in the CREF-Equities column of Table 3.6. The TARs on the Marketable Bonds, Social Choice and Global equities funds are calculated the same way; these are reported in Table 3.6 also.

The CREF-Money Market fund was started April 1, 1988. I constructed a money-market series back to 1978 shown in Table 3.6 from widely available information on the performance of the primary money-market instrument, U.S. Treasury bills. The CREF-Marketable Bonds series was started on March 1, 1990. TIAA recently reconstructed the total returns back through 1976. My series go back to 1952 and earlier. Where needed, I spliced my bonds returns into CREF's actual marketable bonds.[8]

The Social-Choice fund was started March 1, 1990, but no adequate series existed to represent its historical performance. I contacted the three largest such funds—Calvert Managed Growth, Pax World Fund and the Dreyfus Third Century Fund. The historic performance numbers they furnished were used to construct the series in Table 3.6. This information went back only to 1980. The CREF-Global Equities was started March 1, 1992. Information from the Templeton Growth fund, Templeton World fund, the Oppenheimer

---

[8]Robert M. Soldofsky, Performance of Long-Term Marketable Securities: Risk-Return, Ranking and Timing-1961-1984. Charlottesville, VA, Financial Analysts Research Foundation, 1986.

Global fund, the Putnam Global fund and the Morgan Stanley Capital International Index was used to construct a proxy for this series.

The construction of these longer series was essential in order to demonstrate both absolute and relative return, and relative risk. The bottom of Table 3.8 shows the average return on each fund for 5, 10, and 15 year periods ending with 1994. In Chapters 5 and 6, these performances are compared with those of the relevant financial markets and similar funds.

CREF-Equities pensions for retirees are a variable annuity. They are an annuity because they are a continuing series of payments and they are a variable annuity because the amount received after the first year of the annuity will vary in proportion with the price of a CREF unit. The exact calculation is illustrated in the Variable Annuity section of Chapter 10.

Table 3.6 shows the one-year, contractual, announced returns on TIAA for the past 15 years. These returns are announced before January 1 for the coming year and are used to determine the interest that will be paid on or credited to your TIAA account for that year.[9] That rate can be safely "guaranteed" for the coming year because new loans for that year are estimated and reflect the market rate of interest. Furthermore, TIAA, like all insurance companies, makes some advance commitments that is, it makes some contracts to lend money for some months in advance at a specified rate. In addition, the contractual rate is changed every year and could be changed more often if conditions require such an action. The one-year contractual rate moves upward and downward more quickly than the rates earned on the entire portfolio, which are shown in Table 3.4.

The word "guaranteed" or "contractual" return is used in another sense by TIAA and all other life insurance companies. Insurance companies guarantee that their rates of return paid to policyholders will not fall below a minimum, which is three percent in the case of TIAA. The amount they earn and will pay each year to clients is sometimes called a "guaranteed" rate; it is the (basic) guaranteed rate plus dividends. Even if the company does not earn the (basic) guaranteed rate in some year(s), they guarantee to pay it. That payment would have to be made with other sources of funds and in some way be deducted from the owners' equity. Experience from at least the time of the Civil War assures these companies that rates earned below the guaranteed rate are very highly unlikely.

RETURN AND RISK PERFORMANCE
The long-run performance of the securities and investment markets should be the most important point when allocating your investments among the available funds offered by TIAA and CREF. The actual performances of TIAA and CREF-Equities starting with 1979 are given in Table 3.6. The rate-of-return performances of the other six CREF funds are a mixture of their actual performances for the full years they have been in existence and constructions based upon published and publicly available information. The return

---

[9]More recently this rate has been changed more than once a year because of the volatility of market interest rates. The rate in effect January 1, 1993 was 6.0 percent. It was increased to 6.25 percent as of July 1, 1993 and further increased to 6.75 through September, 1994. The rate was set at 7.25 percent for October through December, 1994, and increased again to 7.50 percent for January through June, 1995.

performance back to 1952 for TIAA and CREF, and tables of bond and stock performance back to 1871 are from studies provided in Chapter 6.

The table of the annual returns, provides enough information to calculate the standard deviations for each of the return series. (The calculation of the standard deviation is reviewed in the last section of Chapter 8.) The standard deviation is basic to most measurement of risk. Its use permits a financial analyst to go far beyond the simple statements of risk such as "very low" or "moderate" as used in TIAA-CREF publications. Combining these quantified measurements of return and risk provides insights into some of the likely consequences of your allocation decision.

The lower part of Table 3.6 gives the average returns for these eight series for the past 5, 10, and 15 years. These performances for the TIAA-CREF series are compared with those of similar series and with the financial markets as a whole in Chapter 6.

RISK PERFORMANCE

Perhaps the most popular measure of risk in finance is the fluctuations of the return around its own mean or average. The deviations from this mean are measured in statistics by the universally used standard deviation. The standard deviation is not limited to finance and economics, but is a fundamental measure in all scientific research that uses inferential statistics. One property of the standard deviation is that about 68 percent of the observations fall within one standard deviation of the mean and that about 95 percent of the observations fall within two standard deviation of the mean when the distribution is normal or bell-shaped. This distribution is typical of financial-market data.

The standard deviations for TIAA and CREF funds are reported in Table 3.7. The order in which the returns and standard deviations for the CREF Funds are shown is based upon their relative riskiness from lowest to highest. The one standard deviation range itself depends upon the size of the average for which it is calculated. Thus, for CREF-Equities with a 20-year total return of 13.34 percent; the standard deviation of 16.10 percent is slightly larger than the average itself. For the Marketable Bonds the total return and standard deviation are 10.02 percent and 8.4 percent, respectively; the standard deviation is smaller than the average. To make more sense out of these measures of return and risk, the standard deviation is divided by the return to "standardize" the results in terms of relative riskiness. This measure, the results of which are shown in column 3 of Table 3.7, is called the coefficient of variation.

The outcomes in Table 3.7 are most revealing! TIAA has by far the lowest coefficient of variation, but that results largely from the marked-to-market method of calculating its return. I have less confidence in the mean and standard deviation of the Social Choice fund because they are based on only 14 observations.

Another way of making sense out of the one standard deviation range is to note that the chances are 68 out of 100 that the returns will be within the range of one standard deviation of the average. If the one standard deviation range for CREF-Equities, for example, is 16.10 percent and the mean of the range is 13.34 percent, that range itself runs from -2.76 percent to +29.44 percent.

The story—analysis—has four important points to consider. First, the future market performance may not duplicate the annual or average performance for the past 20 or more years. If you are not yet retired, a time horizon of at least 25 years is relevant for you. Perhaps as long as 50 years may be the relevant period.

Second, a flat or static view of the world omits the compound-growth effect of funds earnings at various rates for 15 years, 25 years, or more. Table 3.6 shows the actual returns for TIAA and CREF-Equities starting with 1979. The other CREF series did not exist back to 1979 so proxy returns were prepared for them from published and publicly available information. Note the range of the average returns for the 5, 10, and 15 years ending at the end of 1994. Also note the declining rates on the money market funds. As long as inflation stays low, the return on such a fund may well remain closer to recent performance.

After making these disclaimers about future rates of return, the rates at which $1 may grow over the coming years are stated in the following brief schedule:

AT RATE SPECIFIED, $1 GROWS TO:

GROWTH RATE	GROWTH PERIOD (YEARS)		
	15	25	35
5 %	$ 2.08	$ 3.39	$ 5.52
10	4.18	10.83	28.10
15	8.14	32.92	131.18

(For further discussion, see the Magical Compound Interest section in Chapter 8.)

Third, a major reason for constructing and presenting the annual returns starting with 1979 was to have enough observations to permit the calculation of a usable standard deviation for each series.   Twenty observations were used, but experiments with some longer series suggested the results were not different enough to change the lessons or investment advice drawn from them.

The fourth point is the Correlation Coefficient Matrix, Table 3.8. This table could not be constructed unless the annual performance data and their standard deviations for each series were available. The correlation matrix means that each series is correlated against each of the other series.

The correlation coefficient establishes the likelihood that the returns on any one series will be higher or lower as compared with any other series in any one year. If two series always move upward or downward in absolute unison, their correlation coefficient would be +1.00. If they move in exactly opposite directions in exactly reversed patterns, the correlation coefficient would be -1.00. These changes would be exactly offsetting. If you had $10,000 invested in a stock that returned +20% and $10,000 in another stock that returned -20 percent that year, your average return would be zero; the returns would exactly offset one another.

In Table 3.8 where TIAA is correlated against TIAA, the correlation coefficient is 1.00. If you had two TIAA accounts, or if you and your spouse had separate accounts, you would get no diversification effect. As you read across the top row, note how different the correlation coefficients are. The Money Market and Marketable Bonds perform most like TIAA, and the Social Choice fund is slightly negatively correlated with TIAA. When the return on the

Social Choice fund goes up, the TIAA return is somewhat likely to go down and vice versa. If you hold TIAA and your primary goal is diversification, your two best options are the Social Choice and Growth Equities Funds.

If you hold CREF-Equities and you are considering gains through diversification, the Global Equities and Index Equities are not good picks because their performances come close to mirroring that of CREF-Equities itself.

The goal of modern portfolio management, Harry Markowitz loves to say, is to seek the right diversification for the right reason.[10] The right reason is to achieve low or negative correlations from this viewpoint.

SUMMARY OF RETURN AND RISK
As a pension fund investor, you must consider (1) return in the very long run, (2) risk as measured by the standard deviation, and (3) diversification as suggested by the correlation matrix. The risk characterizations of TIAA-CREF's investment alternatives presented in The CREF Global Equities Account, are "very low," for TIAA and CREF-Money Market; "low to moderate" for the CREF Marketable Bonds and Social Choice accounts; and "moderate" for CREF Equities and Global Equities. These characterizations are inadequate for those who want to use some of the best tools available to help plan for their financial future.

ATTITUDES TOWARD RISK
The standard deviation as it has been used here measures the variability or dispersion of objective data around its own mean. In this case the performance of returns in the financial markets have been measured. Financial economists and behavioral scientists are also concerned about attitudes toward risk or variability in returns. These attitudes may be measured by simple forms of utility curves.[11]

The drawing below illustrates the three basic forms of utility curves that measure attitude toward risk. Utility is measured on the y or vertical axis and rate of return is measured on the x or horizontal axis. Utility is measured in utiles which have an arbitrary scale in much the same sense as measurements of temperature. One underlying assumption in the drawing is that as the rate of return increases so does risk in the sense that the dispersion around the return becomes larger. That point is made by the objective data in Table 3.6. As one looks into the future the prospective range of returns tends to be wider as the mean return increases.

Attitudes toward risk are characterized most simply as risk aversion, risk neutral, and risk seeking or loving. The straight line or risk neutral curve implies that the individual is indifferent or neutral to risk. Whether the return, for example, turns out to be 10, 15 or 20 percent in any one year is a matter of indifference as long as risk and return change proportionately. A risk averter dislikes risk so much that he will accept a lower return with

---

[10]Harry Markowitz, Nobel Laureate in Economics, is the creative originator of modern portfolio management theory.

[11]For a fuller introduction to this subject see Copeland, Thomas E., and J. Fred Weston, Financial Theory and Corporate Policy, 3rd ed. Reading, MA: Addison-Wesley Publishing Company, 1988, pp. 77-102. Swalm, Ralph O., "Utility Theory-Insights Risk Taking," Harvard Business Review, Nov-Dec. 1966, pp. 123-136.

no risk rather than a higher return with some risk of getting a lower return. The returns on TIAA, in this sense, are the least risky of those available from TIAA-CREF, but they have some risk. Many individual investors prefer short-term U.S. Treasury securities or savings certificates because of the assurance they have of earning their stated rate of return in the short run.

In the drawing at the end of this paragraph, the straight line from the origin represent the risk neutral position: risk and return increase proportionately.[12] The downward sloping curve illustrates risk aversion. A person whose attitudes are represented by this curve will trade off ever higher amounts of return for equal-sized amounts of risk. The higher the additional increment of prospective return, the more skeptical he becomes that it will ever be received. The upward sloping curve represents the attitudes of a risk seeker or risk lover. He enjoys the risk involved so much that he will accept more and more risk for equal sized promised increments of return.

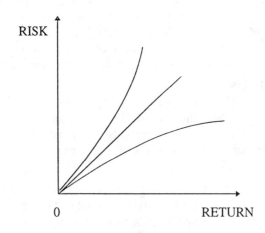

Attitudes toward risk are frequently illustrated in terms of a "fair gamble" format. Assume that you find a lottery ticket for a unique lottery in which you have a 50-50 chance of winning $1,000 or nothing. Then ask yourself quite seriously what the lowest price would be that would induce you to sell the ticket. Remember that your average or anticipated gain from holding the ticket until the lottery is held is $500. That amount is the average of the 50-50 chance of receiving $0 or $1000.

If you would accept $400, for example, for your lottery ticket, you are risk averse. If you would accept $300, your risk-aversion attitude is more intense. If you would require $450 for a 50-50 chance of receiving $500 you are only modestly risk averse. On the other hand, if

---

[12]Risk and return are defined in the sense suggested in Table 3.7. The probability distribution around the mean return is likely to vary as suggested by the standard deviation for each risk class. Also the mean values and standard deviations will change somewhat over time. Note, however that 16 years of data were used in preparing these results.

you would require $600 to give up your ticket, you are a risk seeker or risk lover. The more you required up to the $1,000 amount, the more intense your love of risk.[13]

The combination of short time horizons, neglect of the compounding effects of interest over long periods of time, strong risk-aversion attitudes, and lack of understanding of the basics of finance go a very long way to explain the strong preference by TIAA-CREF participants for TIAA as contrasted with the various CREF equity funds as shown by data presented in later chapters.

---

[13]This discussion of risk measurements is in the last section of Chapter 8, Investment Basics.

CONCLUSIONS

Both TIAA-CREF and Soldofsky have suggested investment-allocation goals for the three-asset class or narrow-framework goal structure. These differ somewhat in that the latter portrays more age-related and nearness to retirement allocation recommendations. Soldofsky also clarifies the distinctions between monthly investment-allocation and retirement-allocation goals.

A retirement real income goal of 60-80 percent of final income is widely recommended. This goal should be specified as the after-tax level for retirement cash flow as is explained later. Inflation hedges should be used to try to keep real income from falling during retirement. The further you are from retirement, the less accurate your estimated benefits will be using the TIAA-CREF suggested method included in your Annual Report. A useful rule of thumb method is suggested to estimate retirement income relative to final salary if you are more than five and certainly more than 10 years from your projected retirement date.

An initial appraisal of the various TIAA and CREF accounts is made. Later in the chapter after the different methods used by TIAA and CREF to calculate return are explained, more sophisticated approaches to measuring risk and return are used. Risk-return measurements are provided for all TIAA-CREF accounts including the two CREF accounts introduced in 1995.

The marked-to-book and marked-to-market methods of determining the returns on TIAA and on the CREF accounts, respectively, are explained and illustrated. These distinctions are essential for understanding the performance of your TIAA and CREF accounts both before and after your retirement. Your monthly investment allocation decision should be reviewed after you understand these differences.

The year-by-year performance for the TIAA-CREF accounts over the past 16 years is provided. As necessary, realistic estimates are made for what the performance would most likely have been for the newer CREF accounts from data available from the financial markets. Average performance for the past 5, 10 and 16 years ending in 1994 are provided in a table. The very well known statistical measurements, the standard deviation and coefficient of variation, are prepared for the eight available funds. The differences in risk among these accounts are quite clear even for those who do not understand the underlying statistical procedures.

Attitudes toward risk as well as objective measurement of risk are important in your investment allocation decisions. On occasion, TIAA-CREF publications use the language of attitudes toward risk. The last section of this chapter introduces the formal notion of risk-return trade-offs, one of the popular measurements of attitudes measured in finance, economics and behavioral science.

TABLE 3.1

TIAA-CREF'S RECOMMENDED ALLOCATIONS BY AGE RANGE

AGE	TIAA	CREF	DISTRIBUTION AMONG CREF OPTIONS		
			STOCK	BONDS	MONEY MARKET
20s and 30s	25 %	75 %	50%-65%	10%-20%	0%-5%
40s to Mid-50s	40	60	30-40	10-20	0-10
Mid-50s to RETIREMENT	60	40	30-35	5	0-5

SOURCE: Guiding Your Retirement Savings TIAA-CREF, 1991.

TIAA-CREF MONTHLY INVESTMENT ALLOCATIONS

43

TABLE 3.2

SOLDOFSKY'S RECOMMENDED MONTHLY ALLOCATIONS TO TIAA-CREF AS A FUNCTION OF TIME TO RETIREMENT

YEARS TO RETIREMENT	TIAA	CREF	INDIVIDUAL CREF FUNDS			
			EQUITIES	SOCIAL CHOICE	MARKET BONDS	MONEY MARKET
11 or more	50%	50%-100%	Up to 1/5 of CREF Equites Total may be in Global Funds	Up to 50%	Reduce TIAA by % in this account	Usually 0
10 to Retirement	40%-75%	25%-60%		Up to 50%		Up to 25% of other CREF items on rare occasions

Comments on Soldofsky Recommendations:

1. TIAA is used to represent all sources of fixed income or wealth—from debt securities, savings accounts and the like prior to retirement.

2. CREF is used to represent all sources of wealth from equity securities including stock mutual funds.

3. The TIAA-CREF allocation of wealth should be placed in a wider context of wealth and retirement income about as follows: CREF (Equities, Global and Social Choices) 25%-50%; TIAA and CREF (Money Market and Marketable Bonds) 20%-30%; Home (and other real estate) 15%-30%; Social Security (OASI) 15%-25%; and Cash (checking accounts, savings accounts, CDs, etc.) 10%-15%.

TABLE 3.3

RATE OF RETURN ON TIAA: AN ILLUSTRATION
(in $ millions, approximate)

ASSETS	
12/31/91	$ 55,600
12/31/90	49,800
	$104,000
(1) AVERAGE ASSETS 1991	$ 52,000
(2) NET EARNINGS[a]	$ 4,763
(3) NET RATE EARNED $(2) \div (1)$	9.16%

[a]After considering both realized and unrealized gains and losses.

TABLE 3.4

**TIAA PORTFOLIO
RATES OF RETURN EARNED**

YEAR	RATE	YEAR	RATE	YEAR	RATE
1974*	7.59 %	1981*	10.11 %	1988	11.72 %
1975*	7.82	1982*	10.88	1989	11.12
1976*	8.13	1983	11.09	1990	9.97
1977*	8.39	1984	11.74	1991	9.25
1978*	8.71	1985	12.43	1992	9.01
1979*	8.97	1986	12.66	1993	8.19
1980*	9.44	1987	11.72	1994	8.02

*Before considering unrealized and realized gains and losses.

TABLE 3.5

TOTAL ANNUAL RETURN ON CREF:
HYPOTHETICAL ILLUSTRATION

WITH CAPITAL GAIN

CREF PRICE, T+1	$ 55.00
CREF PRICE, T	50.00
INCREASE (CAPITAL GAIN)	$ 5.00
DIVIDENDS RECEIVED	1.50
TOTAL INCOME	$ 6.50

TOTAL ANNUAL RETURN $\dfrac{\$5.00 + \$1.50}{\$50.00} = \dfrac{\$6.50}{\$50.00} = 13.00\%$

WITH CAPITAL LOSS

CREF PRICE, T+2	$ 48.00
CREF PRICE, T+1	55.00
DECREASE (CAPITAL LOSS)	$ - 7.00
DIVIDENDS RECEIVED	1.60
TOTAL INCOME	$ - 5.40

TOTAL ANNUAL RETURN $\dfrac{\$7.00 + \$1.60}{\$55.00} = \dfrac{\$5.40}{\$55.00} = 9.82\%$

TABLE 3.6

**PERFORMANCE ON TIAA AND CREF FUNDS INCLUDES
HYPOTHETICAL AND OTHER REAL FUNDS FOR EARLIER YEARS AS
NECESSARY AND AVAILABLE
(1979-1994)**

		CREF						
Year(s)	TIAA (Contractual Annual Rate) [a]	CREF Equities [a]	Money Market [a,b]	Marketable Bonds [a,c]	Social Choice [a,d]	Global Funds [a,e]	Equities Index [a,f]	Growth Index [a,g]
79	11.6	15.8	11.1	1.9	--	11.0	24.1	28.7
80	13.7	26.6	13.1	2.7	28.5	25.7	32.5	36.4
81	12.5	-1.5	16.4	6.3	-0.1	-4.8	-4.4	-7.1
82	13.7	21.9	12.5	32.6	10.5	9.7	20.7	31.1
83	12.5	25.1	8.9	8.4	17.9	21.9	22.7	13.6
84	11.6	4.7	11.3	15.2	4.9	4.7	3.4	-3.8
85	11.7	32.7	8.0	22.1	27.0	40.6	32.2	28.8
86	10.3	21.8	6.5	15.3	10.5	41.9	16.7	-14.4
87	8.7	5.1	6.6	2.8	3.5	16.2	1.9	3.9
88	8.9	17.5	7.6	7.9	15.1	23.3	17.8	12.0
89	9.2	28.0	9.2	14.5	20.3	16.6	29.3	34.7
90	8.6	-5.5	8.2	9.0	4.3	-17	-5.1	-1.3
91	8.7	30.1	6.0	16.0	25.2	18.3	33.7	41.7
92	7.7	6.3	3.6	7.4	11.1	-5.2	9.7	5.2
93	7.3	13.9	3.0	9.8	9.4	22.5	10.9	3.7
94	6.5	-0.1	4.3	-2.9	-1.3	5.1	0.2	2.2
				Averages[g] (%)				
1990-1994	8.3	8.2	5.0	7.7	13.81	3.7	9.1	9.3
1985-1994	9.6	14.3	6.3	10.0	12.85	14.8	14.0	12.9
1979-1994	9.7	15.1	8.5	10.6	12.5	14.4	15.3	15.3

[a]SOURCE: <u>Charting TIAA and CREF Accounts</u>, Spring 1995, NYC, TIAA-CREF 1995.

[b]Started 4/1/88. Hypothetical returns before then from TIAA-CREF publication.

[c]Started 3/1/90. Hypothetical returns before then from TIAA publication.

[d]Started 3/1/90. Earlier realistic returns prepared by Soldofsky.

[e]Started 5/1/92. Earlier realistic but hypothetical returns prepared by TIAA-CREF.

[f]Started 5/1/92. Earlier realistic but hypothetical returns prepared by TIAA-CREF.

[g]Started 5/1/92. Realistic earlier returns back through 1987 prepared by TIAA-CREF.
   Returns 1980 through 1986 prepared by Soldofsky.

TABLE 3.7

TIAA AND CREF FUNDS: 1979-1994
TOTAL RETURNS AND RELATIVE RISK[a]

Fund	Total Return	Standard Deviation	Coefficient of Variation $(2 \div 1)$
	(1)	(2)	(3)
TIAA	9.7 %	.020	0.206
CREF			
Money Mkt.	8.5	.037	0.435
Social Choice[a]	12.5	.096	0.768
Market Bonds	10.6	.087	0.821
Equities	15.1	.122	0.801
Equity Index	15.3	.131	0.856
Growth Equities	15.3	.160	1.046
Global Equities	14.4	.159	1.104

[a]1980-1994 only

TABLE 3.8

TIAA AND CREF FUNDS: CORRELATION MATRIX
1979 - 1994

Fund	TIAA	Mon Mkt	Mkt Bnd	Equities	Soc Cho	Glb Eq	Ind Eq	Grh Eq
TIAA	1.00	.64	.68	.48	.16	.18	.15	.14
CREF								
1. Money Mkt	.64	1.00	.16	.13	.03	- .16	.01	.12
2. Mkt Bonds	.68	.16	1.00	.54	.31	.25	.32	.38
3. Equities	.48	.13	.55	1.00	.45	.50	.52	.47
4. Social Choice	.16	.03	.31	.45	1.00	.60	.90	.86
5. Global Equities	.18	- .16	.25	.50	.60	1.00	.63	.50
6. Index Equities	.15	.01	.32	.52	.90	.63	1.00	.93
7. Growth Equities	.14	.12	.38	.47	.86	.50	.93	1.00

CHAPTER 4

TIAA: INCOME, ASSETS AND SAFETY

INTRODUCTION

- Why should you try to learn about TIAA's operations?

- What is TIAA's rate of return on its assets?

- What are TIAA's major assets?

- How do its income and asset profiles compare with those of the life insurance industry?

- Why have rates of return fallen in recent years?

- How do TIAA and other life insurance companies account for and provide for losses?

- Why have some life insurance companies failed?

- What is the outlook for TIAA?

- How liquid is TIAA?

- Will it be able to pay my pension benefits when it is time for me to collect?

Teachers Insurance and Annuity Association (TIAA) was incorporated in 1918. It received a grant of $1,000,000 from the Carnegie Corporation, which was interested in many aspects of American education. Andrew Carnegie (1835-1919) was a Scottish immigrant who grew extremely wealthy for his time. He believed that he had an obligation to the citizens of his adopted country. His philanthropies included $60,000,000 that helped build hundreds of libraries in middle-sized cities throughout the United States.[1,2]

TIAA's first investment was in 1919 in Liberty Bonds, the name given to the U.S. Government securities issued to help finance World War I. The practice of investing primarily in fixed-income securities has continued. As of December 31, 1994, TIAA's assets had grown to $73.4 billion, which makes it the third largest insurance company in the United States. The allocation of these assets by class such as bonds and mortgages is shown in Table 4.1. Its retirement plans are being used by more than 5,500 colleges, universities and nonprofit organizations.

---

[1]For the authoritative history of TIAA see William C. Greenough It's My Retirement Money-Take Good Care of It. Irwin. Homewood, IL, 1990. Bill Greenough joined TIAA in 1941 shortly after earning his Ph.D. in Economics from Harvard. He is largely responsible for developing CREF. He retired as President in 1972 and died in 1990.

[2]Without the generosity of Andrew Carnegie and the philanthropic organizations he established to further education in the United States, TIAA may never have come into existence or survived. Pages 6-21 of Greenough's book are largely a tribute to Andrew Carnegie. For more information, see Lester, R.M., Forty Years of Carnegie Giving. New York: Charles Scribner's Sons, 1941.

All insurance companies in the United States own some stocks with the sole exception of TIAA, which holds only about 0.2 percent of its assets in stock. The College Retirement Equities Fund (CREF), which was started in 1952, is the companion and parallel organization with TIAA. CREF held $54.8 billion in assets at the end of 1994. TIAA-CREF's combined assets of $128.2 billion make it one of the largest insurance companies in the world. Other life insurance companies do not separate their stocks and fixed-income securities operations.

TIAA PARTICIPANT CONCERNS

You should realize that you and your spouse may be TIAA participants for half a century or more. How long will you have been a TIAA participant when you retire? Add your joint life expectancy when you retire to your years in TIAA to make a good estimate of the number of years you will be relying upon the safety and income-earning capacity of TIAA. (At age 65 for husband and wife joint life expectancy is 25 years.)

A large part of your retirement accumulation depends upon the safety, liquidity, and rate of return of TIAA's assets. Both your accumulation at the time of retirement and your benefits during retirement will depend to a substantial degree upon TIAA's net rate of return, that is, the rate of return after provision for expenses and inevitable losses.

Be assured about TIAA's quality as an insurance company; four of the five major insurance rating agencies in the United States give TIAA their highest rating. Only two of the more than 2,000 insurance companies in the United States have such high ratings. These companies are New York Life and Northwestern Mutual. The four rating companies are Moody's, Duff Phelps, Standard & Poor's, and A. M. Best, which is the foremost insurance rater in the nation.

Insurance companies can and do become bankrupt or sink to the edge of bankruptcy. During the past several years you may have been aware of the screaming headlines about the bankruptcy of First Executive Life and Mutual Life Insurance (New Jersey) in which many policy holders may have lost substantial parts of their investments   Several smaller companies have also been seized by insurance regulators. In 1990, Equitable Life Assurance, one of the nation's largest life insurance companies, lost several billion dollars and was on the verge of bankruptcy. It has reorganized with small losses to its policy holders. Equitable has since reorganized from a mutual to a stock company, and raised over $2 billion to meet capital requirements. The problems of Travelers and Aetna Life were also well publicized.

Uneasy TIAA participant may take comfort from the ratings given TIAA by the highly credible rating agencies. Professor Joseph M. Belth, Professor of Insurance at Indiana University, says that the best thing that most people can do is follow the ratings of the four major independent, insurance-rating companies. One of his criteria is that the insurance company have the highest rating given by two of those four companies. TIAA has the highest rating given by each of the four. When I asked Professor Joe Belth what the individual should read to satisfy himself about the quality of TIAA, he responded that the field was too difficult and too technical.[3] Belth is a long-time, nationally-known, consumer

---

[3]For further information, see Belth, J.M., A Consumer Handbook, 2nd ed., Bloomington, IN: University of Indiana Press, 1985.

advocate in the insurance field. The balance of this chapter reviews the 1991, 1992 and 1993 income, asset, and capital position of TIAA and places them in an intelligible format. Some 1994 data are included also participants may obtain a copy of the latest TIAA Investment Supplement by calling 1-800-842-2733, Extension 5509 and asking for one.   The last Supplement runs about 60 pages. Most of it is a listing of individual investments. TIAA's segmented income is given first and then its assets are discussed. The income and assets by class should help you understand these details.

TIAA'S RATE OF RETURN AND RESERVES

TIAA's rates of return on assets and increases in reserves for the past five years have been as follows:

Year	Net Rate Rate of Return	Increase In Contingency Reserves
1994	8.11%	$ 267.6 million
1993	8.32	-63.4 "
1992	8.96	541.6 "
1991	9.36	231.5 "
1990	9.76	240.1 "

TIAA's declining rate of return on its assets was to be expected in view of the declining market interest rates. As older loans are repaid and new ones are purchased at lower rates, the inevitable result is lower average earnings. The lower earnings do not necessarily reflect inept policies or loans, but asset quality must be examined because it has become the source of trouble and even bankruptcies for other life insurance companies. In 1994 interest rates started upward.

Note the Contingency Reserves have increased more than fourfold from 1989 through 1992. On the one hand these Contingency Reserves are charges against the Distribution of Income; on the other hand, they build up what would be the "Net Worth" or "Surplus" on the balance sheet of a for-profit business using the familiar enterprise accounting principles. TIAA and CREF, of course, are not for-profit operations; they operate like mutual associations. The 1991 increase in the Contingency Reserves amounted to 4.9 percent of the company's investment income of $4,702.3 million; in 1992 it amounted to 10.7 percent of its investment income of $5,037.5. This dramatic increase helps explain decreasing benefits to annuitants in 1991 and 1992.

These data are only the beginning of the story about the quality of TIAA's assets. In the last several years, direct write-downs on asset valuations have been taken that do not show as "charges" against income. These write-downs were $188.7 million in 1990, $326.1 million in 1991, $52.6 million in 1992, and about $40 million in 1993. In 1994 an unrealized gain of $39 million is reported.

In 1991 a new item of $957.7 million appeared on the Changes in Contingency Reserves called "Reclassification of accumulating annuity dividends declared for the following year," served largely to increase the "Net Worth," helped substantially to raise the year end 1991

"Net Worth" to $3,054.8 million. However, the Investment Supplement says the purpose was to conform with "general industry practice." Given the 1991 year-end assets of $55,575.8 million, the Net Worth is 5.5 percent of the assets which the company calls a "strong" financial cushion" for the protection of its participants. At year-end 1992, the Asset to Net Worth ratio was 5.8 percent. Its 1992 capital ratio was 7.64 percent against contractual liabilities as defined by insurance industry practice. In 1993 it fell to 7.35 percent and it rose in 1994 to 7.48 percent. TIAA's capital adequacy is about twice the industry-recommended level.

LIFE INSURANCE INDUSTRY COMPARISONS
The industry average capital ratio in 1992 was 9.30 percent of "Net Worth" or "Surplus." Companies such as Equitable Life Assurance and Aetna Life have 5.3 percent and 6.1 percent respectively in "Net Worth" for each dollar of assets. Both of these companies and Travelers have been very busy raising additional net worth because of their low net worth positions and because their asset portfolios still contain large amounts of junk bonds, real estate, and real estate mortgages of doubtful quality. Northwestern Mutual Life, one of the other companies with triple-A ratings, has 8.4 percent in Net Worth for each dollar of asset.[4]

The failure of Executive Life in 1990 and of Mutual Benefit Life Insurance Company of New Jersey in 1991 sent a strong chill through the industry and its policyholders. Executive Life probably lost over $10 billion. According to a 1993 Wall Street Journal item, policy holders will be lucky to get back as much as 72 cents on the dollar. Annuitants have been receiving 100 cents on the dollar and death claims are being paid in full.[5]

A major strength of TIAA as compared with the life insurance companies that have failed or that are financially troubled is the nature of its clientele. The policyholders of most other life insurance companies can—and did—withdraw their investments, especially in the case of Executive Life. When large numbers of policyholders cancel their policies and withdraw their investments at the same time, the company must liquidate some assets. When the liquidated assets are sold at far below their book value, the losses incurred are soon greater than the company's "Surplus," and it is driven into bankruptcy. Once a run on a company begins, it may be doomed to some degree of failure.

RESERVES AND LOSSES
Public concern with the safety and liquidity of life insurance companies has led to reforms in disclosure rules. The SEC assigned a task force to look into their reporting and disclosure practices. Congressional committees are also investigating these and other matters. The life insurance industry is largely regulated by commissions established under state laws. The National Association of Insurance Commissioners (NAIC) is a voluntary organization that sets rules, but it does not have a legal standing. The rules do become guidelines that

---

[4]These data on average net worth and industry data on the asset mix of life insurance companies are included in, Greg Steinmetz, "Equitable Feels Pressures of a Newly Public Concern," Wall Street Journal, September 23, 1992, p. B3.

[5]Laura Jerski and Frederick Rose, "Executive Life Bailout Springs a Leak," Wall Street Journal, April 2, 1993, p. A5.

insurance companies follow. In that sense it is similar to the New York Stock Exchange, which is self-regulating but has the SEC looking over its shoulder.

Late in 1991 the NAIC announced a new set of rules for establishing reserves against losses. Under a new accounting rule, the market value of real estate will have to be disclosed. The new rules for reserves will not have to be implemented fully until 1994.

Under the old rules life insurance companies had to set up reserves—Mandatory Security Valuation Reserves—against bonds (loans), but not against real estate mortgages and real estate. Under the new system, reserves are called Asset Valuation Reserves; they must be set up separately for bonds, real estate mortgages, and real estate. Interest Maintenance Reserves (IMR) are to be established for realized gains and losses for fixed-income securities due to interest rate fluctuations. However, these new IMR accounts apply only to bonds acquired after January 1, 1991. The detailed calculations are very complex, as they were under the old system.

TIAA adopted the new NAIC system in 1992. Its Investment Valuation Reserve was increased from $683.4 million under the old system to $1,376.2 million under the new system, an increase of $692.8 million or 101 percent. That means TIAA has provided in advance for losses of about 1.9 percent of its assets. In corporate accounting, this account would be somewhat similar to bad debts on long-term accounts receivable.

When bonds, real estate mortgages, and real estate are kept on the books at their purchase price, complexities arise when their market values drift or plummet away from book values. Keeping the accounting records in terms of book value is as old as the life insurance industry itself. The Mandatory Security Valuation Reserve System, the first such system for the insurance industry, was established in 1951, but it was not adequate in a period of price decline such as that experienced in the 1980s.

Companies are reluctant to revalue assets at their market prices for at least seven reasons. First, no exact value or market prices exist for nontraded or infrequently traded notes and bonds. A recent price may not be reasonably representative of what the price would be with more trading. Second, prices would have to be changed frequently to keep up with market conditions. Third, the cost of discovering and recording the market prices would be substantial. Fourth, the exact price placed on the records would always be open to challenge. Fifth, large reserves for losses might have to be established and changed frequently. Sixth, the losses that come about in bunches based more on general business conditions than on problems of a single company or piece of property procedure, are difficult to estimate and provide for. This booked-valued or fixed-value system was tried under the previous Mandatory Securities Valuation Reserve system, but found wanting in a crises. Seventh, an individual company does not want to disclose its problems to the world; it may lose customers or policyholders.

When widely held common and preferred stocks are traded (including those of stock insurance companies) the large volume of daily trades sets the market price for each security. The asset values of the stocks can be kept at market prices; no valuation reserves need to be kept. By separating CREF from TIAA, the problems of CREF are simplified. All CREF-Equities assets can be easily presented at their daily market value.

The downside of CREF's daily price fluctuations is that many people perceive that as the source of unbearable risk. They may also believe that keeping assets at book value as TIAA does with the regular increases in reserves removes them from losses resulting from business and interest-rate risks. In times of crises reality breaks through the facade of book value. The stupendous losses in the savings and loan banking industry starting in the late 1980s was primarily due to the practice of not disclosing market values and not providing adequate reserves bank-by-bank for the declines in market values as they developed.

TIAA'S INCOME

TIAA's 1994 earnings of $5.5 billion on its major classes of assets are reported as follows:

Assets Class	Asset Value (Billions)	Rate (%)[a]
Securities (Bond and Stocks)	$43.90	9.05%
Mortgages	21.20	8.34
Real Estate and other	9.20	5.36
Net Amount (Rate) Earned	- -	8.11

[a] As reported in the TIAA Investment Report, 1994

TIAA'S ASSETS

TIAA's assets passed the $10 billion mark in 1977. They grew at a compound rate of about 12.4 percent per year since then and have grown at almost 14.8 percent per year since 1958. TIAA has considerably more people working in its investment activities than CREF does. Many of TIAA's investment procedures are much more labor intensive than CREF's. TIAA has 20 trustees, the majority of whom are elected by participants like yourself.

In this section, the 1993 and 1994 year-end asset portfolios will be presented. Some comments will be made about the meanings of the terms and the underlying operations. More details about TIAA's asset portfolio and industry data are presented in Table 4.1.

BONDS

The bond portfolio consists of both publicly offered bonds (bonds which are traded in the markets) and direct placements (securities for which little or no public trading exists). No inference should be made that direct placements are of lower quality and are more likely to default than publicly offered bonds.

Sometimes a large corporation will offer a large amount of notes directly to financial institutions. These institutions can include insurance companies such as TIAA and/or state pension funds such as New York State Teachers or California State Pension System. On very large issues, ten or more financial institutions may participate in the purchase.

Both the buyer (lender) and the seller (borrower) may have advantages in direct placements. The large borrower will have much lower issue costs because it does not have to run the gauntlet of federal regulations and because the issue can get to the market much more quickly. The lender may receive a slightly higher than market rate and a very desirable investment. Smaller creditworthy borrowers often find the administrative and legal problems more burdensome than larger borrowers that come to the market regularly. In the case of a smaller borrower, the lender may be able to bargain for something of future, potential value such as warrants (rights) to buy some of the issuer's stock in a future or a convertible security. A convertible security is one that can be converted into common stock at some future date.

Several examples of loans made by TIAA are as follows:

	ASSET VALUE
Coca-Cola Bottling Co. of NY, Inc. Senior Notes (Private Placement)	$40,000,000
Detroit Edison Co. General and Refunding Mortgage Bonds (Public Offering)	$86,900,000
Brocker Manufacturing, Inc., Sr. Subordinated Notes (Private Placement). With this loan TIAA received shares of Class B and Class A Common Stocks which as yet are shown to have no market value.	$13,200,000
Data Documents Senior Subordinated Notes with Warrants (Private Placement). With this loan TIAA exercised warrants for 6,408 shares of cumulative, redeemable preferred stock with a market value of $511,768 and exercised warrants for 61,000 shares of 10.0% convertible preferred stock with a market value of $6,100,000.	$29,374,000

A note is simply a one-name paper; in that sense, it is similar to the note an individual signs when getting a personal loan at a bank. A senior note is one that will be paid before other notes of the same class or series. A subordinated note will be paid only after all other notes of the same class or series. Preferred stock are stocks whose dividends must be paid before any dividends on common stock of the company can be paid. A preferred stock is cumulative when any dividends that have not been paid in the past on that stock must be paid before any dividends on the corporation's common stock can be paid. A preferred stock is convertible when it can be exchanged for common stock on specified terms at the will of the holder. Preferred redeemable stock may be redeemed at the request of the holder if the agreement is written that way.

The public offerings and direct placement held by TIAA at the end of 1994 are summarized as follows:

	$ Billions	%	Gross Yield
Public Issues	25.4	57.9%	9.00%
Direct Placements	18.4	42.1	9.2
	$43.8	100.0%	

Sweetners. Sweetner is the term given to rights, warrants and other securities of value or potential value received as part of a private placement loan. Most of the 22 common stocks held by TIAA at the end of 1992 had such origins. Seven of the 22 were listed in the Investment Report at zero value. Fifteen preferred stocks were held. The 22 common stocks and the 15 preferred stocks were valued at $27.7 million and $135.5 million respectively in the 1994 Investment Report.

One can infer that all of these securities were obtained as equity participations because TIAA does not buy equity securities alone. Twelve of these 37 stocks were carried at zero market value.

Common and preferred stocks are shown at market value when there is a market. A nonpublic stock, that is, a stock for which there was no known public market, may be shown at a positive value if the TIAA analyst determines that it has a positive value. When stocks obtained through equity participations have a positive value, they are typically not held for more than a few years.

All of these common and preferred stocks had a total market value of about 0.2 of a percent of the TIAA's total assets.

Bond Ratings. Quality ratings on the individual, publicly traded bonds held by TIAA and other financial institutions can be found in the publications of such established financial ratings services as Moody's and Standard & Poor's.[6] Ratings can be purchased for private placements, but most of the large financial institutions are quite capable of evaluating the credit quality of companies whose securities they purchase and hold. The four highest quality grades of corporate bonds are deemed to be of investment grade. These grades are designated (in Moody's symbols) Aaa, Aa, A and Baa. Bonds below investment grade are popularly called "junk bonds." Upon analysis, however, many of the best "junk" bonds have only modest default risk, and may pay interest rates that more than offset the higher risk. During the late 1980s and the early 1990s, junk bond portfolios performed exceedingly well in a climate of falling interest rates.

MORTGAGES—COMMERCIAL AND REAL ESTATE
At the end of 1994, $21.0 billion or 27.5 percent of TIAA's assets were in mortgage loans. That percentage was down from 30.2 in 1993. The industry average for 1992 was 19.4 percent. About two-thirds of TIAA's loans were made for office buildings and shopping

---

[6]For an introductory discussion of the criteria for bond ratings, see Robert M. Soldofsky and Garnet Olive, Financial Management, Cincinnati, Ohio, Southwestern Publishing Company, 1974, pp. 74-80.

centers. Although these loans were of undoubtedly high quality when they were made, 5.2 percent of the values were reported to be below investment grade by the end of 1994. The extent to which the values of some of these mortgages were written down is not given in the TIAA's Investment Report. For the nation the vacancy rate on downtown office space hit a new high of 19.9 percent at the end of the first quarter, 1993 and the suburban office vacancy rate remains just over 20 percent.[7]

Realized loss, or losses that occur upon sale of mortgages and real estate, are revealed in the TIAA Audited Financial Statements. These losses and the corresponding Asset Valuation Reserves were as follows:

| Asset | Losses (in millions) | | | AVR[a] |
	1994	1993	1992	12/31/93
Mortgages	103.8	137.3	$122.7	417.7
Real Estate	24.6	(5.9)[b]	10.7	397.4

[a] Asset Valuation Reserve
[b] Gain

The 1993 loss on mortgages was 0.7 percent and the gain on real estate was 0.2 percent of their respective 1993 asset values.

The gross returns on the three major classifications of TIAA's assets were as follows:

Asset	1994	1993	1992	1991
Securities	9.05%	9.30%	10.21%	10.45%
Mortgages	8.34	9.21	9.44	9.82
Real Estate	5.36	4.20	4.12	5.00

If the financial markets worked perfectly and if TIAA were all wise, the net yields on all these asset classes would be the same when adjusted for risk. However, net yields on these classifications are not provided. Losses on mortgages and real estate were as shown above and administrative costs differ. Gains on securities are sometimes realized through price appreciation and through the sweetners obtained through transactions. The 1992 and 1993 gains from stock were $20.8 million and -$8.1 million, respectively.

About 42.5 percent of TIAA's mortgages are "participating," that is, TIAA has the right to receive additional income over the mortgages' life under specified conditions. Such terms could raise mortgage returns before expiration. Generally, such mortgages are initially

---

[7]Jim Carleton, "Downtown Vacancy Rate Hits a Six-Year High," Wall Street Journal, April 20, 1993, p. A2.

written for 30 years but can be shortened to 17 years when specified terms are met. Some inflation protection is built into these long-term mortgages.

Even though direct real estate ownership has the lowest return, it also carries the greatest chance of capital gains.

REAL ESTATE

TIAA had $7.1 billion or 9.7 percent of its assets in directly owned real estate at the end of 1994 as compared with 10.7 for 1993. In 1992 that percentage was 10.0 percent as compared with the industry average of 2.6 percent for that year. The reasons stated are that, in a period of inflation, real estate prices will increase and that most of the company's obligations relate to its very long-term pensions. It can be patient.

At the end of 1994, 12.1 percent of TIAA's real estate had been foreclosed or was in the process of being foreclosed because payments were 90 days or more overdue. In 1991, 1992, and 1993, about $1 billion in property was foreclosed. The 1994 Supplement reports that some $780 million of these foreclosed properties, which are now managed directly, have been reclassified and are providing positive income. In 1994, $300 million in real estate was sold as compared with new foreclosures of $244 million.

The 5.4 percent return on real estate is disappointing but it has risen from its 1992 low of 4.1 percent. TIAA continues to decrease its percentage of real estate holdings.

TIAA owns or has an equity participation in more than 500 pieces of prime property. In 1993 it had a realized real estate loss of $24.6 million which was about 0.14 percent of its real estate assets. Nevertheless, it has come under adverse criticism in the press.

In 1994 TIAA decreased its unrealized losses on real estate to $37.1 million from its 1993 figure of $68.0 million. TIAA has invested more than $639 million in the Mall of America, an enormous shopping center in the Minneapolis-St. Paul, Minnesota area. TIAA has more than $400 million invested in the Seven World Trade Center. It is to receive a percentage of the building's profit, but doubt exists about the building's ability to generate a profit. Probably the value of the investment is less than its cost. TIAA was carrying it as a performing loan in 1992. TIAA declined to tell a Wall Street Journal reporter whether it had established any reserve for possible losses on this property.[8]

Real estate problems plagued other insurance companies such as Travelers Insurance and Mutual of New York. Rating agencies have been criticized for not downgrading such insurers sooner. The agencies defend themselves, but others say that when such companies' ratings are downgraded, the insurers have more difficulty in keeping policyholders.

Losses on large real estate loans continue to hamper large commercial banks as well. Chase Manhattan Corporation, the nation's sixth largest bank, is taking a $2 billion write-down on its real estate loans. The amount charged against its equity base was so large that the bank will have to sell $750 million in common stock to maintain its required capital-to-loan position. First Chicago and Bank America have also recently written down and sold troubled

---

[8]Neil Barsky and Susan Pulliam, "Hidden Risks—Life Insurance Loans on Real Estate Cause Ever-Rising Worries," Wall Street Journal, January 31, 1992, p. A1.

property loans recently after they foreclosed. Chase hopes to get as much as 40 cents on the dollar when it sells some of its foreclosed property. Its spokesman said that liquidity is a problem in the real estate markets. Many other large banks took large charges against earnings in the 1980s to get their problems behind them.[9] One can only hope for the best outcome as far as TIAA's real estate mortgage loans and direct ownership of property are concerned. A substantial part of benefits of present and future retirees depends upon the degree of success of TIAA's policy.

CASH FLOW

Cash flow basically refers to cash in and cash out. The complexities of huge, modern enterprises, whether they are private profit-seeking businesses (such as mutual life insurance companies), quasi-governmental, or governmental organizations, makes calculating cash in and cash out a very difficult process. If the necessary information is not provided, an outsider can make only a crude guess. However, even such a guess may be adequate for many purposes.

The ability of a business to pay its obligations as they come due is the necessary condition for remaining solvent. Cash-flow projections are essential also. Earning an adequate rate of return, regardless of when cash is received and disbursed, is the condition for being economically viable. A less than adequate rate of return—at least over a period of the business cycle—is a strong indication that the economy would be better off without that activity. A strong cash flow will help a business survive even during years when it shows annual losses in accounting terms. TIAA could let its investments be gradually paid off, use the cash received from the payment of those loans, and continue to meet its obligations—mostly pension payments—for a very long time.

TIAA's Statement of Cash Flows for its 1992, 1993 and 1994 activities is given in its Audited Financial Statements, a part of which is summarized in Table 4.2. Essentially, its operating activities provided a positive cash flow of $5.7 billion, $5.8 billion and $5.7 billion in 1992, 1993, and 1994 respectively. TIAA has a very strong cash flow position.

Cash is received from investment activities. These inflows come primarily from sales and redemptions of bonds, repayments of mortgages, and sales of real estate. Cash is disbursed for these same types of assets in order to maintain the asset portfolio and to invest the net cash received from operations. These activities are summarized in a few lines.

---

[9]Steven Lipin, Chase Manhattan Writes Down Chunk of Bad Assets, Plans Big Stock Sale. Wall Street Journal, April 26, 1993, p. A2.

| | 1994 | 1993 | 1992 |
		($ billions)	
Cash from Operations	$ 5.7	$ 5.8	$ 5.7
Cash Received from Investment			
Operations	7.3	9.2	6.5
TOTAL	$ 13.0	$ 15.0	$ 12.2
Cash Paid for New Investments	14.1	14.5	12.3
Increase (Decrease) in Cash Balance	$ (1.1)	$ (0.5)	$ (0.1)

The ratio of TIAA's cash inflows from operations to its policy benefits as calculated from Table 4.2 was 4.8 in 1992, 3.8 in 1993, and 3.7 in 1994. If Investments are added to the inflows, the cash inflow to policy benefits ratio rises to 8.3 for 1992, 7.8 for 1993 and 6.9 for 1994.

TIAA's high and rising cash inflow is based upon the loyalty of its participants, the increasing number of participating institutions, and higher payments from its participants. The very long-term nature and predictability of its obligations makes it highly unlikely that at any time within the foreseeable future—perhaps decades—TIAA will have trouble meeting its obligations.

As long as the structure of higher education and the number of nonprofit organizations such as the Association of University Professors that use TIAA remains essentially the same, as long as the income tax laws stay much as they are, and as long as competitors make no drastic inroads into TIAA's dominant market share, present and prospective annuitants can feel very safe about their continuing income.

The rapid shifting of accounts and funds among companies can be devastating for any insurance company. The problems of Executive Life, which surfaced in April 1991, were related to several factors. The company promised above market rates of return on guaranteed investment contracts (GICs) and attracted clients who could be moved by such a promise. When the company could not keep paying such high rates, these clients began to move their funds elsewhere. The loss of clients occurred at a time when bond and other asset prices were falling. When Executive Life had to liquidate assets to meet its cash-outflow requirements for the running policyholders, the company began to collapse with increasing rapidity. Finally, insurance commissioners called a halt, and the company was put in bankruptcy.

Many people still remember the devastating case of Baldwin-United, which was taken over by Metropolitan Life the mid-1980s. When Baldwin-United became bankrupt in September 1983, tremors shook the entire insurance industry. This very rapidly growing company had large insurance subsidiaries. The claims against the company were more than $33 billion; it was the fifth largest bankruptcy in the United States up to that date. In 1986 Baldwin-

United's 165,000 single-premium, tax-deferred policyholders received less than 10 cents on the dollars they had invested.

These two massive failures, numerous smaller ones, and numerous near failures have badly tarnished the life insurance industry's image. Policyholders are fearful about whether the next failure will be that of a company in which they have a large investment.

The worst that may happen to TIAA's present and prospective annuitants is, in my opinion, lower and declining benefits as interest rates fall, and as losses are absorbed on junk bonds, mortgages, and real estate. For individual annuitants, from 1990 through 1994 TIAA benefits dropped over 10 percent. These problem investments will be worked out of the system over the coming years. Most life insurance companies facing these same problems will experience a comparable future. A great advantage of TIAA is its stable and loyal body of policy holders. The best that may happen is that the 10 percent of assets in real estate will help protect participants and annuitants in the event a serious future inflation.

CONCLUSIONS

TIAA's ability to meet its payment obligation appears remarkably good into the relevant future. Some people now in the system will be drawing benefits well into the middle of the twenty-first century. TIAA's financial policies and clientele are such that the company will continue to be outstandingly successful. Its return on investment is and remains among the very highest in the industry.

The technique of analysis used here should be useful for any life insurance company about which you are concerned.

TABLE 4.1

TIAA'S ASSETS AS OF DECEMBER 31, 1994

ASSETS	$ MILLIONS	IN PERCENT	Industry Average 1992[a]
Bonds	$ 43,779	59.7 %	61.4 %
Stocks (Common and Preferred)	163	0.2	5.0
Mortgages	20,217	27.5	19.4
Real Estate	7,075	9.7	2.6
Other Long-Term Investments	384	0.6	
Accrued Investment Income	1,730	2.3	11.6 [b]
	$ 73,348	100.00 %	100.00 %

[a] SOURCE: Greg Steinmetz, "Equitable Feels Pressures of A Newly Public Concern," Wall Street Journal, Sept. 23, 1992. His industry averages were provided by the American Council of Life Insurance.

[b] Includes 4.9 percent in policy loans.

TABLE 4.2

TIAA'S ASSETS AS OF DECEMBER 31, 1994

	1994	1993 ($ billions)	1992
CASH INFLOWS			
Premiums Received	$ 2.9	$ 2.8	$ 2.5
Transfer from CREF (net)	.2	.3	.5
Dividends Added to Annuities	1.8	2.0	2.0
Investments	5.4	5.2	5.0
TOTAL	$ 10.3	$ 10.3	$ 10.0
CASH OUTFLOWS			
Policy Benefits	1.5	1.3	1.2
Dividends	2.8	2.9	2.9
Operating Expenses and Income Tax[a]	.2	.2	.2
TOTAL	4.5	$ 4.4	$ 4.3
NET CASH INFLOW	$ 5.8	$ 5.9	$ 5.7

[a]Operating Expenses in 1992, 1993, and 1994 were respectively $176.5 million, $192.1 million and $214.0 million.

SOURCE: Teachers Insurance and Annuity Association of America, Audited Financial Statements, December 31, 1994.

CHAPTER 5

CREF AND COMMON STOCKS

INTRODUCTION

- When, why and how did CREF come into existence?

- What two innovations were born with CREF?

- How are losses treated by CREF? TIAA?

- What should you know about the safety, liquidity and income of the CREF funds?

- How well have TIAA and CREF benefits performed for retirees? Have their benefits kept up with the cost of living?

- How well have CREF-Equities performed compared with (1) stock-price indices and (2) stock mutual funds?

- When and why did CREF-Equities adopt the Sharpe-Markowitz Portfolio Management Technique?

- What are the comparative returns and risks of CREF-Equities and TIAA?

- What are the five factors used in traditional security analysis?

- How are the differences of risk and return from CREF and TIAA evaluated?

The College Retirement Equities Fund (CREF) started operations July 1, 1952. The basic idea for the variable annuity that became CREF erupted in Bill Greenough's mind late in 1949. By that time this recent Harvard Ph.D. in Economics had been with TIAA for eight years. He sharpened the idea by talks with numerous academics, many of whom were on the TIAA Board of Trustees.[1] In 1952 the TIAA pension plans were being used by 613 organizations. Initially 334 organizations permitted CREF's use by their employees. After nine months of operations, CREF's assets reached $1.8 million. Several background points are necessary to understand how radical an idea CREF was when it was founded, and how well and creatively the basic questions were solved.

---

[1]For a detailed history of the development of the idea and its implementation, see William C. Greenough, It's My Retirement Money-Take Good Care of It, The TIAA-CREF Story, Homewood, IL. Irwin. 1990, pp. 77-128. This book is especially fascinating to me because I know many of the academics to whom Greenough referred. I have a signed copy of Greenough's 1951 privately prepared research report, A New Approach to Retirement Income. The report included a study of how well a fixed-dollar fund and a common stock fund would have performed from 1900 to 1951. One of the many tables shows that for the 21-year period, 1930-1950, a 50-50 fund would have kept the holder virtually even with the cost of living. The holder of a fixed-income fund would have fallen about 47 percent behind the cost of living and the holder of a common stock fund would have beaten the cost of living by about 41 percent.

CREF

In 1950 insurance companies were not authorized by state regulations to hold more than token amounts of common stock. After the insurance scandals at the turn of the century (New York State's 1906 Armstrong Investigations of the industry), the Great Depression, which started in 1929, confirmed the general view that common stocks were too risky for life insurance companies to hold. The Dow Jones Industrial Average (DJIA) dropped from 381 on September 3, 1929, to 41 on March 8, 1932, for a loss of almost 90 percent. By May 1946, the DJIA had recovered to 213 and after the slump in 1947, the Great Bull Market of the 1950s started.

In the fall of 1949 when Greenough first thought about an annuity tied to stocks, the DJIA was at about 180, and by the summer of 1952 it was about 270, a rise of 50 percent. Greenough's goal was to invent an annuity product that could help protect people's income from the ravages of inflation. There had been bursts of inflation after World Wars I and II.

After World War II pension plans burgeoned and much of the pension-fund administration business was acquired by investment bankers and bank trust departments which were not restricted in their investment policy by insurance company law. A struggle of billion-dollar proportions was taking place between the insurance companies on the one hand and the investment banks and commercial banks on the other hand. Led by the State of New York, eventually laws were changed to allow insurance companies to increase their stock holdings, and other accommodations were worked out to help the insurance companies in their struggle to win a part of the pension business.[2]

CREF: AN INNOVATION

Two of the unique, successful innovations were the variable annuity based upon stock prices and the establishment of CREF as a separate organization. The variable annuity required that life expectancy and the value of a life-expectancy unit be separated. Life expectancies at retirement were to be calculated on the basis of TIAA's 30 years of experience with its clients. The value of a CREF investment unit would float with stock prices. At retirement, a person would have built up some total number of CREF units in his or her account through regular investments. The price of a unit would vary from one purchase to another depending upon stock prices and the dividends received. The process of working out the unit value in a mutual fund of stocks was well known.

If a person invested $100 when the unit value was $11, he was credited with 9.0909 units. If at the next $100 purchase, the unit price was $11.50 because of stock price changes, he was credited with 8.6956 units, and so forth. The value of his account was simply the number of units owned multiplied by the unit price at the time that the calculation was made.

At the date of retirement, life expectancy for the individual and spouse, if any, is calculated and the number of annuity units to be paid each month and year is determined. For actuarial reasons the price of an annuity is kept separate from those of an accumulation unit.[3]

---

[2]See Robert M. Soldofsky, <u>Common Stock Investing 1900-2000</u>, Ann Arbor, MI: University of Michigan Press, 1971.

[3]An example of how the variable annuity calculation works is given below in Table 11.7.

Mortality experience is very stable from year to year but is not absolutely fixed. Life expectancy can increase or decrease for a particular insurance company's clients. Therefore, a reserve is kept in the event adjustments are needed in any one year. Adjustments in the basis of the longevity calculation were to be made by CREF every five years. Once these rules for calculations had been worked out no further changes had to be made.

The second innovation which has proved to be so powerful was setting up a separate organization for CREF. In that way unit prices could be kept readily without the confusions that might be involved when stock holdings are kept at market value as contrasted with the traditional book-value basis of insurance companies. The increases and decreases in the prices of the stocks held are known at the end of each market day.

TREATMENT OF LOSSES
No need exists for complex valuation rules within the CREF organization or from outside any organization such as the National Association of Insurance Commissioners as in the case of TIAA. No outside, independent, safety and liquidity rating is needed. TIAA and other insurance companies' marked-to-book-value assets face the problem of second guessing asset valuations. Insurance companies have been known to "play games" with asset valuations to prevent clients from understanding their most likely, correct asset values for the management's own purposes—to try to cover up poor investments or to prevent runs away from the company.

Some people who read their personal annual reports on their pension-plan accumulations for TIAA or similar companies may feel secure by noting how their asset values are rising regularly. They may never inquire into the underlying values of these assets. In comparison, the fluctuating values of a CREF or stock account appears to be excessively risky. As shown later, those feelings of relative security and riskiness may not be well founded.

INTERNAL POLICY PROBLEMS
Other policy problems and questions had to be worked out for this innovative variable annuity. Once a person starts drawing upon his (her) CREF accumulation for his (her) pension, how often will the value of the annuity unit be changed? The decision was made to revalue the annuity unit once a year. That simplified the record keeping in pre-computer days and tended to give the annuitant a constant, twelve-month budget. The date of the annual revaluation was set as March 31 to reduce any implications for income taxes that might be involved. The annuitant receives the revised payments starting May 1 each year. Originally, an individual was not allowed to allocate more than 50 percent of his (her) monthly investment to CREF. After the initial success of CREF, that allocation limit was raised to 75 percent at the beginning of 1967 and to 100 percent on July 1, 1971.

From the beginning the problem of transfers from TIAA to CREF and from CREF to TIAA were raised. Transfers from TIAA to CREF were impractical because of the virtual impossibility of getting a market price for the amount to be shifted from TIAA to CREF. Shifts from CREF to TIAA might devastate the new organization if the stock market crashed and participants wanted to switch out of stocks when prices were low and questions of liquidity existed. Therefore, transfers were permitted only for those over 60 years of age.

Few participants made such transfers from CREF. The age limit was dropped to 55 and then eliminated entirely in 1984. In 1973 Supplementary Retirement Annuity contracts were introduced for both TIAA and CREF to assist in providing for tax-deferred, personal savings. These supplementary contracts can be cashed out at any time after age 59½ without any income tax penalties.

PUBLIC POLICY PROBLEMS
Early in 1951, the superintendent of the New York Insurance Department clearly indicated that he would not support a variable annuity plan. What New York State did would set the response around the United States because it is probably the leading state for insurance regulation. TIAA decided to seek a charter as a Special Corporation under New York law. Political support was mustered, grudging acquiescence of the Insurance Superintendent was obtained after some changes were made in the proposal, and the College Retirement Equities Fund was incorporated March 18, 1952, as a special corporation.

Meanwhile, the tax status of this unique, variable annuity pension plan had to be worked out with the Internal Revenue Service. Preliminary rulings of the IRS were unfavorable. TIAA went to the Senate Finance Committee for a Hearing on its proposal. Eventually, the IRS relented after encountering Congressional and other political pressure, and the variable annuity pension income was to be treated like any other pension income. Only gains above the original contribution are now taxed, and that tax is at the ordinary income tax rate.

A serious question arose as to whether or not CREF would have to register with the Securities and Exchange Commission.[4] Registration would result in more regulations and expense.

That question was not finally resolved until 1959 by the U.S. Supreme Court in the case of VALIC (Variable Life Insurance Company), another nonprofit company offering variable annuities to public employees and to nonprofit organizations such as colleges and universities. VALIC was started in Washington, D.C. where it did not have to win approval from a state insurance commission before beginning operations.

SUBSEQUENT GROWTH
By the end of 1988 CREF had grown to $30.2 billion, and TIAA was $38.6 billion. The worlds of financial theory and practice had grown and proliferated beyond what anyone could possibly have imagined 36 years earlier. Competition was barking at TIAA-CREF's heels, and academic gadflies were remarkably annoying. CREF undertook to diversify and expand the funds made available to its participants starting April 1, 1988. These funds were started under the CREF corporate structure because they were all, in effect, to be marked-to-market and were transferable among themselves. The marked-to-book valuation of TIAA was still seen as a obstacle to the transfer from itself to CREF. After the initial success of CREF, a few corporate pension funds and insurance companies began variable annuities of their own. By 1967, 27 states approved variable annuities and they were offered by 125 life insurance companies by 1984.

---

[4]CREF finally registered with the SEC in 1988 after a long struggle. The CREF Money Market fund went into operation April 1, 1988.

NEW CREF ACCOUNTS

CREF's Money Market account was started April 1, 1988, after at least six years of delay. The uses of a money market fund are discussed at the end of Chapter 6. On March 1, 1990, both the Marketable Bond Fund and the Social Choice Fund were opened, and on March 1, 1992, the Global Equities Fund was opened. On July 1, 1994, CREF opened two more accounts: the CREF Equity Index Account and the CREF Growth Account. The former is designed to perform like the U.S. equity markets in general, and the latter seeks stocks that have outstanding growth potential. The absolute and relative sizes of the funds are shown in Table 5.1. By the end of 1992 American investors owned $197.1 billion of foreign stock out of a total world value estimated at almost $11 trillion; foreign stock holdings have been increasing at 21 percent per year for the last five years. CREF-Equities or CREF-Stock, as the original CREF is now called, was renamed to distinguish it from the other CREF-sponsored accounts.

Competition and new financial products are the main causes of the widened menu of available funds. Money market funds began in 1975. New funds will likely continue to be established within the CREF family of funds now that the organization has had some experience in setting up such funds. Their competitors have many more individual funds than does TIAA-CREF.

SAFETY, LIQUIDITY AND INCOME OF CREF-EQUITIES

This section concentrates on CREF-Equities for several reasons:

- It is overwhelmingly the largest and the oldest of the CREF family of funds.

- The Money Market Fund has a special purpose portfolio as described in the Money Market Fund subsection of Chapter 6.

- The relative size of the Bond Market account will probably grow, but the account is not at this time available for a pension annuity. It is likely to be a choice that is inferior to TIAA itself as explained in the Return and Risk subsection of Chapter 3 and in the Marketable Bonds subsection of Chapter 6, which discusses reasons that the market prices of bonds fluctuate. The relationship of bond prices, interest rates, and the term to maturity are discussed in a subsection by that name in Chapter 8.

- The Social Choice account is a balanced fund—that is, it holds both marketable stocks and bonds—so that the discussion of what underlies the values of these securities applies to the securities held in this new account. The social-political viewpoint that restricts the companies whose securities the Social Choice Fund may hold are discussed in the Social Choice Fund subsection of Chapter 6.

- The Global Equities account was opened April 1, 1992. The experience with and the modest size of this fund is so little that no special comments will be made about it here. The fund will hold equity securities so what is said about the principles underlying the value of equities applies almost completely to these securities. Insofar as foreign securities are held, the element of foreign-exchange risk is added. The return-risk performance of foreign equities in general was described in the subsection by that name in Chapter 3.

The organization of the discussion of the safety, liquidity and income of the life insurance part of TIAA-CREF is roughly parallel to the discussion of the equity part, CREF. You are either an actual or potential CREF participant as long as you are a TIAA participant.

WHAT SHOULD YOU KNOW?

What do you need to know about CREF to understand the basis of its safety, liquidity, and income?

- What underlies the values of an individual common stock and the entire stock market?

- Where do the values come from that result in the irregularly rising average stock prices as shown in the well known market averages such as the Dow Jones Industrial Average (DJIA)?

- How are stock losses dealt with? Does anything like TIAA's contingency reserve exist for CREF?

- How expensive is it to maintain a stock portfolio? How do the administrative costs of TIAA and CREF compare per dollar of assets?

- How do I know that stocks can be sold—liquidated—by CREF when I and others need to get our money out in the form of pension benefits?

CREF EQUITIES AND/OR TIAA IN RETIREMENT

Reporting in the popular press, financial press, and in special studies indicates a strong aversion to common stocks by a substantial portion of the population. A small sample survey of new employees at the University of Iowa (see Chapter 6) gives the same sort of result. These results are confirmed by questions asked of me at seminars I offer and in conversations with clients. I do not want to overstate the case, however. An appreciable proportion of TIAA-CREF participants do enter retirement with an ample investment in CREF. In 1992 annuity payments from TIAA and CREF Equities were $790.0 and $606.6 million respectively. In 1994 the annuities from all CREF accounts were $789.2 million; the annuities from CREF-Equities were 97.7 percent of this total. The substantial number of people who convert most or all of their CREF to TIAA at the point of retirement further suggests a fear of fluctuations in retirement benefits if they maintain their CREF investment.

Intellectual arguments and empirical demonstrations are usually inadequate to overcome emotional bias. However, the data exhibited in Figures 5.1 and 5.2 on the post-retirement performance of TIAA and CREF for the periods starting in 1972 and 1982 should warn participants to examine their preconceived positions carefully and to make the effort to understand the factual, practical, and intellectual material set forth. The materials in this chapter and the prior chapter are concerned with the operations, investments, and safety of TIAA and CREF. Subsequent chapters deal with the underlying principles of finance and investments that the intelligent person may wish to master sufficiently to make informed decisions.

An alternative to making your own informed decisions is making those decisions on the basis of hearsay, the equally uninformed positions of friends, or the biased and prejudiced opinions of professional persons in various positions of authority. I have met staff benefit advisors, lawyers, bankers, accountants, tax advisors, ministers and physicians who personally believe that common stocks are much too risky for ordinary people to hold. Some TIAA-CREF participants profess such a disinterest in money and income that their decisions are made by default by whomever happens to be around.

Figures 5.1 and 5.2 show the post-retirement income that a person would have received each month from TIAA and from CREF if he or she retired in 1972 or in 1982. Monthly payments start at $1,000 per month from each fund. A separate line tracks the increased cost of living from the same starting dates. TIAA and CREF benefits are adjusted annually based upon the performance of their respective asset portfolios.

CREF'S ASSETS AND PORTFOLIO MANAGEMENT
Though CREF's assets are all in common stocks for all practical purposes, it maintains ample cash balances for operating and liquidity purposes.

WORKING CASH
Some time must pass before new inflows of cash can be invested in stocks, and cash is always being received from dividends and the sales of securities. Cash is held for normal operating expenses such as salaries, and benefits must be paid to annuitants. Working cash balances must be kept to coordinate these and other activities. Most such cash is kept in interest-earning securities and bank balances.

CREF's year-end assets reached $1.5 billion in 1970, $11.4 billion in 1981, and were $62.2 billion by the end of 1994. CREF's assets have grown approximately 16 percent per year for the past 25 years. That exceedingly rapid growth may be attributed to three major factors: increases in stock prices, increases in investments from continuing participants, and the growth of the number of participants as the number of organizations using TIAA-CREF continues to grow. That number is now just over 5,500; it is up about 800 or almost 20 percent from ten years ago.

CREF-Equities holds common stock in about 1,800 U.S. companies and about 840 foreign companies. The 1993 year-end value of its U.S. stocks and foreign stocks were $42.3 billion and $10.6 billion respectively. Although the dollar values involved are astounding, keep in mind that the U.S. domestic traded equities are estimated at $4.5 trillion. The world market for equities is about $10.7 trillion.

CREF acting alone is unlikely to affect stock prices in general. CREF and most other large financial institutions limit their holdings of any one common stock to 5 percent or less of its total market value. Individual mutual funds are limited to holding 5 percent of the common stock of any one company by the Investment Company Act of 1939.

CREF's holdings are so large and so broadly diversified that the company has learned that it cannot hope to earn much above the market return counting both dividends and price appreciation. Up to 1971 CREF relied primarily upon the analysis of individual securities for stock selection, but it was often unable to match the performance of the Standard & Poor's 500 stock average, a very highly regarded gauge of general market performance. It was being criticized strongly for sub-market performance.

CREF PORTFOLIO MANAGEMENT AND NOBEL LAUREATES IN ECONOMICS

In 1971 Professor Milton Friedman, University of Chicago and CREF board member from 1964 to 1968, made the suggestion, according to William Greenough, that CREF give up security analysis and just buy a cross section of stocks represented in the S&P index. Friedman was aware of the revolutionary changes going on in portfolio theory. Friedman became a Nobel Laureate in Economics in 1976.

James Tobin of Yale, who became a Nobel Laureate in Economics in 1981, was a TIAA board member for the 1968-1972 term. He himself made contributions to the modern portfolio, and he was a mentor of Harry Markowitz, the man whose work is the basis of modern portfolio theory. Paul A. Samuelson, who was on the CREF board from 1974 to 1985, became a Nobel Laureate in 1970. He also made contributions to the development of portfolio. Perhaps most importantly, William F. Sharpe was on the CREF board from 1975-83. Sharpe was doing some of his best work in portfolio theory as applied to common stocks during these years. He too was awarded a Nobel Laureate in Economics in 1990.

In 1977 CREF implemented a part of the Sharpe-Markowitz capital asset pricing model for most of its stock portfolio and reduced its administrative costs from .41 to .31 percent per $100 of assets.[5] These expenses include the costs of its Advisory Services.

STOCK INDEXING AND PORTFOLIO MANAGEMENT

In 1981 CREF adopted a stock-index model for about 80 percent of its domestic stock holdings. Users of such plans will have stock portfolios that perform almost exactly the same as the stock-market average they pick as their model. Studies have shown that index funds will perform better than about two-thirds of all equity funds in any one given year. Equity funds that rely on stock selection rarely have the best performance as many as two or three successive years. CREF's performance, when compared with widely known stock averages and largest mutual funds, is excellent, as shown in Tables 5.2 and 5.3.[6]

Comparative Performances. CREF compared its performance with the S&P 500 index from 1981 through 1991. In 1992 it changed to the Russell 3000 index because it represents a much broader picture of stock performance.

In 1973 CREF started to purchase foreign stocks. It set a target of 10 percent for foreign securities in 1978 and has since raised that to 15 percent. Experience in investing in foreign stocks was one of the things that encouraged it to start a global fund in April, 1992.

---

[5]For a delightful review of the developments that comprise capital market theory, see Bernstein, P. L., Capital Ideas. New York: Free Press, 1992. Peter Bernstein was a member of the CREF Board also from 1977 to 1988. This book may be heavy going in parts for some people, but is well worth the effort. The first part of the book reviews and evaluates traditional security analysis also.

[6]Vanguard, one of the largest mutual fund companies, started an index fund in 1976. Most other large mutual fund companies did not start index funds until 1990. Vanguard's expense ratio on its Index Trust 500 Portfolio is 0.20 percent. CREF-Equities ratio is 0.32 percent, but it includes the costs of running an annuity program and the costs of related research programs.

Table 5.2 shows the performance of various stock market indexes and averages. CREF's performance is generally below both the S&P 500 and the Russell 3000. However, the performance of the indexes does not include any administrative costs.

Table 5.3 compares CREF's performance with those of the nation's five largest stock mutual funds and the five best performing stock mutual funds based upon their most recent ten-year history. Large size is generally thought to be a handicap in seeking higher performance as larger funds have less flexible portfolios; they must consider the impact on the day-to-day market of any large trades they make. Nevertheless, two or three of the larger funds have outperformed CREF over the past five and ten years. Given that there are almost 2000 stock funds, CREF's record is excellent—especially for consistency. The Vanguard 500 Index fund's performance is slightly better than CREF's. Two differences between CREF-Equities and Vanguard's 500 Index should be noted: first, CREF has about 15 percent of its market value in foreign stocks and Vanguard has none; second, CREF indexes only about 80 percent of its domestic portfolio.

CREF'S SAFETY, LIQUIDITY AND BENEFIT PAYMENTS

HOW SAFE IS CREF?
The question could be rephrased to ask, "How safe is CREF relative to what?" And over what time horizon? Table 3.7 included the following for CREF-Equities and TIAA for their 1974-1993 return and risk performance:

	CREF-EQUITIES	TIAA
Total Return	13.34 %	9.30 %
Standard Deviation	16.10	1.90
Relative Riskiness*	1.20	.24

*Standard deviation divided by the mean. (See Table 3.7 and the Return
-Risk Performance subsection of Chapter 3.)

Obviously, on a year-by-year basis, CREF-Equities is riskier, but does the difference in return have more importance than the difference in risk for the annuitant? Sum of $1 growing at 9.30% and 13.34% for 20 years will grow to $5.92 and to $12.37 respectively. CREF's much higher rate of return overwhelms TIAA's lower standard deviation for the long-run investor.

CREF AND TIAA BENEFITS COMPARED
The actual benefits for a CREF and a TIAA hypothetical annuitant are shown in Table 5.4.[7] The surprising result for TIAA follows from its marked-to-book procedure and the way in which each new year's investment in your TIAA account is handled. For a discussion of TIAA's "vintage-year" procedure, see the section by that name in Chapter 10. The decline in

---

[7]As a matter of fact, increases (changes) go into effect on May 1 of each year for CREF and on January 1 for TIAA.

TIAA benefits starting with 1990 reflects the impact of declining interest rates working their way through the TIAA accounting system. Some parts of the decline in TIAA benefits represent charges for realized and anticipated declines (losses) in the market value of bonds, mortgages, and real estate.

Even though TIAA is shown in statistical terms as being relatively much less risky than CREF, TIAA's payments are not fixed. They rise and fall slowly to reflect changing interest rates and realized and unrealized losses. The changes in the CREF variable annuity payments reflect the performance of the CREF portfolio in the prior year. The percentage changes for CREF in Table 5.4 will not quite correspond with those implied in Table 3.6 because those in 3.6 are based on annual changes through December 31, while those in Table 5.4 are based on changes for the year ending March 31.

INCOME AND LIQUIDITY
As CREF's price rises and dividends are received, the price of a CREF unit rises. When stocks are sold, income is realized. (Of course, if a stock's price falls and it is sold, a loss is realized.) When stocks continue to be held after their prices rise, those gains are reported as an unrealized gain on investments. Any of those realized gains could be used to pay benefits to annuitants. Furthermore, if it were necessary to do so, stocks could be sold to realize cash to pay benefits. When an insurance company sells stock, it does not pay the income taxes itself. Eventually, beneficiaries pay ordinary income taxes on their gains.

CREF receives cash premiums from participants each year. Some transfers are made also from CREF each year to TIAA as some participants reallocate their accumulations. Furthermore, funds may flow on a net basis from CREF-Equities to the other CREF accounts: Money Market, Marketable Bonds, Social Choice, and—more recently—Global Equities. The net outcome of these transactions for CREF-Equities for 1992, 1993, and 1994 are shown in Table 5.5.

On the basis of these data, CREF does not now have nor is it likely to have notable problems in meeting its benefit payment obligations. In fact, an innovative feature of CREF when it was incorporated was that it was organized in such a way that it could never become bankrupt.

STOCK SELECTION AND PORTFOLIO MANAGEMENT
Insofar as CREF just buys a market basket of stocks to match the S&P 500 average or the Russell 3000 average, only a modest knowledge of security analysis would seem to be necessary. However, numerous changes are made in the stocks included in these averages each year because of such events as mergers, poor performance, and even impending bankruptcy. When poor stock performance is observed or anticipated, it would be folly to keep a given stock in a portfolio rather than replace it with another that might perform better.

About 20 percent of the domestic stock portfolio is still based upon individual selection. Even greater skill and information is needed to pick foreign stocks for the CREF portfolio because foreign security laws about disclosure are different from ours and because accounting rules differ as does the whole organization of each country's financial system. In a portfolio of foreign securities, one must be ever vigilant about changes in exchange rates.

HOW ARE STOCKS PICKED?

Five of the most important considerations in stock selection are introduced at this point. They include:

1. the price/earnings ratio;
2. the dividend yield;
3. earnings dating;
4. earnings growth; and
5. the quality of earnings.

One must be aware of both the past history and prospective performance of a company. The price-to-earnings ratio and the price-to-dividend ratio embody much of the essential information condensed into two ratios.

Price/Earnings Ratio. The stock price is a given from market trading. Earnings are the outcome of all the firm's regular business operations and unusual ones that occur irregularly, such as the sale of property at a gain or a loss. The ratio of price to earnings (P/E), say at 15 to 1, is a conventional way of looking at the approximate rate of return. If the P/E is 15 to 1, the earnings to price is 6.67 percent. Such a rate of return can be compared with interest rates, which are more fundamental. If interest rates are rising and a conventional relationship exists between the P/E or its inverse, the E/P, the E/P would typically rise. For example:

	P/E	E/P	Long-Term Interest Rate
Beginning position	15/1	6.67%	8.50%
Interest rate rises to 9.0% P/E and E/P adjust to	14/1	7.18%	9.00%

Assume nothing else of importance occurred, which is unlikely. As the earnings are assumed to be unchanged in the short-run, the stock price must fall to result in the higher rate of return and lower P/E ratio. (The very short-run may be a week, but not more than three months.)

Dividend Yield. Assume a company is paying dividends that amount to 3.0 percent when the long-term interest rate is 8.5 percent. If the interest rate rises to 9.0 percent, investors will seek a higher dividend rate (yield) to keep their dividend rate roughly in line with the higher interest rate. The dividend per share will not change in the short run. Hence, the price must fall. If the dividend was $1.50 per share and the stock price was $50, the beginning yield was 3 percent. If the dividend yield rises to 3.33 percent in the market, the price must fall to $45 because $1.50 divided by .033 is $45. Of course, these changes usually take place quite slowly on both the interest-rate side and on the stock-market side.

Earnings Dating. Another factor related to earnings is the dating of the earnings. Conventionally, the P/E is based on past or _trailing_ earnings. Theoretically, one should be more concerned with prospective or <u>leading</u> earnings.   These days at least two firms specialize in collecting and publishing the leading earnings estimates prepared by security analysts of brokerage houses, investment banks, mutual firms, commercial banks, and other organizations. As many as 100 leading earnings estimates may be gathered and summarized for popular, individual stocks. Be aware of whether you are looking at trailing earnings, leading earnings, or some combination of the two when you are looking at a stock's earnings or its P/E ratio based on those earnings. P/E ratios and dividend yields are prepared for collections of stocks and are summarized by some average or index such as the S&P 500 or the DJIA 30 stocks. One must be careful to ask about what is used for the dividends or earnings underlying these series.

Earnings Growth. A fourth factor in stock selection is the growth rate of earnings. If earnings growth is expected to be 6 percent per year and the P/E is 15, that P/E is already adjusted by the market for the anticipated growing earnings. If analysts increase that expected growth to 8 or 9 percent, the stock becomes more attractive and its P/E ratio will rise perhaps to 16 or 18. Generally, higher prospective growth rates are associated with higher P/E ratios. P/Es of 30 or more are not rare. The lower the growth rate, the lower the P/E might be.

For the last 20 years the composite earnings for the S&P 500 Index has moved irregularly upward. For the whole period it grew at 5.23 percent. The lowest earnings were $6.42 for 1972 and the highest were about $30.00 for 1994. The P/E and dividend yield were 12.5 times and 2.9 percent at the end of 1994. The ranges for these items are discussed in Chapter 8. No compelling reason exists to believe the <u>growth</u> of earnings and prices will differ much over the coming 20 years.

Quality of Earnings. The final factor is the quality of earnings. The same reported dollar amount of earnings per share may be of better or poorer quality. Better quality earnings usually means that more anticipated or likely costs or expenses are deducted sooner rather than later. Other things being equal, higher quality earnings usually merit a higher price-earnings ratio. Two examples of what makes earnings quality "higher" or "lower" among several dozen possible cases are given.[8]

Machinery and equipment can be depreciated more rapidly or more slowly and still be in compliance with the <u>Internal Revenue Code</u>. Say that a $100,000 machine could be depreciated either over five years or as long as ten years. (Further assume for simplicity that there is no salvage value.) Annual depreciation over five years would be $20,000 per year, while annual depreciation over ten years would be $10,000 per year. Net income would be of better quality if the five-year schedule were used, because costs would be higher and net income would be lower in each of those five years. The firm would tend to recoup its initial

---

[8]Section 2's "Market Place" in <u>Wall Street Journal</u> carries newly released corporate earnings summaries. Reading a few of these summarizes will illustrate the variety and complexity of adjustments to corporate earnings statements.

[9]For a convenient introduction to interest theory and its application to bonds, stocks, and many other types of securities, see James C. Van Horne, <u>Capital Market Rates and Flows</u>, 3rd Ed. Englewood Cliffs, N.J. Prentice Hall, 1990.

investment faster and could reallocate the funds elsewhere when they were recovered. Furthermore, if income before taxes is lower, the income tax bill will also be lower, which is a distinct advantage.

Charges for medical benefits are news. In 1991 the Financial Accounting Standards Board, a non-governmental organization that makes rules for accounting and audits by certified public accounting firms, decreed that starting in 1993 each firm should recognize as costs the probable medical benefits for retirees that would have to be paid in the future. These charges are properly allocated to the years in which the now retired employees or to be retired employees actually were working. Recognizing these charges for current and past service, estimates said, could cost American business as much as $400 billion annually. Most companies are now starting to recognize these costs. More detailed examples are given in the Quality of Earnings section in Chapter 8. Corporate profits will be lower as the promised, future medical liabilities are recognized as expenses, but the quality of earnings will be higher. The process of recognizing and adjusting for quality of earnings is well understood by security analysts and stock pickers.

THE REINVESTMENT PROCESS FOR COMMON STOCKS
The startling results for annuitant's CREF benefits shown in Figures 5.1 and 5.2 and Table 5.4, are largely the result of the income reinvestment process. The results of this process are illustrated by the irregular jumps of the stock averages to new highs every few years. The cyclical low on the DJIA of 1739 on October 19, 1987 just after the October crash was higher than the cyclical, all-time high of 1286 to that date on February 6, 1984. A low of 1087 was made July 24, 1984, before a run up in 1987 pushed the DJIA to a new high of 2722 on August 25, 1987. From that point the DJIA fell almost exactly 1000 points in two months including a 508 point loss on October 19, 1987, the biggest one-day loss ever. During most of 1994 the DJIA was in the 3500-3900 area or up to 1200 points above the 1987 high. The DJIA in 1994 was about 40 percent higher than its highest point just seven years ago. In December 1995 the DJIA pushed through the 5200 level for the first time.

The explanation of periodic new highs for individual stocks and stock averages is the fact that corporations regularly reinvest a part of their earnings in the business at a positive rate of return. The amount reinvested adds additional earnings themselves, and this process continues year after year. The reinvestment process named after two academics, Professors Gordon and Shapiro, who popularized it while they were students at MIT, is discussed and illustrated in the Common Stock Growth Model section in Chapter 8.

PRESENT VALUE, COMPOUND INTEREST AND SECURITY VALUATION
A sum of money to be received in the future has a lower value today than the same amount to be received at that future date. A future sum is discounted from the date it will be received to the present date at a fixed or determinable rate of interest. If the amount to be received is the interest on a U.S. government debt, that debt will be discounted at the lowest or (virtually) riskless rate of interest. If that interest rate is 6 percent, $100 to be received exactly one year from now is worth $94.34 or $100 discounted at .06 is $94.34. As an equation that is: $100 ÷ 1.06 = $94.34. If you have $94.34 today and invest it at 6 percent, it will be worth $100 one year from today.

Two fundamental things tend to increase the interest rate above the riskless rate which is judged to be 3 to 3.5 percent by financial economists. These fundamentals are the anticipated rate of inflation and the degree of assurance that the future payment will be made exactly as anticipated and on time. If the anticipated inflation rate is 3 percent, the riskless rate will be about 6 percent or the riskless rate plus the anticipated inflation rate. If the anticipated inflation rate is 8 percent, as it has been in our recent past, the inflation-adjusted interest rate will be about 11 percent.[9]

The second factor is the degree of assurance that the payment will be made in the amount anticipated and on time. In the case of a U.S. government bond, that assurance is as close to being absolute as anything is in the world of finance. As one looks down the assurance scale from U.S. government bonds to corporate bonds—AAA, AA, A, BAA, and so on down to D—the discount (interest) rate rises. As one looks down the scale to riskier and riskier securities and observes history, the riskier securities do fail more frequently. If the financial markets were perfect, the chances of default would just exactly explain these default-related increases in interest rates.

Preferred stocks clearly can be and are graded for quality just as bonds are graded. Preferred stocks, stocks on which the dividends must be paid before any dividends can be paid on common stock, are often extremely safe investments; that fact is reflected in their relatively low returns.

Common stocks are valued also on the basis of their anticipated dividends and the assurance the market has that those dividends will be paid. Almost all successful corporations whose stocks are traded in the market have rising dividends. Those dividends will rise less or more slowly depending on the company, its industry, the ability of its managers, and so forth. As the income left after paying dividends is reinvested and put to work at a positive rate of return, earnings and dividends will both grow.

As with bonds, these stocks are priced in the market depending upon how high and assured that growth rate is and the assurance that the anticipated rising dividends will occur as anticipated. What the market does in a deeper analysis is to discount these anticipated, rising dividends just as it discounts interest payments in the case of bonds to determine a present value or market price. The less the confidence in the dividend growth rate, the higher the discount rate will be relative to somewhat similar securities.

The process one usually observes in the market place is that of prices being set by trading on the basis of very similar securities. At the more basic level, however, the anticipated cash-flow stream is being discounted.

For a further, modest introduction to compound interest, see the Magical Compound Interest section in Chapter 8.

CONCLUSIONS

CREF, a stand-alone company, brought out the first successful variable annuity in 1952. The company is very safe and highly liquid from the viewpoint of investors and beneficiaries. One of the important differences between TIAA and CREF that is not generally understood is the way in which losses or declines in the value of their respective investments are handled. Losses are provided for in advance as far as possible in TIAA by charges against income, as they are in all life insurance companies. TIAA may sometimes have long-term gains from the sale of real estate. CREF units change in value every day with the prices of the stock it holds. The results of these gains (losses), whether accounted for in TIAA's marked-to-book procedure or CREF's market-to-market procedure, are reflected in the participant's accumulation values and in their retirement benefits. TIAA benefits respond more slowly to market forces than do CREF benefits, but they both do respond.

TIAA's rate of return has been quite high for a life insurance company, and CREF's rate of return has generally been superior to those of most stock mutual funds. The mostly fixed-income securities that TIAA holds are inherently less risky than the stocks CREF holds. However, for the long-term investors the higher return on stocks overwhelms the return on the less risky TIAA portfolio. The result, as shown, is that TIAA benefits have not kept up with the cost of living while CREF benefits about equaled or exceeded the cost of living in the long run. However, these results are not assured in each and every year or even over a period of two or three years. The future patterns of benefits are very likely to be similar to those of the past 40 years.

The five major factors of stock analysis were introduced as was the basic topic of compound interest. These topics are pursued further in Chapters 7 and 8.

TABLE 5.1

**TIAA-CREF FUNDS
AS OF DECEMBER 31**
($ MILLIONS)

ACCOUNT	YEAR		$ as a % of 1994 Total	% of Increase by Fund 1993-94
	1994	1993		
Equities	$ 54,761.1	$ 55,319.3	88.0%	-1.0%
Money Market	2,918.9	2,576.4	4.7	13.3
Bond Market	618.7	619.8	1.0	a
Social Choice	781.8	713.0	1.3	9.6
Global Equitiesa	2,745.1	1,509.0	4.4	81.9
Growth Equities	309.3	-	0.5	b
Equity Index	72.2	-	0.1	b
Totals	$ 62,207.1	60.737.5	100.0	2.0

[a]Decreased by about 0.02 percent.
[b]Not meaningful.

TABLE 5.2

CREF AND THE PERFORMANCE OF STOCK AVERAGES[a]

	AS OF 12/31/94			
Fund (Index)	1 YR	3 YRS	5 YRS	10 YRS
CREF	-1.0%	6.2%	8.2%	14.3%
DJIA	5.0	9.9	10.3	16.2
S&P 500 Average	-1.3	6.3	8.7	14.4
S&P Mid Cap (400) Average	-0.3	-	16.3	13.1
Russell 200 Index (Small Company)	-1.8	11.2	9.7	11.2
Russell 3000 Index	0.2	6.4	10.7	15.3
Wilshire 5000	2.1	11.4	12.2	13.7
Value Line[b] - Timeliness #1				
Class I - With Changes in Rank	-2.6	6.7	11.1	16.3
Class I - Without Changes in Rank	4.6	10.1	14.4	17.6

[a]Dividends have been included even though they are omitted in the Averages as published daily.

[b]An outstanding stock-picking service.

NA=Not Available

SOURCES: TIAA-CREF and various issues of the Wall Street Journal, Barrons, and Business Week.

TABLE 5.3

CREF AND MUTUAL FUND PERFORMANCE
AS OF 12/31/94

	Size (Billions)	1 YR	3 YRS	5 YRS	10 YRS
CREF-EQUITIES	48.3%[a]	1.0%	6.6%	8.2%	14.3%
Five Largest Funds:					
Fidelity-Magellan	36.0	-1.8	9.4	12.0	
Investment Co. of America	19.2	0.2	6.1	8.8	14.2
Washington-Mutual Fund	12.6	-0.8	15.0	8.1	13.9
Vanguard-Windsor	10.9	-0.1	11.6	8.6	
Income Fund of America	10.5	1.2	-2.5	8.0	14.4
Five Best Performing Funds - 10 Yrs:					
20th Century Gift Trust	0.3	13.5	20.7	22.0	25.6
Seligman Communication	0.3	35.3	29.2	24.6	22.7
Fidelity Select, Health	0.2	-10.2	18.5	12.3	12.1
GAM: INTERNATIONAL	0.7	21.4	0.9	18.5	21.5
Invest. Co.: Strategic Health	0.5	0.9	-7.3	14.0	20.6
GROWTH AND INCOME FUNDS*		-0.6	7.0	8.7	12.8
S&P 500 (WITH DIVIDENDS)*		1.3	6.3	8.7	13.8

SOURCES: Wall Street Journal, January 6, 1995 and BUSINESS WEEK, February 14, 1994.

*Expenses, of course, are not considered.

TABLE 5.4

TIAA AND CREF ANNUITY BENEFITS COMPARED

1982-1994

Year	TIAA[a]	CREF[b]	Cost of Living
1982	$1,000	$1,000	100.0
1983	1000	1390	103.2
1984	1000	1509	107.6
1985	1000	1625	111.5
1986	1003	2203	113.6
1987	1003	2709	117.7
1988	1003	2515	122.5
1989	1003	2696	128.4
1990	975	3013	135.4
1991	975	3252	141.4
1992	948	3450	145.3
1993	882	3778	149.7
1994	869	3834	154.2

[a] Assume payment of $1,000 per month in 1982 from each fund for a person who retired late in 1981.

[b] Basic data furnished by TIAA-CREF and rearranged for the purposes of this table.

TABLE 5.5

**CREF-EQUITIES CASH FLOW
($ MILLIONS)**

Inflows:	1994	1993	1992
Investment Income less Expenses	$ 1,128.2	$ 1,073.5	$ 1,025.0
Net Realized and Unrealized Gains (Losses) on Investments	-1,177.6	5,492.9	1,761.8
Premiums Received	2,196.9	2,046.0	1,862.4
Net Transfers to TIAA	-190.6	-220.6	-381.2
Net Transfers Among CREF Accounts	-912.1[a]	-734.2[a]	-2.5
TOTAL	$ 1,411.7	$ 7,657.5	$ 4,265.5
Outflows:			
Benefits Paid and Other Outflows	$ 1,411.7	$ 1,281.1	$ 1,061.6
NET INFLOW	$ -366.9	$ 6,439.4	$ 3,203.9

SOURCE: CREF Annual Reports
[a]Largely to the Global Equities Fund.

FIGURE 5.1

**TIAA AND CREF BENEFITS
1972-1994[a]**

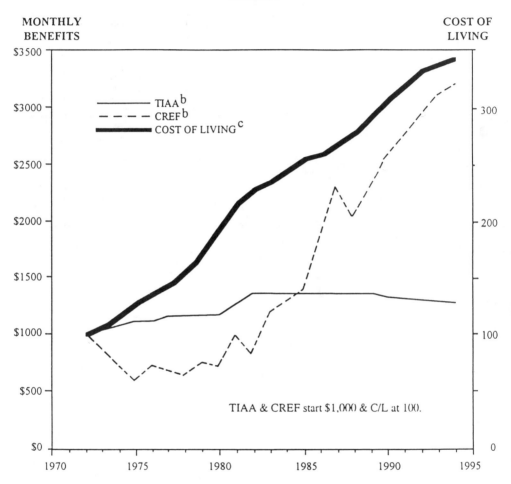

MONTHLY
BENEFITS

COST OF
LIVING

TIAA & CREF start $1,000 & C/L at 100.

---

[a]Basic data furnished by TIAA-CREF and rearranged for the purposes of this table.

[b]Assume payment of $1,000 per month in 1972 from each fund for a person who retired late in 1971.

[c]Adjusted to a base of 100 for 1972.

CHAPTER 6

TIAA-CREF RETURNS AND NEW EMPLOYEES' ALLOCATION DECISIONS

INTRODUCTION

- What are the basic characteristics and differences between TIAA and the CREF accounts?

- How do new employee allocate their monthly investments among the eight available choices?

- How reasonable are those choices on the basis of the information presented—or that should have been presented—before making that investment allocation decision?

- How reasonable are these decisions in view of the rate-of-return performance of these available alternatives?

- What other information or prejudices may influence these allocation decisions?

- What are the advantages and disadvantages of the available alternatives?

About 100,000 new participants open TIAA-CREF pension accounts each year. In this chapter some of the basic information that is or should be presented to new employees who are joining the TIAA-CREF system are reviewed. Some organizations will hold information meetings for new employees, provide them with TIAA-CREF information booklets, or both. In Chapter 3 TIAA-CREF's and Soldofsky's preferred allocations were discussed. In this chapter actual allocations of new employees and the recommended allocations are compared.

Before moving to a small study of new employees' investment decisions, some of the basic rate-of-return information will be summarized for TIAA and four of the five CREF accounts. The allocation decisions of new University of Iowa employees are described and analyzed. These employees, I believe, are not greatly dissimilar from new employees entering the system or corporate 401(k) systems anywhere in the country. A few of the leading advantages and disadvantages of each fund will be included in the comments about these allocation decisions. Finally, the procedural differences in computing TIAA and CREF returns are set forth. These differences are an essential element in understanding the risk and return characteristics of your investment accounts both while you are working and building your accumulation and after you retire. The amount earned and the level and stability of your benefits depends to a surprising degree upon your understanding of these basic procedures and your allocation decisions.

The returns on the CREF-Money Market account, which are determined on a third basis, will be described later.

NEW EMPLOYEES' ALLOCATIONS

The question of what allocation decisions new employees make and the basis of those decisions is of great interest. Once the employee makes that decision, he or she may not review or change it for many years. Only a small percentage of the general public have the information needed to make prudent and informed decisions about their long-term investment decisions among eight different and diverse choices starting in 1994. That allocation decision is made more complex by the difference in the ways that returns are measured and accumulations grow. These differences are described in the last section of this chapter. Only a rare individual is likely to understand these differences and their implications when they are presented in a few minutes along with a large amount of additional information on other employment subjects. At the fringe-benefits information and decision meetings several matters such as life and health insurance decisions are also likely to be presented. Information and decision overload exists. The TIAA-CREF allocation is very likely to be of less immediate concern to the employees than sick leave and vacation policies. Few people understand the differences between the TIAA, CREF-Equities and CREF-Money Markets valuation procedures.

I have no reason to believe that the TIAA-CREF counseling that new employees receive at the University of Iowa is greatly different from what is received at other large participating employers. My experience in providing seminars at smaller schools and non-profit organizations convinces me that much less is done at most of these places. Even their staff benefits people are generally less well informed. Personnel officers have many functions to perform and the turnover in such jobs may be quite rapid.

During the month or so between the date of employment and the first formal benefits meeting, informal conversations of the new employees with their immediate co-workers provides some information about what to expect at the benefit meetings and the decisions that will have to be made. In terms of financial decisions, many poorly informed employees just tend to pass on their own beliefs to their new coworkers. Perhaps less than one-in-ten of their fellow employees owns any common stock directly or indirectly through a mutual fund. Within the whole country only about 15 percent of people own any common stock directly. Most of that 15 percent rarely trade or buy shares. From these and other data I infer that only a very small percentage understand or follow the securities markets.

Once the TIAA-CREF allocation decision is made, it is not likely to be changed for years. Colleagues who made their allocation choices before the new CREF funds were opened in 1991 and 1994 may not even be aware of the six new funds. They are even less likely to be aware their performance characteristics, and they are unlikely to consider switching to any of them.

New participants in TIAA-CREF must allocate their monthly investments among the TIAA and the seven available CREF funds. The decision cannot be delayed. There is no way to punt. Allocating all of their required monthly investment to TIAA is an investment decision.

Hence, at an information meeting new employees are or should be presented with adequate information for making their decisions. Much of that information is sketched in the next few pages.

BASIC CHARACTERISTICS OF TIAA AND CREF ACCOUNTS
TIAA and CREF are separately incorporated, but they cooperate and coordinate their activities in providing financial services to their participants. For historical and logical reasons TIAA invests only in fixed-income investments. Any stocks it hold are received as a result of its lending operations. They are never purchased directly in the market place. Those

stocks it does hold are not intended as permanent investments. All of the CREF accounts with the exception of the Money Market account hold stock except for small amounts of "cash" and debt held for operating purposes.

TIAA

TIAA invests almost exclusively in non-marketable, fixed-income securities. Non-marketable means that no ready market with a publicly quoted price exists. Corporate bonds and notes are about 57 percent of its portfolio; mortgages about 30 percent; real estate about 10 percent; the balance is in miscellaneous items. Sometimes large financial institutions negotiate prices on such securities and trade among themselves.

An advantage of buying securities (lending) directly rather than on the open market is that slightly higher rates of return may be obtained. Some issues are too small to trade in a public market. Also, rights, warrants, or other valuable options may be obtained that help increase the lender's rate of return. Hence, a gigantic insurance company such as TIAA with an assured, stable clientele has been able to earn rates of return in the long run significantly above the average market return. TIAA's rate of return has been among the highest in the life insurance industry for decades.

Such directly purchased financial instruments are recorded and kept at book value (cost or purchase price) because they have no readily determinable market price. The amount in each participant's account is reported on this stable, book-value basis. Switching accumulations from TIAA to CREF is extremely difficult because market prices do not exist for the great bulk of TIAA's investments.

CREF

Each of the seven CREF accounts is invested in instruments which are marketable and for which publicly quoted prices are readily available. Hence, switching among these eight funds presents little problem, but a small administrative cost is involved. The Global Equities account was started on July 1, 1992 and two index accounts were started July 1, 1994.

Equities, that is, common stocks or the ownership interests in publicly-held corporations, bear the most risk of price fluctuations. The enormous diversification within the CREF portfolio greatly reduces the risk, but price risk remains. Over long periods of time--10 years and more—stock portfolios have outperformed fixed-income portfolios such as TIAA and marketable bond funds. In all probability, stocks will continue to outperform—earn a higher rate return—than bonds.

The **Marketable Bond Account**, which was started in March 1990, and the equity funds hold the securities of many companies that could not be owned by the Social Choice Fund because of its environmental or other policies, or because of the nature of their products. For example, MMM was the twenty-second largest polluter of air and water in the United States according to the National Wildlife Federation's Toxic 500 list. The Marketable Bond account itself holds bonds and mortgages of Commonwealth Edison, Florida Power and Light and Philadelphia Electric which were cited as nuclear lemons by a Public Citizen's study because of the way they either maintained their nuclear facilities and/or because of the ways they handled their nuclear wastes. The Marketable Bond Fund also held notes of RJR Nabisco, one of the nation's leading tobacco manufacturers.

The **Social Choice Account** was started in March 1990 to provide an opportunity for participants to direct their investments to the securities of corporations that have less objectionable—"socially correct?"—policies and products. In November 1993 the screen against South African securities was removed after sanctions against that nation were lifted earlier in the month. The sizes of these newer funds as of January 1, 1995, are as follows:

	($ millions)
Marketable Bonds (6/30/91)	$ 618.7
Social Choice (9/30/91)	781.8
Global Equities (7/1/92)	2,745.1
Money Market (5/1/88)	2,918.9

These amounts are small compared with CREF-Equities, which is worth more than $54.8 billion.

The Social Choices fund has 61 percent of its assets in corporate stocks, 37 percent in corporate bonds, and the balance in "cash" and miscellaneous investments. Even with its relatively small size, it has more than 150 stocks, which provide it with wide diversification.

Through the end of 1994, the Social Choice account has earned a total return very slightly higher than that of CREF-Equities largely because of the strong performance of its corporate bond component during that period. The corporate bonds in turn performed very well because the inflation rate was falling, which results in lower interest rates and rising bond prices. Over a decade or two, the return on the Social Choice fund will inevitably be smaller than that of CREF-Equities because of its bond component, as illustrated in Table 3.6. On the other hand, the relative risk of a balanced fund such as the Social Choice fund will be lower than that of a 100 percent equities fund as shown in Table 3.7.

The past performance and prospects of international funds and index funds were discussed in Chapter 3.

Global Account. The Global Account has risen rapidly since it was started on July 1, 1992. Its rapid growth is largely explained by the wide-spread favorable publicity these types of funds have received until late 1994. However, the fact remains that their performance has been very volatile as was shown in Tables 3.6 and 3.7. The Equity Index and Growth accounts were both started July 1, 1994 so their assets are still small and their performance over their first six months is not long enough to be useful. Equity Index accounts have become popular issues for mutual funds because their administrative costs are very low and their performance mirrors the general performance of the stock markets. Growth accounts hope to out-perform the markets by holding excellent growth stocks. However, as shown in Tables 3.6 and 3.7, the long-run performance of mutual funds of these types has been very similar to that of CREF-Equities.

Money Market Account. The CREF Money Market account was started May 1, 1988, to allow participants to move funds from CREF-Equities or the other CREF accounts to the Money Market when they believe equity prices are too high, and to switch back to equities when they believe the prices of equities were sufficiently low. Timing switches to seek substantial gains is and will remain a goal for very confident people. Some will succeed. But academic research has shown that market timing schemes are rarely successful.

The Money-Market account invests in U.S. government and corporate securities that have maturities up to two years. Such securities are extremely safe because of their short maturities and because of their minimum price fluctuations. If held to maturity, they are paid at their par or contractual maturity value. The returns on such securities are almost always less than the returns on long bonds of the same quality because short-term securities have minimal price risk. The yield on the CREF Money Market fund as of January 1, 1995 was 4.07 percent. At the end of 1995, 30-day U.S. Treasury bonds were yielding about 5.3 percent, and 30-year Treasury bonds were yielding about 6.0 percent. At times this spread between bill and bond yields has been six percentage points or more.

A few words on the high rates of return on corporate bonds and money market funds since about 1980 are in order. Since inflation and interest rates peaked about 1980, they have both been falling. As interest rates fall, bonds with fixed payments such as $9 per year rise in price; the market price adjusts to return the market rate of interest to the bondholder. When interest rates rise a bit, as they did in 1987, the total return on bonds falls and may even be negative. In other words, marketable bonds have substantial price risk, but less than that of common stocks as demonstrated in Table 3.6 and below in the long-term performance section of this chapter.

NEW EMPLOYEE ALLOCATIONS

In August and September 1991 tabulations were made at the University of Iowa of investment allocations selected by new employees.[1] Richard Saunders, Staff Benefits Director, provided the raw data from which numerous forms of summaries were prepared. The tabulations were made for 203 professional and scientific (P&S) staff, 109 Merit staff, and 29 new faculty members for a total of 341 people.

One of the most revealing features of the analytical tables was that 55 people or about 16.1 percent of the total of 341 allocated 100 percent of their funds to TIAA. These percentages differed substantially by the three broad groups as follows:

P&S Staff	31.4%
Merit Staff	14.3
Faculty	9.1

---

[1] I wish to thank Richard Saunders, Staff Benefits Director, and his assistants for collecting this anonymous information. I alone am responsible for the summaries made from it.

Thirty-four percent of the Merit staff, 75 percent of the P&S Staff, and 91 percent of new faculty allocated some of their monthly investment to CREF-Equities. Almost 20 percent of the new faculty members allocated all of their monthly investments to CREF-Equities.

The Total Allocations Table, Table 6.1, shows that 31.7 percent of the new employees directed exactly 50 percent of their monthly investments to TIAA. That was the largest grouping by far. I can surmise that good luck, common sense, and the coaching of employees in their immediate work groups led to these satisfactory results. Perhaps a 50-50 choice between TIAA and CREF was selected as prudent in view of the lack of knowledge. Many new employees took the position that a "no brainer" decision meant allocating about equal percentages to each of the choices presented. The 50 percent TIAA allocation group will be examined further.

Table 6.1, Allocations of New Employees, may not be immediately clear. Examine the 75 percent row. These who allocated 75 percent of their monthly investment to TIAA had another 25 percent to allocate. As it happened each of these allocated their remaining 25 percent to a single CREF account.

Fifty-one people allocated 55-74 percent of their monthly investment to TIAA. A number of these people allocated their remaining monthly investment to two or more accounts. For example, one person allocated 70 percent to TIAA. 15 percent to Social Choice, and 5 percent each to Equities, Money Market and Marketable Bonds. Thirty-six of the 341 did not allocate any of their monthly investment to TIAA.

ACTUAL ALLOCATIONS TO CREF
Thirty-three of the new employees made a 100-percent allocation to CREF-Equities. Another 15 allocated 51-99 percent to CREF-Equities. Almost 80 percent of the new employees directed some of their money to go into one or more of the CREF accounts. The many combinations of allocations to TIAA and the four then available CREF accounts selected for investment are too scattered to report in detail. Fifty percent was the most frequent percentage allocated to TIAA; some 108 of the 341 new employees made that allocation. Table 6.2 shows allocation decisions of those who placed exactly 50 percent of their funds into TIAA. Sixty-one employees or some 52 percent of this group also selected 50 percent in CREF-Equities. That 61 people represents almost 18 percent of the entire sample.

The proportion of this group that ordered half of their monthly investments to go to the Money Market account or the Marketable Bond account is surprising and strongly suggests a lack of information about the implications of those decisions. A number of people who picked 50 percent for TIAA spread their monthly investments into two or three of the CREF funds.

Comments about the probable undesirable consequences of these decisions are made in the last section of this chapter after the most likely relative returns on each option are discussed. Comments on return and risk of the Global Equities account were made in Chapter 3.

LONG-TERM TIAA AND CREF PERFORMANCE
Table 6.3 sets forth the actual returns on TIAA and CREF-Equities for the 5, 10, 20, and 30 years ending December 31, 1994. Note Well. The annual returns on TIAA are always positive because the marked-to-book method is used. When the marked-to-market method is

used, as it is for Marketable Bonds, Social Choice and CREF-Equities, the Total Annual Returns are negative some years.

The magic and majesty of an accumulation growing at compound rates of interest takes more than five years to be clearly seen. The different accumulations at different rates and for different time periods are suggested in Table 6.4, a little but vital table to help you maintain a very long-run perspective. (For a discussion of the basics of compound interest, see the Magical Compound Interest section, Chapter 8.)

The relative extent of the returns as calculated on TIAA and the four oldest CREF accounts is suggested in Table 6.3, Performance Table. In some years the total return on CREF-Equities—and common stock in general—has been negative. (The total annual return is the dividends plus the change in price divided by the beginning of the year price.) In ten of the 41 years that CREF has been in existence, the returns have been negative. The only two consecutive years of negative returns were 1969 and 1970. Such a run could occur again. The returns have been positive in 11 out of the last 13 years; the returns were minus 5.5 percent in 1990 and minus 0.1 in 1994. During the past 13 years the average returns have been better than they have been over a comparable period since 1871, the earliest year in stock performance in the total annual return format available.

The prices of existing single-family houses rose 3.6 percent in 1969 and 7.8 percent in 1970. As noted in Chapter 1, the prices of stock and real estate typically move in opposite directions.

Both bond and stock yields may be negative in some years in the total annual return procedure as shown by the following summary:

1953 - 1994

Number of Years with Total Returns That Are

	Positive	Negative
CREF	32	10
Ba Bonds[a]	34	8

[a]Bond quality just below the top four investment grades.

The first full year for CREF was 1953. Only in five years since 1953--1957, 1966, 1969, 1973, and 1974--were the total returns on stocks and bonds both negative. Stock and bond market data in the total return format are available back to 1871. The frequencies of annual positive and negative returns are summarized in Table 6.5.

For the years 1910 through 1952, stock and bond returns were both negative only three times: 1917, 1920, and 1933. The total rates of return for stocks and bonds for the 42 years, 1911-1952, and the 38 years, 1953-1992, are reported in Table 6.6.

These data for the earlier periods back to 1871 are added for the skeptic who may believe that the information was biased by the selection of the year 1953, the first full year for CREF.

These data also confirm that, in the long run, the total returns on stocks are very likely to be one-fourth to one-half higher than those on bonds.

ADVANTAGES AND DISADVANTAGES OF TIAA
AND THE SEVERAL CREF FUNDS

Most of the relative advantages and disadvantages of TIAA and the several CREF funds can be inferred directly from the display of their returns as shown in the Performance Tables 3.6 and 6.3. Only major advantages and disadvantages are stated at this point. Other important points were made in the formal discussion of risk in Chapter 3.

TIAA

A major advantage of TIAA is its return stability which is based upon the marked-to-book procedure used to calculate its return. This procedure, which is almost universally among insurance companies, was described in Chapter 3.

An illustration will help to make one point about the advantages of a stable return. If the return for each of the previous five years had been 9.0 percent, the average return was 9 percent. However, if the returns had been -1 percent, 4 percent, 9 percent, 14 percent and 19 percent, the average return is only 8.8 percent when it is calculated as it actually is using compound interest. (Just multiply 0.99, 1.04, 1.09, 1.14, and 1.19, and take the fifth root of that product on your calculator. The result is 1.0877 or 8.8 percent.) The arithmetic average remains 9.0 percent.

If you use the series of returns of -11 percent, -1 percent, 9 percent, 19 percent, and 29 percent, the actual return is 8.5 percent even though the arithmetic mean (the sum of the five items added and divided by 5) is again 9 percent.

The total returns on the Marketable Bond account at times could be as widely dispersed as suggested in the above illustrations. The fact that the total returns on the Marketable Bonds are figured on a marked-to-market basis is a disadvantage for this fund relative to TIAA. The same holds true for CREF-Equities. The disadvantage of the marked-to-market funds is the opposite side of the coin for TIAA's marked-to-book procedure.

An obvious advantage for TIAA is the relative stability of pension payments for the retiree.

Three disadvantages of TIAA must be understood. First, during retirement benefits are not fixed. They will rise and fall slowly to reflect changes in market interest rates. Second, once you commit large parts of your accumulations to TIAA and are getting close to your likely retirement date, switching funds to one of the CREF funds is awkward. Until 1991 no funds could be switched from TIAA to CREF. Now, you can make an irrevocable contract to switch funds from TIAA to CREF in equal amounts over a ten-year period. You should make some detailed calculations and estimates if you utilize this procedure.

If you start such a contract when you are 55 and plan to work to 65, what happens if you later decide to retire at 62 for whatever reason? (See the discussion of switching from TIAA to CREF in Chapter 11.)

The third disadvantage of TIAA relative to CREF-Equities is the lower, long-run rate of return from fixed-income investments made in the bond market as shown in Tables 6.3 and 6.6. Table 6.4, "The Amount to Which an Annuity Will Grow," will give you some insight into the likely implications of these lower returns for your retirement benefits. These differences are elaborated in more detail later.

CREF-EQUITIES

Two major underline{advantages} of CREF-Equities are largely mirror images of the relative disadvantages of TIAA. First and most obvious is its higher rate of return. Second, despite CREF's irregular increases, its (total) rate of return or performance has been higher than TIAA's return and higher than the rate of inflation. This assertion was further demonstrated in Table 5.4.

Several underline{disadvantages} are cited for CREF. First, its wide fluctuations in annual returns are hard for many people to live with. During the last 22 years these returns have ranged from -31.0 percent in 1974 to +32.7 percent in 1985. In 1954 the increase was 48.8 percent. Second, it does include securities that many people find objectionable because of the products and/or policies of some of the corporations whose stock are held. This same objection is applied to the TIAA portfolio.

A third objection is that because of the way CREF works as a variable annuity, the benefits in the first year of retirement are about 40 percent less than they would be from an equal investment in TIAA. Only after 5-10 years of retirement are the CREF benefits likely to equal the TIAA benefits available in the first year. Fourth, the CREF benefits may fall as well as rise in the years immediately after the annuity is started. What some people view as a disadvantage, the more or less irregular rise in CREF-Equities benefits after retirement, is eulogized as its major benefit by others. CREF's post-retirement increases over the past 20 years and more have far exceeded the rise in the cost of living.

MARKETABLE BONDS

At least 26 of 341 people in the new employee sample elected to place some of their monthly investment allocations in the Marketable Bond account. Two of these 26 chose to place half of their total monthly investment in this fund.

What are the underline{advantages} of the Marketable Bond account? Why did TIAA-CREF decide to offer it to participants?

Two major attractions for the Marketable Bond account are suggested, but I doubt that either of them motivated its selection.

First, the bond account is marketable. It has a daily price; it may be exchanged by participants for any of the other CREF accounts at any time. Second, the other CREF funds can be exchanged for the Marketable Bond account at any time. That flexibility is an advantage. (See Table 7.3 on the extent of the exchanges among the TIAA and CREF Funds.)

In order to time exchanges among the CREF funds successfully, one would have to have a deep and current understanding of how the financial markets work and how the complex, changing forces move the price of each fund upward or downward. Substantial amounts of time would have to be spent at the task, and even then losses and gains are equally probable. I doubt that new employees will have enough invested in these accounts to make the effort worthwhile. Of course, participants may enjoy the learning process and some may have little else to do with their time when they are not working at their job.

The correlation coefficient on the total returns between good quality equities such as those held by CREF-Equities and Ba quality bonds, which I use here to represent the marketable bond portfolio, is 0.37 over 20 years and more. (The correlation coefficient is a nice statistical way of summarizing the degree to which increases and decreases in returns correspond. If they correspond exactly, the correlation coefficient is +1.00. If their movements are exact opposites, the correlation coefficient is -1.00.)[2]

Some people may believe that because a financial instrument is called a bond, it is safe. Two things should be understood. First, the quality of an individual bond may deteriorate and it may become virtually worthless. That was the experience with a significant percentage of the "junk" bonds. Second, the Ba bond yields, figured on the same total return basis as the common stock, fluctuate through a wide range. From 1953 through 1994 their range was   -11.3 percent to +25.6 percent. That range is smaller than the -31.0 percent to +32.7 percent range quoted for CREF-Equities for the same period.

Perhaps some of those selecting the Marketable Bond account did not like the idea that funds in TIAA could not be transferred at will from TIAA to any of the CREF accounts. Perhaps, some of those selecting Marketable Bonds did not understand that TIAA holds mostly corporate notes, which are for most purposes equally as safe as the bonds issued by the same corporations. Or, perhaps, the word "bonds" was more glamorous, more familiar, or implied minimal risk.

Five disadvantages of the Marketable Bond fund may be cited. First, if they have an arithmetic average return one or two percentage points above the TIAA return, the actual yield as illustrated in financial calculations may be lower than that of TIAA. Second, over the 20- and 30-year periods shown in the Performance Table 6.3, the yields on marketable bonds prepared from TIAA and other sources are below those of CREF. Over the 1911-1952 period and the 1871-1910 period, bond yields were much lower than stock yields as shown in Table 6.6.

The high yields achieved by Marketable Bonds for 1988 through 1991 are the visible effects of declining interest rates during those years. Third, these calculations do not allow adequately for any deterioration in the quality of individual bonds which happened with some frequency from 1987 through 1991.

Fourth, the lower yields very likely to be earned by corporate bonds as compared with TIAA, result in a smaller accumulation at the point of retirement. Finally, CREF-Bond annuities are not available; all accumulations will have to be transferred to another CREF account or to TIAA in order for benefits to be received.

WHY DID CREF OPEN A MARKETABLE BOND FUND?
My personal speculation is that other insurance companies and mutual funds, that arrange through insurance companies to provide annuities, offer bond funds. TIAA-CREF was feeling the competitive pressure. It developed this product for participants who were being

---

[2]For further information, see Table 3.7.

offered bond funds and a variety of other funds by companies trying to increase their share of the college and university pension-fund market. A few very vocal individual critics of TIAA were demanding a marketable-bond account. TIAA-CREF, I believe, caved in to these forces and offered such a fund.

If the market rate of interest remains at about the 1995 level for the next few years, the rate earned by the Marketable Bond account may be slightly below that of TIAA. On the other hand, if interest rates rise, the total returns on the bond fund will fall, and so will the market value of its units. Any person who wants to "repurchase" his TIAA contract if he leaves the TIAA-CREF system and has part of his investment in the Marketable Bond account, will be surprised to find that its cash value may be less than the amount he invested.

In conclusion, I perceive no long-run financial advantage for the participant in holding the bond account. Modern financial portfolio theory might argue for the bond fund because of the added diversification, but I believe that this advantage is overwhelmed by the higher returns from equities when the participant is likely to be in the system for many years.[3]

SOCIAL CHOICE ACCOUNT

Fifty-six people or 16.4 percent of the sample of new employees allocated some of their monthly investment to the Social Choice account. Of these, 17 people allocated 50-75 percent and five ordered 100 percent of their monthly investment be placed in the Social Choice account.

Public concern with the nature, cleanliness, and preservation of our physical environment has been growing for several decades. The employment and political policies of American companies operating abroad as well as at home are a legitimate concern. People working in colleges, universities, and nonprofit organizations may be more sensitive to such issues than the general public.

A few mutual fund companies have responded by offering several environmentally purified and politically concerned funds. These dedicated funds include Dreyfus' Third World Fund, Parnassus Fund, and several funds in the Calvert family. In fact, if you have millions to put into the financial markets, Calvert will design a fund to reflect your particular environmental, social, and political preferences.

When I obtained the performance records of these funds a few years ago, their yields were all less than that of the average, matched funds that did not select securities of the basis of environmental, social, and political criteria. Several of these were balanced funds; that is, they held both stocks and bonds, just as the new Social Choice account does.

The performance of CREF's Social Choice account through its short history has been acceptable, but because of restrictions upon what it may purchase and because of its stock-bond mix, participants should anticipate that its performance will average several percentage points below that of CREF-Equities.

---

[3] I have been in TIAA-CREF for 41 years and am still in quite good health. My wife may be in the system for 70 years or more if she lives her expected life span.

I have no quarrel with anyone who elects to place any or all of his pension investments in the Social Choice account. In fact, I have a strong admiration for people who place the quality of the world in which they live ahead of personal financial concerns. My point is that those investing in the Social Choice account should know what they are doing. The diversification among the stocks and bonds of the companies that are being purchased and held is great enough so that no disaster is likely to occur because of the restrictions on security selection.

I have personally checked the securities portfolio in the Social Choice fund against lists of several hundred companies whose corporate issuers have transgressed the cannons of good citizenship in one way or another. I did not find any of these securities among those held by the Social Choice fund.

MONEY-MARKET ACCOUNT
More than four percent of all employees new to the University of Iowa in August and September 1991 allocated some of their investment for the Money Market account. I can only speculate on their reasons for that decision. Whatever their reasons for doing so were, that allocation decision is most unlikely to work to their financial advantage.

I do not believe anyone should have a part of his accumulation in the CREF-Money Market account except as a temporary holding place until he believes the time is ripe to redeploy these funds into another account.

Money market accounts sponsored by mutual funds came into existence in the 1970s. TIAA was late bringing out its money-market account; it did not open its money market account until April 1988. It was opened six months after the Stock Market crash of October 1987, which included the record drop in price of 508 DJIA points to 1739 on October 19th. The DJIA had been above 2200 earlier that month.

When one is quite certain that stock prices are about to fall, he/she can move some of his/her investments into the Money Market account to keep the value of his/her investment from falling, earn a modest rate of interest, and then move the funds back into CREF-Equities at a lower price. He/she may have a considerable gain in the sense that he/she owns more shares and has reduced his/her investment per share. The same sort of maneuver can be made with investments in the Marketable Bond and the other CREF accounts.

Some participants may realize that the tops and bottoms in the bond market prices generally do not coincide with tops and bottoms in the equities markets. If one knew enough—or thought he knew enough—he could move his funds through all three accounts to seek the maximum advantage.

If you want to try that, good luck! The chances are very great that you will lose in that process. But you now have the opportunity to try! The opportunity to trade between the Money Market account and the other CREF accounts is usually said to be an advantage.

A second advantage of the Money Market account exists: the participant may have an assured gain when the CREF Money-Market rate is higher than the TIAA new-money rate for the year. As will be explained later, TIAA sets the rate it pays on new money once a year at the beginning of the year for the entire year.[4] If the money-market rate is above the TIAA's announced, new-money rate, you may have the new investment that you would otherwise have allocated to TIAA sent to the Money Market account and gain the difference between these two rates. When the money-market rate falls to the level of the new money rate, you can then order your investment in the Money Market account to be transferred to TIAA and change your monthly allocation. The gain in any one year from this tactic is likely to be small.

The only times that the money-market rate is likely to be above the TIAA rate is during a period of or just after a period of rising inflation. Since the CREF-Money Market account was established in 1988, this rate differential has appeared only once and lasted for a few months. This advantage is not large and occurs very infrequently.

Two disadvantages of the Money Market fund are clear. The lower rate of return on the money market account relative to TIAA or even to the Marketable Bond account will produce a much lower accumulation for your eventual pension. Second, I have observed people have transferred money from CREF-Equities to the Money Market account when they are absolutely convinced that the stock market prices had to go down. They were confounded when the stock prices fell very little and even rose. Then these participants become frozen in place for years waiting for stock prices to fall and to vindicate their judgments. One day prices will fall, but even a large fall may not bring the price of a CREF unit back to the level it was when they transferred relatively large amounts in terms of their accumulation in their Money Market account.

GENERAL APPLICABILITY OF ALLOCATION COMMENTS

What has been said about the investment allocation for new TIAA-CREF participants applies equally to all participants. These principles apply also to those in other pension plans wherein participants have some allocation choices. Finally, the principles described and rates of return received apply to do-it-yourself investors as well.

---

[4]Recently, TIAA has changed this more frequently than once a year.

CONCLUSIONS

TIAA is basically a fixed-income fund and four of the seven CREF funds are wholly equity funds. One of the CREF funds, Social Choice, holds both bonds—fixed-income securities—and stocks. The Marketable Bond account holds bonds only and the Money Market account holds debt securities that mature in two years or less. TIAA and the Money Market account are marked to book and the others are marked to market. This difference in techniques alone makes TIAA's value far more stable than that of the other accounts.

These differences should be understood by both new and continuing TIAA-CREF participants. Most new employees in TIAA-CREF, like those in similar corporate pensions, exhibit a general lack of understanding of these differences and a conservative bias. Less than 20 percent of new employees allocate half or more of their regular investments to the various CREF equity accounts. Another 20 percent allocate all or nearly all of their investments to TIAA.

Allocations among the available accounts should be made after considering the likely very long-run nature of these investments, their likely future rates of return, and their relative riskiness. Even those who make prudent decisions may not well understand what they have done. Good decisions are sometimes made on the basis of very incomplete or erroneous information.

The speed with which the initial allocation decision must be made after employment and the very concentrated information that may be present about the elections that must be made helps to explain some of the imprudently conservative decisions such as 100 percent allocation to TIAA and other imprudent decisions such as allocating 23 percent or more of new investments to the Money Market account.

Tables and charts based on past performance show that equity investments have far outpaced TIAA and Marketable Bonds. In general terms, CREF-Equities benefits for retirees have exceeded the cost of living and TIAA have not. TIAA adds stability to post-retirement income.

TABLE 6.1

NEW EMPLOYEES' ALLOCATION DECISIONS
(MONTHLY INVESTMENT ALLOCATIONS OF NEW EMPLOYEES
UNIVERSITY OF IOWA - FALL 1991)

TIAA		CREF							
		Equities		Social Choice		Marketable Bonds		Money Market	
Allocation %	% of New Employees	Allocation %	% of New Employees	Allocation %	% of New Employees	Allocation %	% of New Employees	Allocation %	% of New Employees
100	16.1	-	-	-	-	-	-	-	-
76-99	4.4	5-20	2.3	5-20	1.5	25	0.1[a]	25	0.1[a]
75	3.8	25	2.3	25	0.1	5-40	0.1[a]	5	0.1[a]
55-74	15.0	0-4	10.3	10-45	2.3	30-50	0.1	25-50	0.1
50	31.7	50	17.8	45-50	1.2	5-30	2.3	10	0.1[a]
26-49	8.6	50-65	1.1	5-60	5.6	5-30	2.3	10	0.1[a]
25	6.5	50-75	4.7	25-75	2.6	25-50	0.1	25	0.1
10-20[b]	3.2	20-80	2.3	10-50	5.6	5-50	3.2	5-50	2.3
0	0.0	50-100	11.4	100	0.1	50-100	0.1[a]	100	0.1[a]
Number Selecting This Allocation	305		204		56		26		15
% of Total	89.4%		59.8%		16.4%		8.9%		4.4%
Total New Employees	341								

[a]Less than 0.1%

[b]No one elected a TIAA allocation between 1 and 9%

NEW EMPLOYEES' ALLOCATION DECISIONS

105

TABLE 6.2

**NEW EMPLOYEE ALLOCATIONS TO CREF ACCOUNTS
FOR THOSE ALLOCATING 50% TO TIAA[a]**

% To All CREF Accounts	Equities	CREF (Number of Persons)		
		Money - Market	Social Choice	Marketable Bonds
50	61	3	11	2
40	-	-	2	-
30 & 35	2	-	4	4
20 & 25	15	2	13	7
10 & 15	3	3	3	4
Number of New Employees[b]	81	8	33	17

[a]Allocations for 108 of the 341 people who selected any of the CREF accounts.

[b]Numbers do not add to 108 because some people allocated part of their pension investments to two or three of these CREF accounts.

SOURCE: August and September 1991 study of new University of Iowa employees.

TABLE 6.3

**PERFORMANCE OF AVAILABLE TIAA-CREF INVESTMENT FUNDS
1966-1994[a]**

		CREF			
YEAR	TIAA	EQUITIES	SOCIAL CHOICE	MARKETABLE BONDS[a]	MONEY MARKET[b]
1994	6.5%	-0.1%	-1.3%	-2.9%	4.3%
1993	7.3	13.9	9.4	9.8	3.0
1992	7.7	6.3	11.1	7.4	3.6
1991	8.7	30.1	25.2	16.0	6.0
1990	8.6	-5.5	4.3[c]	9.0	8.2
1989	9.2	28.0	20.3[c]	14.5	9.2
1988	8.9	17.5	15.1[c]	7.9	7.6
1987	8.7	5.1	3.5[c]	2.8	6.6
5 years	8.3	8.2	9.3[c]	7.7	5.0
10 years	9.6	14.3	12.6[c]	10.0	6.3
20 years	8.8	14.2	--	8.0[b]	7.9
30 years	7.4	9.9	--	4.6[b]	7.4

CREF-Bonds account started March 1, 1990. Hypothetical returns to and including 1976
prepared by TIAA-CREF. Total returns for early years drawn from Soldofsky's published
studies.

CREF Money-Market account started April 1, 1990. Hypothetical returns back to and including
1953 prepared by TIAA-CREF.

Hypothetical returns for years prior to inception of these funds prepared by TIAA-CREF.

SOURCE: Charting TIAA and CREF Accounts, Spring 1995. TIAA-CREF, New York City.

ADDENDUM

Information reporting the 1995 performance of the CREF Accounts was received too late to be
incorporated in the text and tables of this book. These 1995 total return performance in
percentage terms are as follows: Equities, 30.9; Money Market, 5.9; Marketable Bonds, 17.8;
Social Choice, 29.5; Global, 20.1; Equities Index, 36.2; and Growth Index, 35.2.

TABLE 6.4

**AMOUNT TO WHICH $1000 PER YEAR WILL GROW
AT SELECTED INTEREST RATES**

YEARS	6%	9%	12%	15%
10	$13,181	$15,192	$17,548	20,303
20	36,786	51,160	72,052	102,444
30	79,058	136,308	241,333	434,745
40	154,761	337,882	767,091	1,779,090

Compare the rates used in this table with those actually achieved, as shown in Tables 3.6 and 6.6.

TABLE 6.5

**POSITIVE AND NEGATIVE TOTAL RETURNS
ON STOCKS AND BONDS: 1871 TO 1952**

		1871-1909	1910-1952	1871-1952
Stocks				
	Positive	29	29	58
	Negative	9	14	23
Bonds				
	Positive	35	34	69
	Negative	3	9	12

TABLE 6.6

**TOTAL RETURNS ON STOCKS AND BONDS:
1871-1992**

	1871-1910	1911-1952	1953-1992
Stocks	7.3%	7.7%	10.9%
Bonds	4.0[a]	4.9	4.6

[a]U.S. Government bonds to 1900; Railroad bonds from 1901-10.

CHAPTER 7

ENHANCING YOUR TIAA-CREF RETIREMENT BENEFITS

INTRODUCTION

- What are the four major strategies for enhancing your TIAA-CREF retirement benefits?

- How does each of these strategies work?

- How much could each add to your retirement benefits?

- What distinct advantages and disadvantages does each strategy have?

These strategies are independent of one another. The summation of all of them could have a surprisingly large and very welcome effect upon your retirement benefits.

TAX-DEFERRED SALARY OPTION

The first of these strategies is the tax-deferred salary option. Most individuals use this option which is provided for in pension plans that are qualified by the Internal Revenue Code (IRS). The Tax-Deferred Arrangement (TDA) shifts the part of your salary that you voluntarily contribute to your pension from an immediate tax-paying status to a deferred tax-paying status. That is, you will not pay any income taxes on your investment in your pension plan until that money is received bit by bit in your eventual pension. This TDA status applies to your contribution only. Your employer's contribution is not subject to income taxes when it is paid in. However, because it has never been taxed, you will also be required to pay income tax on your employer's contribution and everything earned on that contribution as it is received bit by bit in your pension.

The TDA and its companion, the TSA or Tax Sheltered Annuity, are no small things. They are two of the greatest ways still left in tax code to bolster your pension, and they cost employers nothing.

Be sure to ask your employer whether or not these valuable advantages are available to you. Most employers do, but sometimes they do not check carefully to be sure that employees utilize them. When new employees join an organization, so many options are made available to them in various programs that they sometimes select an option that is least beneficial. I have known cases in which employees have been with a university for 20 years and never realized that they were not using this wonderful TDA option that could easily have increased their eventual benefits by 10 percent or more.

The TDA is easier to illustrate than to state in words. Assume that a faculty member is paid $36,000 per year in 12 equal monthly amounts of $3,000. He must invest 5 percent of his own money or $150 per month toward his pension. (Obviously, the percentage may differ with the employer's rules.) If the applicable federal income tax rate is 28 percent, the income tax on that $150 is $42. State income taxes must be paid also. Assume that they are $9 for a total of $51 per month or $612 annually on the 12 monthly payments. (Your applicable state and federal income tax rates may differ from those used in the illustration.)

With your permission, your employer can shift your $150 per month or $1,800 per year from a taxable to a nontaxable status when that payment is made.[1]

You can do either of two things at this point. You can take the additional $51 monthly and spend it, or you can have your personal payment into your pension plan increased by $51 per month and have the same take home pay as before. You would probably have this additional amount invested for you in TIAA-CREF through a Supplementary Retirement Annuity (SRA) which is discussed later.

Placing the $612 in an SRA account amounts to a substantial increase in your annual pension-fund contribution. In this case, it is a 34 percent increase or $612 divided by $1,800.

TAX-SHELTERED ANNUITY (TSA)

The second strategy is the tax-sheltered annuity. In a tax-sheltered annuity (TSA) the income on the amount in your pension accumulation is also not taxed until you start to receive your pension benefits. Column 2 of Table 7.1, <u>Power of Tax Shelter and Deferral</u>, shows how your first year's pension allocation would grow assuming an 8 percent interest rate. Only TIAA is illustrated for simplicity, but the process works the same way for income on CREF investments. The earnings at 8 percent on the initial $1,800 are $144 per year so that at the end of the second full year the accumulation would have grown to $1,944.[2] The second column shows the amount continuing to grow at 8 percent. Realistically, that interest would vary somewhat year by year.

If the tax shelter did not exist and if your $1,800, initial-year investment earned 8 percent, interest would be $144. However, after federal and state income taxes, you would have only $95 to reinvest at the assumed 34 percent rate.

The amount set aside for your pension, $1,800 and the $95 earned and reinvested on it, would grow as shown in Column 1. After 20 years your accumulation from the first year's investment will be $4,785, which is about 62 percent less than it would be with tax-sheltered reinvestment through your pension account.

Both of these tax advantages, the tax-deferred arrangement and the tax-sheltered annuity, work to your considerable advantage. Instead of taking the $612 in cash made available by using the TDA, you could invest it in your TIAA-SRA and achieve a very substantial

---

[1] As soon as the pension investment is deducted from your paycheck it is vested--that is, the funds are yours and do not revert back to your employer. Your employer must send them on to TIAA-CREF where they will be credited to your account. However, some employers will hold your money for 15 days or even one month and use it for their own purposes. When you receive your TIAA-CREF quarterly reports, note the date that the money is deposited in your account. The employer must get social security taxes deducted from paychecks deposited within three working days. If your employer takes much longer than that to deposit your money with TIAA-CREF, you have a legitimate question to raise with your business office.

[2] Actually, some interest would have accumulated by the end of the first year. This amount is not considered for the sake of simplicity.

additional advantage to yourself. At the end of the first year you would have $2,412 invested rather than $1,800. That larger amount growing for 20 years would accumulate to $10,409, which is 34 percent larger than without the investment of the TDA saving and 117 percent larger than the amount you would have at the end of 20 years without using either the TDA or the TSA.

Some people allege a downside to using one or both of these tax shelters. First, they believe that they are such superior investors that they can do better than a leading insurance company. They feel they can do so much better that they can overcome the income-tax disadvantage and still have a better performance. Second, some people believe that their income tax rate will be so much higher when they retire that they will be better off investing the added cash income from the TSA themselves in a tax-exempt security.

SUPPLEMENTAL RETIREMENT ANNUITY (SRA)

Under the IRS code, people using Section 403(b)--that is, plans such as TIAA-CREF which are available to public employees and employees of nonprofit organizations—may put an amount equal to 20 percent of their salary into their pension plans. This percentage declines under a complex formula after you have been with your employer for a number of years. Your staff benefits director will compute the maximum amount that you can place in an SRA for you.

If your employer contributes 10 percent of your salary to your account, and you are required to put in another 5 percent, you could still volunteer to invest up to another 5 percent. The total contributed by both yourself and your employer would be 20 percent. All of your contributions, of course, would be tax sheltered and tax deferred if you want them that way. Almost every one utilizes these shelters when their advantages are explained.

Currently your individual contribution to your pension plan may not be more than $9,500 per year. If you earn $150,000 per year and you are required to invest 5 percent or $7,500 per year, you can volunteer only another $2,000 even though that total investment, $9,500, is only 6.3 percent of your salary. Corporate pension plans of the 401(k) type have a similar limitation. The employer is putting in $15,000 per year or 10 percent in this continuing illustration.

If you have never used an SRA, you have the right to exceed the $9,500; you could invest up to $12,500 for some years until you use up a past-service entitlement. Again, your staff benefits person would have to calculate the exact amount and time limitations for you.

If you believe that TIAA-CREF can invest to earn a higher rate than you can yourself, especially given the tax-shelter advantages, you may want to invest some additional amount in your pension fund regularly. If you and your employer are now putting away 15 percent per year your tax-deferred salary, investing another 5 percent would increase your pension benefits by one third. If you and your employer together contribute 10 percent, you can put in another 10 percent and double your pension benefits earned after that date.

A formal SRA policy contract was added by TIAA-CREF in 1973. Until then the participant could always invest more in his or her regular TIAA-CREF plan. The advantage of the SRA, which may be either invested in TIAA or CREF, is that at age 59½ without any income-tax penalty you can start drawing upon these funds for whatever purpose you wish, even though you remain fully employed. That withdrawal may be in the form of an annuity or a lump sum. If it is a lump sum, you will have to pay income tax on all or most of the amount withdrawn. You will not have to pay income taxes on any amount you invested without using the tax shelter because income taxes were already paid on this investment. You will have to pay income taxes on (1) the earnings on your investments and (2) the earnings on your employer's investments to your account because income taxes have never been paid on these amounts.

The income taxes on an SRA are meaningfully contrasted with those on your regular accounts. If you make a lump sum withdrawal on your regular account before you stop working, you will have to pay a 10 percent penalty for that withdrawal in addition to your regular income taxes. A few exceptions exist to the 10 percent penalty. If you become disabled or encounter a defined hardship such as medical expenses that exceed 7.5 percent of your adjusted gross income, you may make a withdrawal. Of course, you can start drawing a regular annuity that will pay out over the rest of your expected lifetime, but that amount is likely to be much smaller than if you had waited. The SRA contract provides you, the holder, with much more flexibility than the regular contract. At age 59½ you can start drawing upon it as an annuity without income tax penalty. If you should no longer want to teach summers, for example, you can draw upon all or part of your SRA to help maintain your annual income level. Under your employer's program you may be able to start a partial retirement program and utilize your SRA to supplement your income while still building your regular retirement annuity. Your SRA contracts can be further divided into smaller parts which can be started at times that are convenient for you. SRA benefits from TIAA accounts and CREF accounts are treated separately. You can start receiving benefits from one of these without starting to draw from the other.

The TDA and TSA advantages apply to the SRA accounts as well as to the regular TIAA and CREF accounts. A disadvantage of the TIAA-SRA is that the annual contractual interest rate is now about one-half percentage point below what it is on the regular contract. That has not always been the case. SRA contracts are being widely used, as suggested by the numbers in Table 7.2.

UTILIZING HIGHER EARNING FUNDS

Chapters 3 and 5 discussed the differences in the past rates of return between TIAA and CREF-Equities. As suggested by tables in those chapters, retirement benefits can be greatly enhanced by allocating your funds to those accounts that are very likely to earn higher rates over the long run. The recommended mixes suggested by TIAA-CREF and by Soldofsky were given in Tables 3.1 and 3.2.

What can you do if you believe that you have been allocating too large a proportion of your monthly investment to TIAA? You can do either of two things or both of them, depending upon your age and preferred strategy. You can change your monthly allocation to favor the equities, or you can (under the 1992 TIAA-CREF rule) contract to shift some of your TIAA funds annually to either CREF Equities or to Global Equities. The following sections refer to CREF-Equities as preferred to Global Equities because CREF-Equities is notably less volatile even though its rate-of-return performance is slightly less (See Table 3.7). Reallocation of your monthly investments is the third of the four strategies for enhancing your retirement benefits.

REALLOCATING YOUR MONTHLY INVESTMENT

If you are on the younger side, switching your monthly allocation to 75 or even 100 percent Equities is a good strategy for several reasons. First, as the years go by, you will be able to observe the changing proportion of your TIAA and CREF accumulations. When you reach your total accumulation allocation goal, you can readjust your monthly investment to the proportions that you would prefer to maintain. Second, with monthly investments you are more likely to be utilizing dollar cost averaging more fully than with one transfer from TIAA to CREF each year. When stock prices are low, you buy more units, and when prices are high, you buy fewer units. If you select a 10-year contract to shift TIAA funds to CREF, you are less likely to be using dollar cost averaging as fully. Three, you may not need 10 years to reach your desired TIAA-Equities balance.

REALLOCATING YOUR ACCUMULATION FROM TIAA TO CREF

Starting April 1, 1992, TIAA-CREF announced a way that participants could shift funds from TIAA to CREF. To utilize this plan you must sign a 10-year, irrevocable agreement about the amount to be shifted once a year for ten years. Such a long-term shift will likely have little impact on the fluctuations of TIAA's total assets. In all probability, no asset sales will be required to make such shifts. These transfers may be made also to other insurance carriers if permitted by your employer. Through early 1993, about 9,500 such transfer agreements to switch to CREF had been made. Given the approximately 900,000 CREF participants in the accumulation stage, the number making switching contracts is just over 1 percent so far.

To date no special limitations have been placed upon TIAA and CREF transfers. For example, they can be started at any age. Even if you are beyond 60, you can start such a contract. If you die before your 10-year contract is completed, your accumulation at the date of death must be annuitized, and your beneficiary can start drawing from it.

Several advantages and disadvantages exist for the 10-year switching contract. One advantage is that changes in your monthly allocation may be too small for you to reach your TIAA-CREF accumulation allocation goal even if all of your monthly investments are made to CREF. Second, these annual shifts from TIAA to CREF can continue even if you are retired as long as you leave a CREF accumulation account open and a large enough balance in your TIAA account for the transfers to be made. Third, you could use the 10-year contract and shift your monthly allocation if that appears to you as the better thing to do in your circumstances.

Two disadvantages are suggested. First, the contract is inflexible. Second, reaching your desired goal is much more complex. In setting the amount to transfer annually from TIAA to CREF, consider the items that would go into the calculation. Your TIAA-CREF allocation goal for the accumulation must be established. Your likely TIAA accumulation ten years hence would have to be estimated. That estimation would require that you deduct the amount transferred out each year from your initial amount. Next, you would have to estimate for each year the amount to be added to your TIAA balance from your monthly investment and also the interest earned each year. That calculation would have to be repeated ten times to estimate your TIAA balance ten years hence. Your CREF accumulation at the end of the tenth year would have to be estimated. You would have to add the amount transferred each year and the increase (decrease) in the CREF balance each year based upon CREF's performance. If you make investments monthly into CREF, those amounts and also the annual likely performance of those directly added funds would have to be included. If you overshot your target—that is, had a larger proportion of CREF than you desired—you could still transfer funds back from CREF to TIAA even though the TIAA-CREF switching contract was still in effect. If you overshot your goal, you could adjust your monthly allocation toward more monthly investment in TIAA. During the ten years your switching contract is in effect, TIAA-CREF could develop new investment vehicles.

TIAA-CREF does not release figures on the dollar value of transfers from TIAA to CREF, but the College Retirement Equities Fund audited financial statements do report the net amount of transfer from CREF to TIAA. These transfers for 1992, 1993, and 1994 are shown in Table 7.3.

The extent of these transfers is very small in percentage terms, but is large—hundreds of millions of dollars—relative to the wealth and income of TIAA-CREF participants. These CREF-to-TIAA transfers, whether well advised or not, are an important option for the individuals utilizing them.

WORKING LONGER

The fourth major strategy is working longer. If one of your main goals is to improve sharply your retirement income, working longer is one of the very best courses of action available to you. Your TIAA-CREF benefits will grow almost 10 percent per year for each year you continue to work beyond what is now the typical retirement age of 65. Remember that this rate is 10 percent per year compounded so the added benefits run as follows:

Years Longer	Benefits Increase
1	10.0%
2	21.0
3	33.1
4	46.4
5	61.0

Your social security benefits will also increase several percent per year depending upon your age (see Early Retirement section, Chapter 2), but only above the maximum available which relates back to the maximum amount taxed for social security benefits.

Three sources explain the approximate 10 percent per year increase from working to an older age. First, you will be paying into your account each year. Second, both your accumulation and the added payments into your account will continue to earn tax-deferred income. Third, in actuarial terms, your most likely number of years from retirement to death is shorter, so your annual benefits per year are larger.

Starting January 1, 1994, mandatory retirement age for professors was removed. It had been 68 years for about a decade. However, the IRS rule that requires you to start drawing pension benefits by April 1 of the year after the year in which you become 70½ remains in effect. You can start drawing retirement benefits even though you are still paying into TIAA-CREF to increase your ultimate benefits.

The exact percentage your CREF benefits will increase each year is problematical because CREF-Equities is a variable annuity that relates to the price of a CREF unit. Nevertheless, the number of annuity units you are due will increase each year based upon your decreasing life expectancy. Whether you want to work longer or are capable of working longer because of your health, changing working conditions and other personal circumstances is another question.[3]

On the other side of the coin, retiring early reduces your retirement benefits at the same rate as retiring later increases them. Retiring as early as age 62 reduces your social security benefits by about 6.7 percent per year for each year early that you retire. If you retire before 59½, your annuity will be subject to a 50 percent income-tax penalty, unless you retire because of health-related or other specified conditions.[4]

Another consideration is the likely retirement income of the married couple, both of whom may have substantial pensions. When their ages are different, they may both choose to retire in the same year. I have known a few couple who both worked to age 70 because they feared the $200,000 per year or so they would have in pension and social security income would not be enough to continue to support them in the style to which they were accustomed.

CHANGING EMPLOYERS

Another possibility for some individuals is changing employers for the sake of finding one that has a more generous pension plan. However, if you are changing employers and have several different opportunities, looking closely at the retirement plan of the prospective employers is wise. Few academics stay with the same employer throughout their careers. Three-to-five changes are not unusual. If you move from a TIAA-CREF eligible employer to a private employer that has a 401(k) plan, the counterpart of your present 403(b) plan, the

---

[3]I have written about this question in the style of a labor economist and behavioral scientist in Robert M. Soldofsky, "On Determining the Optimal Retirement Age," Academe, July-August, 1986, pp. 17-23. Also see Ending Mandatory Retirement for Tenured Faculty, Washington, DC: National Academy Press, 1991.

[4]The question often arises about how the age of 59½ was established as the lower limit for the retirement-age penalty tax. The penalty tax applies now to retirement before 59½ and after April 1 of the year after the year the individual becomes 70½ . The age 59½ first appeared in the 1962 law P.L. 87-792, which is popularly known by its House title as the "Keogh Plan" after the congressman who sponsored it. Before that law, no penalty for early retirement existed. Prior to that Congress, there had been discussions of what the age brackets for penalty taxes should be for early or late pension-fund withdrawals. Congress had earlier suggested the brackets of 60-65 as the lower age. The age of 59½ was the result of several compromises. Age 60 was set, but age 59½ represents the "insurance age" of 60. Insurance age is a commonly used age in life insurance practice. For a discussion of the upper limit of 70½, see Footnotes 3 and 5, Chapter 11. (Source: Letter of September 19, 1994 from Ray Schmitt, Specialist in Social Legislation, and Louisa Hierholzer, Technical Information Specialist, Education and Public Welfare Division, Congressional Research Service, Library of Congress, Washington, D.C.)

same principles discussed here apply to your monthly investment allocation and your accumulation allocation goals.

MONTHLY CONTRIBUTIONS TO TIAA-CREF

A modest amount of information is available about the monthly contribution percentages of TIAA-CREF participants and their employers. About 60 percent of all employers use level contribution plans. The rest of them have steps in their plans whereby the percentage paid is related to such things as age and/or length of service.

Contributions information is available for the faculty of four-year colleges and universities, the professional and technical staffs of educational and scientific research organizations, the faculty of independent schools, and the faculty of junior and community colleges. The number of covered participants of the four-year colleges and universities is about three times as large as the total of the other three classes of organizations. Independent schools are schools that run from Kindergarten through the twelfth grade.

Table 7.4 shows the contribution percentages paid by the participant and the percentage of the contribution percentage paid by the employer for the four-year colleges and universities. In general, for all four classes of organizations, the contribution percentage is higher for the larger organizations within that class. In those cases in which the contribution level is under 10 percent, the employer is more likely to make the entire payment. The highest contribution rates, 15 percent and above, are paid more often by the other educational and scientific research organizations (33 percent of participants) and junior and community colleges (36 percent of participants), and four-year colleges and universities (37 percent of participants).

CONCLUSIONS

Four major strategies for increasing your TIAA-CREF were named and discussed. Each could add very substantially to your retirement benefits.

Almost all participants use the tax deferred salary option (TDA), but only about 20 percent use a Supplemental Retirement Annuity (SRA). The importance of the TDA and the companion tax sheltered annuity (TSA) on income earned on your investment is illustrated in Table 7.1. Depending on your selections, the rates earned on investments, and the length of time you are in the plan, you could well double your benefits as suggested in the illustration.

The extent to which you can increase your benefits with an SRA depends upon the difference between the present required contributions as a percentage of your budget-line salary and the (approximate) 20 percent maximum contribution permitted by the Internal Revenue Code. If the total required contribution made by yourself and your employer is 15 percent, for example, the additional 5 percent you could place in an SRA would add one-third ($.05 \div .15$) to your benefits from the date you started that strategy.

Shifting your allocation more in line with those recommended by TIAA-CREF (Table 3.1) and by Soldofsky (Table 3.2) could either increase or decrease your retirement benefits depending upon the direction of your reallocation, and the length of time the adjustment has to work for you.

Most participants have allocations that are too conservative. In my view, in most cases 100 percent in TIAA is imprudently conservative for a person who has at least 10 years until retirement and a life expectancy of more than 10 years after retirement. The data discussed in Chapters 3 and 6, and which will be discussed in subsequent chapters strongly suggests that benefits 20 years out could easily be double or more what they would have been if no change had been made toward the recommended allocations.

Clearly, working longer will increase your TIAA-CREF retirement benefits at the rate of about 10 percent per year. As pointed out, your social security benefits will increase about 3 percent per year after age 65, but only on your salary base up to the maximum amount counted toward those benefits.

The added benefits mount up quickly at 10% per year, but personal circumstances or short-sightedness may lead to early and—in retrospect—an imprudently early retirement.[5]

Other considerations for improving your funded benefits relate to the selection of an employer if you are in the fortunate position of having more than one comfortable employment option. If your present employer's salary level and total benefit package are inadequate in your view, carefully evaluate the pension and other benefits offered by another employer. Being patient until an acceptable opportunity arises may turn out to be better than making a move that only slightly increases your retirement-benefit prospects.

---

[5]See my Supplemental chapter on the experience of early retirees, and an extended discussion of the implications of your retirement age, which is available from the publisher.

TABLE 7.1

POWER OF TAX SHELTER AND DEFERRAL[a]

End of Year	No Tax Shelter & No Tax Deferral (Col. 1)	No Tax Shelter & Tax Deferral (Col. 2)	Tax Sheltered, Money Invested & Tax Deferral (Col. 3)
1	$1,800	$1,800	$2,412
2	1,895	1,944	2,605
3	1,995	2,100	2,813
4	2,100	2,267	3,038
5	2,211	2,449	3,281
10	2,860	3,598	4,822
20	4,785	7,768	10,409
30	8,004	16,771	22,473

[a]Assume interest at a constant 8 percent and combined federal and state taxes at about 34 percent amount taxable each year.

TABLE 7.2

**HOLDERS OF ACTIVE TIAA AND CREF ACCOUNTS
AUGUST 31, 1991**

	TIAA		CREF	% of
	NO.	%	NO.	TIAA
Accumulation Stage (Paying In)				
Regular	1,023,345	100.0	870,691	85.1
SRA	199,384	100.0	168,696	84.6
SRA/Regular		19.5		19.4
Annuitant Stage (Paying Out)				
Regular & SRA	223,886	100.0	120,312	53.7

TABLE 7.3

**NET TRANSFERS FROM CREF-EQUITIES TO TIAA
(IN $ MILLIONS)**

	1994	1993	1992
Net from CREF to TIAA	$ 190.6	$ 220.7	$ 381.3
Total CREF-End of Year	53,251.4	53,618.2	47,178.8
% Transferred	0.36%	0.42%	0.81%

TABLE 7.4

LEVEL CONTRIBUTION RATES FOR FACULTY
FOUR YEAR COLLEGES AND UNIVERSITIES[a]
1989

REQUIRED LEVEL CONTRIBUTION ONLY

Rate	% of Participants[b]
Under 10%	10.3%
10%	15.4
10.1 - 14.9%	38.4
15% and Above	35.9
	100.0%

EMPLOYER'S CONTRIBUTION

Rate	% of 4-Year Colleges[c]
Less than Half	0.3%
Half	30.0
More than Half	43.4
Entire Premium	24.3
	100.0%

[a]Level percentage plans only. Rates are expressed as a percentage of budget-line salary.

[b]About 331,000 employees.

[c]About 1,050 employers.

SOURCE: Documents provided by TIAA-CREF

CHAPTER 8

INVESTMENT BASICS

INTRODUCTION

Chapters 8 and 9 together provide a brief introduction to the field of investments. Chapter 8 covers Investment Basics and Chapter 9 covers Investment Background—that is, information and procedures that most people need to know. Some individuals know parts of this background from years of wide reading, but they rarely find systematic, clear and complete discussions of such topics as stock-price indexes.

The eight major sections of this chapter may be expressed as questions; these questions have a natural progression from the simple ones to the most complex. The last four questions have less clear cut and precise answers than the first four. The second topic or question dealing with compound interest and the cost of living may seem to be slightly out of place, but it highlights an aspect of compound interest that needs to be stressed. This topic is very generally omitted. Perhaps no better place exists to insert this topic than after the introduction of compound interest. The topics or questions are:

- What is the magic of compound interest?
- How is the compound interest procedure related to the cost of living over time?
- How is the understanding of bond prices, interest rates, and the term to maturity directly dependent on compound interest?
- How is compound interest the basis of understanding the common stock price growth model?
- How do the price-earnings ratio and dividend yields help to explain stock prices? How do these items relate to interest rates?
- What is the importance of the quality of earnings in the price-earnings ratio?
- Are trailing or leading earnings used in the price-earnings ratio?
- What methods are used to quantify risk? How are objective and subjective risk distinguished?

This chapter presents these basic investment processes and relationships that people in a market economy should know about investments in general and about financial markets in particular. As a TIAA-CREF participant you now have—or in a few more years will have—your largest single investment in TIAA and CREF. They invest in the financial markets for you, but you still have important decisions to make. You now have eight alternatives to chose among and more choices are likely to be added.

Although the term "investment basics" is used, most of these investment basics refer to processes that take place through time. The term "basic investment processes" might suggest even more clearly what is going on. The processes of compound interest are difficult—impossible—to disentangle from institutional developments such as the reinvestment of a part of its earnings by a corporation.

These investment basics are set forth in a stark, lean format. You can add your own embellishments to these bare-bones presentations. As a mature, capable adult you have a wide and deep experience upon which you can draw for such embellishments. For some participants these basics will serve as a systematic review; for others, much of the material will be new. I hope that it will provide you with a permanent reference on investments in securities.

The materials selected are basic to investments in stocks, bonds, and short-term securities. This material will be useful to your TIAA-CREF allocation decisions. Its applicability is not limited to TIAA-CREF investments. If you have increased confidence that you understand the fundamentals, including the role of a long time horizon underpinning your allocation decisions, you may feel much more comfortable about your financial future. Of course, you can make—and have made—investment decisions without being current on the basics. Your investment allocation decisions both within TIAA-CREF and outside of it may not work out any better with an understanding of the basics. However, an increased understanding will most likely have a strong, positive relationship with better decisions, and will provide higher and growing benefits during your retirement.

The material introduced does not include real estate investment and it is not directly applicable to mutual funds. A section in Chapter 9 deals with short-term investment instruments and the relative advantages of tax-exempt securities.

In this book, basics of security valuation are applied to corporate stocks and bonds. The ownership or equity of a corporation is divided into equal-sized units called shares or shares of ownership. Shares of stock are referred to as common stock because the stockholders own the corporation in common and share in the corporation's value on a pro rata basis. Several classes of stock such as preferred stock may be created. A preferred stock may be preferred with regard to dividends or assets or both in the event of dissolution. The total equity, in the simplest cases, is the net worth or owner's equity divided by the number of shares issued and outstanding. Bonds are formal "IOUs" of a corporation and notes are less formal "IOUs." The interest and principle on bonds and notes outstanding must be paid on time or the corporation is bankrupt. Dividends on common stock are charged against the past accumulated earnings of the corporation. Somewhat more detailed descriptions of bonds, mortgages, and preferred stock were given in the Bond section of Chapter 4.

MAGICAL COMPOUND INTEREST

Most people were first introduced to compound interest or geometric progressions in high school. Some have studied it further in college, and a few use it in their profession.

The fact that the arithmetic and algebra of compound interest are easy to understand does not make the explanation of the underlying source from which interest comes easy to explain. The mathematics of compound interest—sometimes described as geometric progressions— are taught in junior high school, but only advanced courses in economics and financial theory try to explain the underlying processes which give rise to causes of the existence of interest. To inquire into the underlying basis of interest would take the discussion a level deeper than Investment Basics as that term is being used.

Most people have heard that the sustainable growth rate for a developed economy such as that of the United States is about 2.5-3.0 percent per year. That growth rate, which is dependent on a balanced use of labor, management and capital goods, and upon annual savings and investments of goods, can produce an increase in the value of the product over what was produced the previous year. In an idealized world as pictured in economic theory this increase is called "interest." In the real world this idealized "interest" appears as interest on debt instruments, rents on property, and dividends and capital gains on stocks. Parts of this theory of real interest are attributed to the early nineteenth century English economist, David Ricardo, and other parts to the great, early twentieth century American economist, Irving Fisher.

The most basic topic in investments is compound interest. I have called it "Magical" because of the extent of growth of a sum of money invested over longer and longer periods of time. In its simplest forms compound interest and its twin, present value, are easy to calculate. The explanations of why interest exists in the first place quickly become complex and profound. Most of these explanations are driven back to the productivity of our natural resources combined with capital goods, labor, and management. Another explanation is the shortsightedness or impatience of human beings. These discussions can become as technical and philosophical as the "Big Bang" theory in cosmology.

INFLATION AND INTEREST RATES

The lowest or riskless market rate of interest is also linked to this idealized or "natural" rate of interest. This natural rate is also thought of as the lower limit to which the "real" rate of interest may fall. The real rate, in turn, is defined as the rate on the most nearly riskless securities in our society, U.S. government 30-day Treasury bills, less the anticipated rate of inflation. If the anticipated rate of inflation is steadily approximating zero, the market rate of interest—the real rate plus inflation would be close to 3 percent. As discussed in Chapter 9, longer term U.S. government securities have higher market interest rates because of the added risks which are associated with the anticipated, fluctuating inflation rates. For example, as I write the 30-year Treasury bond rate is 6.8 percent. A real interest rate of 3 percent plus an anticipated inflation rate of 3-4 percent, plus an allowance for the uncertainty in and fluctuations of that anticipated inflation ratio "explains" the market rate 6.8 percent. Increases or decreases in anticipated inflation and its uncertainty very largely explains the changes in the market rate.

This basic topic is included in this investment basics section as a very brief refresher, but may be skipped by those who know the subject. The bits of tables provided will be useful for other parts of the discussion of investment principles.

AMOUNT OF $1

Compound interest is just interest on interest. For example, if an investment earns interest at 6 percent per year, the amount of $1 will grow as follows:

Initial investment	$ 1.00
1st year's interest	0.06
End of 1st year	$ 1.06
2nd year's interest	0.0636
End of 2 years	$ 1.1236
3rd year's interest	0.0674
End of 3rd year	$ 1.1910

In general terms the amount of 1 or

$$s=(1 + i)^n$$

where i is the rate of interest

n is the number of periods

s is the amount of $1

PRESENT VALUE

The present value of $1 is the companion concept of the amount of $1. This concept is very useful in understanding how bonds work and for financial language in general.

The present value of $1 is the amount invested today that will grow to $1.00 by the end of a year or n periods.

$$v = \frac{1}{(1 + i)^n} = (1 + i)^{-n}$$

The present value or value of $1 today to be received one year from today when the interest (discount) rate is 6 percent is:

$$\frac{\$ 1}{1 + .06} = \$ 0.9434$$

An annuity is a series of payments. The present value of an annuity is given by:

$$a_{7} = \frac{1 - v^n}{i} = \frac{1 - (1 + i)^{-n}}{i}$$

The value of a bond is the present value of the sum of the interest payments (annuity) to be received until the bond matures plus the present value of the principal or par (face) value of the bond to be received when the bond matures.

When the interest rate rises, the present value of $1 falls as does the present value of an annuity. For example, in the above numerical illustration the present value of $1 when the interest rate is 6 percent is $0.9434. If the interest rate rises to 7 percent, as illustrated:

$$\frac{\$1}{1 + .07} = \$ 0.9346$$

The increase in the interest rate from 6 to 7 percent decreased the present value of $1 to be received at the end of the year by $0.0088 or $0.9434 - $0.9346. Table 8.1 gives the amount to which $1 will grow for various rates that are relevant for this book.[1]

AMOUNT OF $1 PER PERIOD

For some purposes the amount that would be accumulated by $1 invested at the beginning of each year is extremely useful.

The amount of $1 invested per period for three years with interest at 6 per cent is illustrated as follows:

Years Each $ is Invested		
1	$	1.00
2	$	1.06
3	$	1.1236
Total	$	3.1836

The lower panel of Table 8.1 gives some useful, selected values for the amount of $1 per period. Modern hand calculators can compute the amount for almost any period of years at whole and decimal rates as quick as a wink. (A whole rate would be 6 percent and a decimal rate would be 6.18 per cent, for example.)

The equation for the amount of $1 per period is:

$$s_n = \frac{(1 + i)^n - 1}{i}$$

where s_n stands for the amount of $1 per period.

Hence, one mystery that confuses most people who are not familiar with the language and operations of finance is solved: Interest rates and the price (present value) of a bond move in opposite directions as shown by the very simple, numerical example.

---

[1] The detailed explanations of compound interest equations may be found in many finance and investment books. My favorite is Moore, Justin H., Handbook of Financial Mathematics, New York: Prentice-Hall, 1929.

Modern hand calculators can compute the amount of $1, the amount of $1 per period, the present value of $1 and the present value of $1 per period as quickly as you can enter the rate and number of periods. Financial calculators can do bond prices and yields almost as quickly. Books of bond tables are also available in libraries.

COMPOUND INTEREST AND THE INFLATION RATE

The cost-of-living indexes are a part our intellectual baggage; they have been well known for half a century, but they hardly existed at the beginning of the twentieth century. For actively employed people, people planning for their retirement, and people in their retirement years, the prospective increases in the cost of living is a topic of lively interest and deep concern. What is overlooked is the extent of the compounding effect. Have you ever groaned when some older relative said, "When I was starting out I was only earning XXX per hour."? Have you every been tempted to say the same thing to your children or younger relatives?

Inflation growth rates have a compounding impact exactly like that of the compound-interest model. Over the 50 years since the end of World War II, the price level has risen almost ten fold.

This section has two major points:

- A steady, low rate of inflation has a stealth effect upon your ability to get along on your retirement income.

- Serious inflation in the United States has come in 3-4 year bursts. Each burst has a permanent effect.

Popular, technical and esoteric articles on inflation abound.[2] The point of this section is to emphasize the impact of inflation rates over a period of 10-25 years or more. You are likely to be in good health for at least 10 years after your retirement. If you and your spouse are the same age and retire at 65, your joint average or expected life span is about 25 years. If you retire earlier than 65, the length of your anticipated retirement is even longer. And you may be the one who lives well beyond the average expectation.

If inflation rises at the rate of 3 percent per year, for example, you will recognize there is a compounding process of exactly the sort demonstrated in the previous section. To construct a common-sense demonstration, the top panel of Table 8.2 repeats some of the information of the 3 percent and 6 percent columns from Table 8.1. Over the past 25 and 50 years ending in 1991, the inflation rate has averaged 5.8 percent and 4.6 percent, respectively.

The first two columns of Panel B show the extent of the increase in the years 10, 20 and 30. The second two columns express that increase as a percentage of the first-year increase. For example, in the tenth year at the 6 percent rate, the cost-of-living index increases 10.7 index points which is 78.3 percent more than the increase in the first year. The calculation is as follows:

---

[2] Two examples of such articles are: Davis, R.G. "Inflation: Measurement, and Policy Issues," Quarterly Review, Federal Reserve Bank of New York, Summer 1991, pp. 13-24; and "How Reliable Is the Consumer Price Index," Business Week, April 29, 1991, pp. 70-71.

Increase in index points
       year 10   10.7
       year 1   6.0
       Increase in index points   4.7

Increase in index points as a
percentage of first year's increase is $4.7 \div 6.0 = 78.3\%$

The lesson is clear. If the steady inflation rate is 6 percent and the news media keep stating that it is 6 percent, you may tend to lose track of the fact that your outlays in the tenth year of your retirement have gone up about three fourths. Even at the 3 percent inflation rate, your outlays will be up about one third in the tenth year.

Fifteen-20 years or more after your retirement, you are likely to be hard pressed by the lower purchasing power of your income. Try to take steps to protect yourself from the stealth effect of inflation long before your retirement.

CPI AND THE STANDARD OF LIVING

Other aspects of the Consumer-Price-Index (CPI) calculation need clarification and exposition beyond what is found in official explanations. Changes in federal income taxes, state income taxes, and social security taxes (FICA) are not included in the CPI. Changes in sales taxes get into the calculation through the prices of consumer purchases. Automobile license taxes and similar outlays are included as they are a part of the price paid for consumer services. However, as new fees for local services such as trash pick up are expanded in more localities, they are not included until the market basket underlying the CPI is revised. The last revision was done for 1982-84, but changes were not incorporated in the CPI until 1987. The next market basket revision may not occur until about 1995 or 97, depending upon the availability of funds.

Property taxes and increases thereon are not included directly in the CPI. One of the items in the market basket is rents on houses and apartments, but how far and to what extent property taxes are reflected in rents paid is an open question. The improving quality of homes, furnishings, and appliances are not included.

Medical insurance paid by employers is not included, but the employee's insurance cost is included. New medical services and medicines are slow to be included in the market basket. The CPI accurately reflects increases in the cost of goods and services <u>in</u> the market basket, but not the expansion of the market basket with the things we keep putting into it. Our outlays go up as we purchase more of the same items and new ones that are developed. But the CPI reflects the prices only of things in the old and occasionally revised basket. The CPI does not track what most people would call the cost of living and the standard of living.

Two things CPI users misunderstand most frequently are that it does not reflect asset values of things we own such as houses or employer-provided health care.

INFLATION SINCE WORLD WAR II

Since World War II the United States has had five bursts of inflation lasting up to three-four years. After World War II and the end of price controls in 1946, the inflation rate was 8.5

percent in 1946 and 14.4 percent in 1947. The war-time low was 1.7 percent in 1944. In 1951, during the Korean War, the inflation rate rose to 7.9 percent from 1.6 percent in 1950. The annual and cumulative increases in the Consumer Price Index are shown in Figure 8.1.

The inflation rate moved up during the Vietnam War years to just above 5 percent before it fell back again to a low of 3.2 percent in 1972. Next, after the effective formation of the Organization of Petroleum Exporting Countries (OPEC) and the rise in petroleum product prices, the inflation rate averaged above 10 percent for 1974 and 1975. The inflation rate calmed to a low of 5.8 percent in 1976 before rising above 10 per cent for three consecutive years--1979, 1980 and 1981. That most recent burst of inflation was caused by the second round of petroleum price increases and was accented by an essential change in monetary policy initiated by Paul Volcker when he became Chairman of the Federal Reserve Board in October 1979. His action was believed then and now to have been correct economically and it prevented a longer, higher, growing wave of inflation.

No one can accurately project—except by chance—when the next wave of inflation will strike, how high it will rise, or how long it will last. But you will surely experience at least one or two more such waves during your life time. The historical record shows that the process that wipes out very large or overwhelming debts accumulated by nation states has been inflation. Many hyperinflations have led to social and political revolutions.

Just for fun I have reproduced in Table 8.3 some price information from a 1991 catalogue.

BOND PRICE, INTEREST RATES, AND THE TERM OF MATURITY
The discussion of bond prices and interest rates cannot usefully be conducted unless one realizes how the present values of the interest-payment stream and the amount to be received at maturity on a bond are built up from the operations of compound interest. The current and changing prices of bonds are directly related to the changes in interest rates and to the date the bonds mature.

The Magical Compound Interest section contained several observations related to bond valuation:

- The present value of $1 is the reverse image of the growth of $1 compounding at same stated rate.

- The value of a bond is the sum of the present values of the interest payments to be received until it matures plus the present value of the par value to be received at maturity.

- The market price of a bond with a given contractual (coupon) interest rate will vary inversely with direction of the change in the interest rate.

The term to maturity is very important with regard to the change in the bond price for a given change in the interest rate.

For most people this inverse relationship between the change in market price and the change in the interest rate is mysterious. Though financial advisors and market analysts mention these changes frequently, people buying individual bonds or bond funds seldom ask what the remaining term to maturity is. Investors who do not understand the mechanics of bond prices may experience unexpected, substantial losses or gains. Those investors who do understand the mechanics may be able to achieve the gains and avoid the losses by changing the maturity on their bond portfolio as appropriate.

BOND PRICES AND INTEREST RATES MOVE INVERSELY

This inverse relationship is easily demonstrated by the data in Table 8.4. Assume that a $1,000 bond has five full years to maturity and has a coupon rate of 7 percent. You purchase the bond at par when it is issued. What would your gain or loss be if that rate quickly moved up to 8 percent or down to 6 percent?

Observe first in Table 8.4 that the present value of the $70 interest payment at the end of the first year gets lower as the interest rate rises. That is just the reverse side of the coin that something growing at 8 percent per year will grow faster than something growing at 6 percent per year. Something declining at 8 percent per year declines faster than something declining at 6 percent per year.

When the 7 percent coupon or contractual rate bond is issued and the market rate of interest is 7 percent also, the value of the bond is $1,000 as shown in the 7 percent column. The present value of the bond (price) is the sum of the present values of the interest payments for the five years until the bond matures plus the present value of the principal to be received at the end of the fifth year which total exactly $1,000.

If the market interest rate should unexpectedly and swiftly fall to 6 percent, the market price would rise to $1,042. Such an increase of $42 in a few days or even as long as one month amounts to a huge rate of return on an annualized basis. A 4 percent rise in one month would amount to more than 50 percent annualized when compounded monthly.

The rise in price occurs because the present value of each of the interest payments and that of the principal rises as the interest rate falls. The fall in rates does not cause the price rise; the price rise is the other side of the same event, the fall in rates. The fall in the bond price of about $40 as the interest rate rises is demonstrated in the 8 percent column.

INTEREST RATES MAY MOVE QUICKLY

Do market interest rates ever move very quickly? Yes, they do sometimes.

- When Iraq invaded Kuwait on September 19, 1990, the interest rate on U.S. government bonds maturing in 2018 was 8.38 percent and their price was $1,068.75. Fifty days later the market interest rate was 9.07 percent and the price of that same bond was $992.81. Bondholders lost $76.06.

- On January 13, 1993, just before Bill Clinton was inaugurated as President of the United States, the interest rate on long-term U.S. government securities was 7.35 percent and their average price was $1120.00. By March 3, 1993 the rate and price on that same bond series were 6.61 percent and $1208.00, respectively. A holder of this series would have earned $88.00 in less than two months.

- From mid-October 1994 to the end of that year, 30-year Treasury bonds lost almost 24 percent of their principal value as interest rates rose during that 2½ month period.

That loss was greater than the 22 percent loss in the DJIA on Black Monday, October 19, 1987.[3]

U.S. government bonds do not have default risk, but they obviously do have price risk. That price risk is a function of the remaining term to maturity as represented in Table 8.5.

The Table 8.5 demonstration assumes a 7 percent fixed or contractual rate on a series of bonds whose remaining term to maturity ranges from 1-30 years. The market interest rates in the table range from 5-10 percent. Note how sensitive prices are to a change in market interest rates as a function of the term maturity. A decline of one percentage point from 7 percent to 6 percent will result in a gain of almost 1 percent on a one-year maturity bond and a gain of almost 14 percent on a 30-year maturity bond. If the market rate of interest should rise from 7 percent to 8 percent, the declines in price are almost as large.

Professional investors and investment institutions are keenly aware of the fact that price risk increases as a function of the term to maturity. Hence, the market return is usually higher for long-term bonds. The reward from bond ownership is a combination of the interest earned and the capital gain or loss that may be experienced. Most bond analysts and financial advisors suggest that individuals hold bonds or bond funds with about a 5-10 year maturity.

The return on the marketable bond portfolio for CREF's Marketable Bond fund is evaluated periodically and at the end of the year. In 1994, the bonds in its portfolio matured anywhere from 1995 to 2031; the weighted average maturity was 8.9 years. Such an average maturity provides the participant with a higher average return, but it also results in wide year-to-year variability. The average maturity of TIAA's marked-to-book portfolio was 21 years.

The market return or yield to maturity on long-term U.S. government bonds has ranged from 5.53 percent in December 1972 to 13.28 percent in December 1981. Since then bond yields have generally fallen as the inflation rate subsided. The Marketable Bonds column of Table 3.6 reflects the annual total returns on corporate bonds from 1979 through 1994.

COMMON STOCKS AND HIGHER INTEREST RATES

Prices of common stocks are also strongly influenced by rising and falling interest rates for the same reasons as bonds. When stocks are purchased, you are buying the present value of the anticipated, future dividends and the future market price. When that interest (discount) rate falls—as it has generally since the early 1980s—market prices rise. When interest rates rise—as they surely will again—stock prices will fall.

The reinvestment process is another key to irregularly rising stock prices. The price of a CREF-Equities unit was $10.00 when the fund was started in 1952. In April 1995 it went above $75.

THE COMMON STOCK PRICE GROWTH MODEL

The halting growth in stock prices, especially the prices of a group of stocks such as the DJIA or S&P 500, is another mystery to most people. That mystery is easily resolved with a little understanding of the reinvestment process which is another use of compound interest.

---

[3]Thomas T. Vogel, Jr., "Lingering Pain," Wall Street Journal, December 30, 1994, p. C1.

Reinvestment refers to a portion of a business's earnings that are not paid out in dividends each year, but which are retained and reinvested.

On September 5, 1897, the DJIA was 77.61. It reached 352.86 on October 10, 1929, just before the panic on Black Thursday, October 29. By January 3, 1960, the DJIA topped at 685.47. Another important top of 2722 came on August 25, 1987, just before the crash on Black Monday, October 19, 1987, dropped the DJIA 508 points in one day. The low reached in that bear market cycle that day was 1739.[4]

The DJIA rose just above 4700 in July 1995, and rose above 5200 briefly before year's end.

- What explains such irregularly rising stock prices?

- How high is too high for common stocks as measured by some index such as the DJIA, the Standard & Poor's 500, or the Russell 3000--which is the one CREF now prefers to use as an index or measuring stick for the performance of CREF-Equities.

Following the lead of a nineteenth century actuary, Ralph Todhunter, Robert Gordon and Eli Shapiro worked out and popularized a reinvestment model in 1956. The reinvestment process is easier to demonstrate in tabular form than to explain in the form of increasingly complex equations. Part of the higher-and-higher price levels reached by the various stock-price indexes is explained by inflation, but much of the higher price is explained by the reinvestment process.[5]

An ancient practice of business corporations is to pay out only a part of earnings in the form of cash dividends. The difference between the amount paid out and the earnings, the retention, is reinvested in the business. The retention is invested at a positive rate of return, and this process is repeated day after day, week after week, month after month, and year after year. The exposition of this process is simplified by assuming annual reinvesting and compounding as illustrated in Table 8.6. In this table the skeleton or model of the reinvestment process is exposed. The daily ups-and-downs of a business, seasonal cycles, and business cycles are omitted. All that remains is the scaffolding on which the idealized, steadily-growing earnings, prices, retentions, book value, and dividends appear.

In this idealized world, each of the four variables is shown on a per share basis: EPS is earnings per share, DPS is dividends per share, RPS is retention per share, and BVPS is book value per share. In this idealized world, the BVPS is always the same as the market price. The DPS divided by EPS is the pay-out ratio, and EPS minus RPS is the retention. In recent

---

[4]The drop in the DJIA on October 19, 1987, was 22.6 percent of the market value of the beginning of the day. The market closed at its daily low. The drop in the DJIA on October, 1929 was 30.57 points or 11.7 percent of the opening value of 260.64. The intraday low on October 29, 1929 was 212.33, which amounted to a drop of 48.31 points or 18.5 percent. More information on the extent of the bull and bear markets in this century is reviewed in Chapter 9.

[5]For an introductory exposition of the Gordon-Shapiro model and some of its complications and limitations, see Soldofsky, R. M. and Olive, G. Financial Management, Cincinnati, OH., Southwestern Publishing, Co., 1974.

years the dividend pay-out ratios for industrials and public utilities have been about 54 percent and 69 percent, respectively. One other assumption is needed to make the model operational: the rate of return on investment. A reinvestment rate of 15 percent, which is very reasonable in the world of business corporations, is used.

This framework set in Table 8.6 provides a growth rate of 6 percent because the 15 percent return on investment is reduced by the pay-out ratio which is assumed at 60 percent. The RPS of 40 percent times the rate of return of 15 percent gives 6 percent per year. With these assumptions, the process is nothing but the amount of $1 growing at 6 percent a year.

The process is illustrated by the rows (years) in the table. During and at the end of Year 1, the BVPS is $6.67. That amount earning at 15 percent produces EPS of $1.00. The DPS paid is $.60 and the RPS is $.40. In the second year, the added RPS of $.40 invested at 15 percent earns $.06 (rounded), bringing the income up to $1.06. Another approach is that the BVPS is up to $7.09 in the second year. That $7.09 invested at 15 percent provides an income of $1.06 (rounded). For the second year, $.636 is paid out in dividends and $.424 is retained. That retention brings the BVPS up to $7.51, which invested at 15 percent generates earnings of $1.127.

The procedure goes on as long as you wish to run the model. Each of the four columns in the model is growing at 6 percent per year compounded.

For the 15 years through the end of the 1992, the earnings of the Dow Jones Industrials and those on the S&P 500 have grown at about 4.9 percent and 4.1 percent, respectively.

THE PRICE-EARNINGS RATIO AND DIVIDEND YIELD

Two of the most widely used rules of thumb for stock-market investors are the price-earnings ratio and the dividend yield. The latter may be reversed or called the price-dividends ratio. These two rules of thumb can easily be related back to market interest rates and the rates at which corporate earnings are growing. The latter relates back to the processes of compound interest.

The price-earnings (P/E) ratio and dividend yield (DY) are used for analyzing the stock market in general, and for analyzing and comparing the performance of individual stocks. The P/E ratio is the reciprocal of the E/P ratio. If the S&P 500 or the Composite Index stands at 500,[6] and the earnings on those stocks is $25, the P/E is 20 or 20 times the earnings. The E/P is .05 or 5 percent. The E/P in this form can be related to both the market interest rate and to the dividend yield. When the S&P Composite is 500, the dividends may reasonably be $15; the DY is 3.00 percent or $15 divided by 500.

As an important aside, you may wonder why the S&P 500 is being used at this point rather than the more popular DJIA average of 30 stocks. Three important reasons for using the S&P 500 are easily stated. First, it is technically far superior in terms of its construction. Second, because the DJIA consists of only 30 stocks, the composite earnings on these stocks can and do fluctuate violently. The DJIA is so loaded with petroleum and heavy industry company stocks that it had negative earnings for the third and fourth quarters of 1982 and for the fourth

---

[6]The use of the S&P 500 Index with the index itself at 500 may be confusing but as of March 1995 that index stood at 499. An index level of 500 is convenient to use.

quarter of 1991. Third, the S&P is more representative of all segments of American industry including public utilities, transportation and finance company stocks. A virtue of both of these series is that both have companion earnings and dividends series. Most of the other well-known averages such as the New York Times and NASDAQ have no such companions.

Nevertheless, the P/E on the DJIA is useful and more easily located. It is published in the Monday edition of the Wall Street Journal and in Barrons. The S&P 500 P/E is published regularly in Business Week and Fortune. The S&P Outlook, which is in most libraries, carries both the S&P 500 and the DJIA P/Es. The Outlook also has projected P/Es.

The P/E ratio is a gauge from which you may infer whether prices are relatively high or low compared with earnings. Experience shows that the typical range for the P/E is between 10 and 20 times earnings for the past 25 years as shown in Figure 8.2, Panel A. When the P/E gets up to about 20, stock investors become concerned that the market in general is "too" high. When it is below 12, it is quite low and may represent a buying opportunity.

The DY, closely related rule of thumb for investment decisions, is displayed as Figure 8.2, Panel B, for the same period for the same index directly below the P/E chart for convenience. Any DYs above about 5 percent are quite attractive to stock purchasers. Those below about 3.25 percent are seen as warning signs that prices are too high relative to dividends. The DY will be discussed later in this section.

PRICE-EARNINGS
Under the idealistic, simplified circumstances of the stock-price growth model, the P/E would be constant.

Why then does the P/E migrate within such wide boundaries?

Two sets of interrelated forces help explain its range. The first is a general set of economic conditions. They are, first and most importantly, the forecast for the Gross Domestic Product two quarters ahead. Second, the Leading Economic Indicators prepared monthly by the Department of Commerce.[7] More properly, the P/E is sensitive to anticipated changes in these variables.[8] The other set of factors are specific to individual companies. Most important are the expected earnings in the next quarter and the longer run growth prospects for the company and the industry.

Obviously, with reference to the processes of compound interest, the higher and more certain the likely earnings growth rate of a company, the higher its P/E will be. The next quarter's projected earnings change is more important than progressively more distant earnings because investors have more confidence in the accuracy of next quarter's projection.

---

[7]The Leading Economic Indicators are often reported after they are released once each month in the five-minute news summaries. The LEI consists of 62 series, 45 of which are based upon the realm of real series such as production, factory orders, and construction. The other 17 are based upon the realm of financial series such as stock prices and interest rates.

[8]For the background on this subject, see Soldofsky, Robert M. Performance of Long-Term Marketable Securities: Risk-Return, Ranking and Timing, Financial Analysts Research Foundation, University of Virginia, Charlottesville, 1988.

The clear tendency of the three variables, long-term interest rates, E/P ratios, and DYs, is suggested by observations from 1967, 1981, and 1991. The years 1967 and 1981 have the lowest DYs and highest long-term interest rates, respectively, in the past 25 years. These data are as follows:

Years	Long-Term Bonds[a]	E/P[b]	DY[b]	(P/E)[b]
1967	4.65%	5.6%	3.03%	18.00 times
1981	13.28	12.3	5.41	8.12 times
1991	7.56	5.5	2.84	18.05 times

[a]Long-term U.S. Treasury bonds for December of that year.

[b]S&P 500 for the last quarter of that year.

Current conditions always provide added explanatory power at each point. For example, in 1991 and throughout 1992 and into 1993, the P/E ratio rose to extraordinary heights and the DY fell very low as large numbers of people moved funds out of very low yielding certificates of deposit and into common stocks in search for higher current income and in the hope of some price appreciation.

EARNINGS PROJECTIONS AND THE P/E RATIOS

The first part of the fifth introductory question was, "What is the P/E Ratio." That question can now be further specified to ask, "How accurate is the E or earnings part of that ratio?"

- How accurate and timely are the P/E ratios?

- Why do the P/E ratios as published differ for the same date?

The P/E ratio for the DJIA as published in the Wall Street Journal and Barrons are always based upon the latest 12 months' earnings available. Those earnings are always 3-5 months behind the current date because of the time it takes to prepare and publish corporate earnings and because not all corporations have their quarters end at the same time. For example, a few companies have their quarters ending on January 31 or February 28 as well as the more popular December 31. The investor usually assumes the earnings data and the P/E are current. He would like to have the next 12 months' estimated earnings and have it accurate.

Standard & Poor's Outlook, a weekly advisory service, publishes estimates of what they and others believe the whole year's earnings will turn out to be for both the DJIA and its own 500 Index. For example, they started publishing their 1992 earnings estimates in October of 1991. However, the final or actual 1992 earnings were not available until almost June of 1993. The 1992 estimates changed six times as shown in Table 8.7

The S&P's Outlook published the P/E ratio each week in 1992 based upon their latest estimate of what those earnings would turn out to be for the whole year. Obviously, the P/E on the DJIA as published in the Outlook and summarized in Table 8.7, would have doubled based upon the same average DJIA from January 8 to October 7, 1992 as the estimated earnings fell by more than one half. The projected earnings on the S&P 500 fell about 16 percent during 1992. Not until about April 1993 were the published earnings on the S&P 500 close to the eventual, actual, 1992 earnings.

The changes in the 1994 estimated earnings in the Outlook for the DJIA and the S&P 500 were not nearly as large and dramatic as they were for the 1992 estimates. The estimate for the DJIA 1994 earnings started with $185.76 on October 10, 1993 and rose irregularly to $221.19 on October 12, 1994 and were up to $254.98 on June 28, 1995; they had increased 37 percent above their original estimate. The earnings on the S&P for 1994 were estimated at $31.49 on October 20, 1993, fell to $29.17 on March 3, 1994, rose again to $30.42 on November 9, 1994, and were at $30.65 on June 28, 1995.

Using Dow Jones' own latest published DJIA 12 months' earnings on the 30 stocks in its average leads to equally large problems during a period of rapid economic change. The DJIA earnings are published about 4-6 months after the fact. Their earnings available to the user were as follows:[9]

Quarterly Date	Last 12 Months' Estimated Earnings Amount	Used in the DJIA P/E ratio until about
Sept. 30, 1991	$ 100.91	March 1992
Dec. 31, 1991	49.27	June 1992
March 31, 1992	60.62	Sept. 1992
June 30, 1992	71.60	Dec. 1992
Sept. 30, 1992	84.35	March 1993

Hasty decisions made on the basis of published DJIA P/E ratios in the Outlook or the Wall Street Journal could easily turn out to be wrong. The DJIA's P/E based upon the estimate of the current year's earnings is much more useful than one based upon the trailing DJIA's P/E published in the Wall Street Journal, in my opinion. Nevertheless, the P/E boundary guidelines for switching investments from CREF-Equities to its money market fund are fuzzy, to say the least. Rapid changes in the P/Es should be examined further to determine the extent to which that change is the result of a change in the stock index itself or in the earnings element.

Changes in the DY are typically smaller because dividend pay-outs are generally held steady or changed in only small increments. Analysts should review both the P/E and the DY in discussions of the state of the stock market and before recommending any switching between stocks and other investments.

---

[9]The estimated DJIA earnings published in The Outlook for three dates in 1992 as shown in Table 8.7 may be compared with those in the tabulation below. Note how different the estimated earnings were from the actual trailing, published earnings.

DIVIDEND YIELDS

The dividend yield (DY) on a stock as defined is the (cash) dividend divided by the market price. The decision rules that corporations use to make their dividend payment decisions are discussed in all financial management textbooks. Those rules are of little concern for this statement of investment basics because of its focus on the aggregate of individual company dividends by the financial organizations that prepare the stock market indexes.

As noted earlier, the dividend-to-earnings or pay-out ratio for industrials and for public utilities are about 54 percent and 69 percent, respectively. Faster growing companies with less stable earnings such as industrials typically pay out a lower proportion of their earnings in the form of dividends. Public utilities, which are slower growing with more stable earnings than industrials, usually have a higher dividend-pay out ratio. Very rapidly growing companies often pay out little or nothing in dividends. These companies usually have the highest rate of return on reinvestment opportunities; their P/E ratios are the highest in the market. They can sell additional stocks if they need more funds to finance expanding operations at a price several times the book value of a share. They are often reluctant to do so, however, because new stock issues "dilute" or lower earnings per share. Dilution occurs because the same earnings must be divided by a larger number of shares outstanding.

But as a long-term investor in your pension fund, and perhaps one or more mutual funds holding common stocks, you may be less concerned with the performance of individual common stocks. You may be intellectually curious about the forces that move the overall market quickly in one direction or another. More likely you are concerned about your holdings of CREF-Equities. Should you adjust your monthly investment allocation or shift some of your accumulation from CREF-Equities to its money market fund?

Generally, individuals who make such adjustments are likely to lose because they delay the adjustment decisions to shift into the money market funds too long and then delay the decision to shift back to stocks too long. Academic studies show that such timing and switching is most likely to result in no gains or losses in the aggregate. However, switching does have an out-of-pocket cost in most cases, as well as the cost of the time, energy, and personal trauma that may be involved. Other studies show that regular, monthly investing and dollar-cost averaging is likely best for most people who have little or no knowledge of the financial markets.[10]

CORRELATIONS AMONG THE VARIABLES

As a key to switching, many "experts" look to the DY and P/E ratios. Note that the P/E and DYs panels of Figure 8.2 are placed so that you can review the movements of these two

---

[10]See Clements, Jonathan, "Market Timing Is A Poor Substitute for a Long-Term Investment Plan," Wall Street Journal, January 17, 1995, p. C1. This item reviews the performance of market timers and market-timing funds with stock market averages. Most recently a National Bureau of Economic Research studied the investment strategy of 237 investment advisory services for the 1980-92, and came to the same conclusion. See John Graham and Campbell Harvey, "Marketing Timing Ability and Volatility Implied in Investment Newsletters' Asset Allocation Recommendations," NBER Working Paper No. 4890, National Bureau of Economic Research, Cambridge, MA, March 1995.

variables for the same time periods. The correlation coefficient for these two variables is .852; it is so high that one can argue it represents two views of the same thing. Variables that help explain the movement of funds between the stock market and other markets are the Treasury bill rates and long-term interest rates. The correlations of these four variables against one another since 1967, based on semiannual data, are shown in Table 8.8.[11]

But one would really like to know before shifting funds out of CREF-Equities is what these variables are likely to do over the next 6-12 months. At this point economic and financial soothsayers all stumble. Of course, given enough expert opinions, some forecasters are bound to be correct, if only by chance. No one has a long record of being correct most of the time.

For more than a decade, just after the first of the year and just after midyear, the Wall Street Journal has published the projections of highly respected forecasters for the coming six months and 12 months. The projected variables include interest rates on three-month Treasury bills, 30-year Treasury Bonds, the Gross Domestic Product, and the inflation rate. The range of forecasts is startling. If you had accurate projections of these variables you might be able to time switches from CREF—or other indexed stock funds—into a money market fund. However, if the projections were more accurate, less opportunity would exist for increasing your return from timing your switches "correctly."

QUALITY OF EARNINGS

The price part of the price-earnings ratio is a reading of the results of the competitive pricing processes of the stock markets, but the earnings part of that ratio is the subject of numerous rules and conventions that have developed largely during this century. As will be explained by illustrations and surveys, the price itself reflects the "quality" of the earnings. Even somewhat more titillating is the importance of using past or trailing earnings as contrasted with future or leading earnings in the price-earnings ratios. Ideally, economists and financial analysts want to know future earnings with absolute certainty, but can only get projections of differing likelihoods. Interest payments on bonds can be projected with much more assurance than can the earnings of common stock. Hence, the risk in bonds is lower than it is in stocks, and bond returns are generally lower to reflect that lower risk.

Another level of detail is the quality of earnings and its influences on the P/E of individual stocks and on stock indexes. The quality of earnings topic represents the concern with how accurately and how timely underlying business reality is reported in published profit and loss statements. Economic theorists have no trouble defining net income as the difference between revenue and costs and expenses when the balance sheet values remain unchanged. For these economists, all revenues and costs and expenses are priced at their market values at the moment exchanges take place.

---

[11]Several different multiple correlations were tried, but the results were of little additional help. They did suggest that the markets are highly segmented. Some investors responded sharply to changes in Treasury bill rates and others more to changes in long-term interest rates.

The reality underlying accounting procedures is amazingly complex and becoming increasingly more complex each year.[12] The continuing, astounding changes over the past 40 years are as great as those in medicine and physics.

A Wall Street Journal article of October 18, 1990, quoted Susan Lakotos of Kidder Peabody and Co., an excellent investment banking firm, and Steven Einhorn of the redoubtable Goldman Sachs and Co., on the topic of quality of earnings.[13] Susan Lakotos is acknowledged to be an outstanding Wall Street analyst on the quality of earnings. She said that corporate earnings overall were about 25 percent higher than they should be if more conservative figures were used for such things as the cost of materials and depreciation that are charged against sales.[14] Steven Einhorn, a frequent guest on Louis Rukeyser's Friday evening Public TV program, Wall Street Week, said true earnings were as much as 40 percent below reported profits in 1940 and as much as 50 percent below in 1986-87.

When a more detailed analysis is undertaken, the earnings estimates are shown to be different over different industries and at different times. The quality of earnings problem compounds the timing of reported earnings problems discussed in the prior section. Knowing just what the reasonable range is for the P/E ratio is much more subtle both for stock averages and for individual corporations than it appears to be when the subject is first introduced.

The classifications useful to the discussions of quality of earnings are usually set out in categories that are not mutually exclusive; they overlap and interrelate among companies and industries. The impact of price-level changes is the most widespread category. The most important sub-category is the effect of price-level changes upon depreciation. A distant second is the cost of inventory as it enters into the cost of goods sold. Some deterioration in the quality of earnings from items such as depreciation can be anticipated. Others are recognized over a few years as the result of changes in accounting or income-tax rules, and still others may come as almost complete surprises. These surprises have the greatest effect upon the prices of stocks and stock funds that concentrate their holdings in companies that are affected by similar problems. High write-offs for real estate loans by insurance companies and the delayed recognition of pension liability cost are two examples that come to mind.

Deterioration in quality of earnings from depreciation is most often discussed at the aggregate level. The most important cause is depreciation expenses gradually getting further from the true or current cost of that expense as price increases. Fixed assets may last 10-20 years or more. Depreciation is charged on the original purchase price. As replacement prices rise, production costs of older machines that flow into the expenses of the company do not increase. Such old costs can easily become 50 percent or more too low. Industries that use

---

[12]Glover, T.G. Quality of Earnings, New York: The Free Press, 1987.

[13]Donnelly, B. "Profit Quality Erodes Making Them Less Reliable," Wall Street Journal, Oct. 18, 1990, p. C1.

[14]By "conservative" is meant at prices closer to the current market prices. Accounting numbers (prices) always reflect actual prices at the date of purchase and are never changed.

more heavy, long-lasting equipment (such as public utilities) have the worst problems. P/E ratios of public utility stocks take such things into account.

Depreciation leads to additional problems because a building or piece of machinery can be fully depreciated over a long or shorter period of years as permitted by the tax code. Furthermore, even the same total purchase price to be depreciated over 10 years can be charged off in a way that has the highest depreciation in the first year and lower charges thereafter. Sometimes a reverse tactic is used with lower charges first and higher charges later. Or depreciation can be charged to some extent each year. However, each company's policy on such matters are well known.

On other occasions, changes in accounting rules are necessary to keep up with changed circumstances, as in the field of medical costs. Over the past decade or two companies have agreed to pay some part of retiree's medical bills. At first these amounts were small, but they have grown to enormous proportions. The payments for post-retirement medical insurance are properly a charge or cost during the employee's working years.

In 1985 the Securities and Exchange Commission (SEC) asked the Financial Accounting Standards Board (FASB) to study these post-retirement medical costs. FASB decreed after several years of study that those costs (benefits) should be placed on the books in the periods they were earned by employees. Costs not recorded in earlier years will also have to be accounted for by charges against revenues in the coming years. In other words, the quality of earnings had deteriorated; reported earnings were "too" far below the full costs incurred.

The FASB Statement Number 101 of 1991 said that all such medical costs would have to be recognized on the books when they were incurred, starting no later than 1993. Past costs can be recognized a little each year. At the time, analysts said that these costs might be as much as $400 billion per year. That sum was larger than all corporate profits in a single years. Later estimates said the costs could be as much as $1 trillion over a few years. In 1989 Chrysler estimated that recognizing health-care costs for active employees would add about $260 million to its costs; that was about half of its pretax net income.

The Chrysler case is not unique. For corporations such as AT&T and DuPont, these required accruals could be one-fourth or more of their respective owners' equity.[15]

The Financial Accounting Standards Board, a non-governmental board organized and financed by the accounting profession, has made hundreds of rulings that have the effect of law. It was organized in 1973 to succeed a prior self-regulating body for the accounting profession. FASB is one of several self-regulating bodies operating under the general oversight of the Securities and Exchange Commission. The SEC also oversees such other self- regulating bodies as the New York Stock Exchange (NYSE) and the National Association of Securities Dealers (NASD).

INDIVIDUAL CORPORATE EARNINGS ADJUSTMENTS
The Wall Street Journal probably publishes the most extensive newspaper summaries of individual corporate earnings reports. These summaries bunch 15-45 days after the end of each calendar quarter. The earnings summaries for more than 200 companies for the last

---

[15]Burton, L. and Brennan, R. J. Wall Street Journal, April 22, 1992, p.C1.

week of July 1990 were reviewed. The reported adjustments to earnings were catalogued into 11 different classes as shown in Table 8.9. The effects of these changes upon reported earnings per share were estimated where it was possible to do so.

The accounting profession is sensitive to complete disclosure of non-routine business transactions and presentations of the facts in accordance with FASB rules. Within these rules, alternatives are sometimes sanctioned. Accounting Trends and Techniques, an annual study of the reports of 600 large industrial and merchandising firms, reviews these changes in a 500 page book.[16] I reviewed the AT&T summaries of adjustments to income statements and included them in Table 8.9 using the same classifications. The meaning of most of the classifications is self explanatory.

One point of this review is that such adjustments to earnings are quite commonplace. Another point is that only the very informed stockholder is likely to take the time to study these adjustments for the stocks he or she owns. Unexpected disclosures about earnings can and do affect stock prices. Unanticipated events such as mergers, natural disasters, or changes in international exchange rates affect stock prices. Mutual funds and insurance companies sometimes hire investment houses and consulting companies to study the accounting policies of firms before they make a decision to buy, sell, or hold a stock. In such circumstances, the individual investor, who does not spend considerable time and money on stock investment decisions, may well be at a disadvantage.

In my July 1990 survey of the earnings summaries for the 31 companies for which I could calculate the impact of the adjustments upon earnings the results were as follows:

Effects on Earnings as a Percentage of Preadjustment Earnings		Percentage of Companies
101% or more	up	9.7 %
51% to 100%	up	6.4
26% to 50%	up	3.2
11% to 25%	up	25.8
00% to 10%	up	19.4
Losses		35.5
Total		100 %

RISK AVERSION

The term, risk aversion, or risk-averse, has been part of the language since the 1960s. It is used in the TIAA-CREF 1992 publication, The CREF Global Equities Account. Although most people give the term instinctual meaning based upon their own experiences, in finance

---

[16]Shobet, J. and Rikert, R. (eds.) Accounting Trends and Techniques. New York, American institute of Certified Public Accountants, 1990. (Published annually).

it has at least two distinct meanings. The degree or intensity of risk aversion can be and is measured.

Two approaches are regularly used. In the first approach, rates of return are functionally related to utiles, which are units of arbitrary, subjective but internally consistent measures of satisfaction.[17] In the second case, the utiles of satisfaction are held constant, but risk is increased. The experimental or intellectual reaction of the investor (respondent) to the increased risk is measured. In the second approach, risk is usually measured in terms of the standard deviation. These approaches are represented in the two panels of Figure 8.3. The utility approach to risk measurement is presented next and the chapter concludes with three statistical measures of risk.

UTILITY FUNCTIONS

Panel A in Figure 8.3, shows utiles on the vertical axis and rate of return on the horizontal. The values for the utiles are arbitrary; they could just as easily be at a much lower or higher level. The rates of return are scaled to reflect levels experienced in the financial markets.

The risk-neutral line, BB, demonstrates a proportionate increase in return and satisfaction expressed as utiles. Risk aversion is demonstrated by the downward bending curve, CC, which shows that proportionately larger increases in return are required by this investor for equally-sized increases in satisfaction. A built-in assumption is that added risk and added return are very highly correlated. Hence, more and more return is required for accepting equal-sized increases in risk.

This downward-bending, risk-aversion curve may be established by any one of several techniques used to measure attitudes toward risk. Assume that a certain or 100 percent safe return is 6 percent. Point A on Figure 8.3 represents 100 utiles and a 6 percent return. Now an investor is asked to choose between (1) a 50 percent chance of getting a 12 percent return and a 50 percent change of getting zero and (2) 6 percent certain return. Even though the average or mean value of the first choice is 6 percent, most investors would choose 6 percent certain; that is, they are risk averse.

Next assume the same investor has a 12 percent certain return. Perform another fair gamble exercise. He has (1) a 50-50 chance of getting a zero return and (2) a 50-50 chance of getting a return just exactly high enough for him to give up the 12 percent certain. How high a return would he require?

If he responds 30 percent when the mean of the 50-50 gamble outcome is 15 percent, he is stating that a 3 percentage-point gain above the 12 percent certain outcome would just barely induce him to take the gamble. An entire risk aversion curve can be traced out in such a fashion.

The risk-aversion curve for Investor D is shown further to the right than that for Investor C; that is, Investor D is more risk averse than Investor C, as suggested by curve DD.

---

[17]For an introductory discussion see Swalm, R. O. "Utility Theory -Insights Into Risk Taking," Harvard Business Review N-D 1966 pp. 123-136, or McFarlane, D. D. and Horowitz, I. "Risk and the Business Decision," Business Horizons, Summer 1969, pp. 88-95.

Another investor, E, enjoys the excitement of the game or the risk. Investor E might be willing to accept a 50-50 chance of a zero or 10 percent return rather than 6 percent certain; the average is 5 percent. Investor E would be called a risk taker or a risk seeker; his utility function is shown by EE in Figure 8.3.

In the second framework for establishing the attitude toward risk, the rate of return is shown on the horizontal axis, and risk measured by the standard deviation is shown on the vertical axis, as shown in Panel B of Figure 8.3. The number of utiles is set arbitrarily at 100 for a 6 percent return where the standard deviation is zero. In other words, there is no risk. If risk increases—as measured by the standard deviation—as suggested by the vertical curve AA, the person is indifferent to the risk; he is said to be risk neutral.

The curves BB and CC represent two successively more risk-averse individuals. At 2 standard deviations of risk, Investor B believes her combination of an 8.5 percent return gives her the same number of utiles as a 6 percent return and no risk. In fact, Investor B is equally well satisfied with each and every combination of risk and return along the curve, BB.

Curve BB is a form of indifference curve. Of course, the investor would prefer a combination such as a 7 percent return and zero risk because that would increase her utiles of satisfaction above 100. Investor C may also have 100 utiles of satisfaction from a 6 percent return at zero risk. However, he is more risk averse as suggested by curve CC; he requires a higher return for a given level of risk than Investor B.

The risk-seeker curve bends to the left in this framework. As risk increases, the Investor D would accept a lower and lower return. For example, Investor D would be indifferent to a 1 standard deviation chance that might put her earnings between 0 and 10 percent with a 50-50 chance of earning 5 percent. Experiments have shown that such individuals do exist—at least for a part of the relevant range.

STANDARD DEVIATION AND VARIANCE

Many advanced methods of dealing with risk are developed and used in finance. Only three of the most widely used methods are mentioned and presented.[18] The standard deviation, coefficient of variation, and correlation coefficient are used to a very limited extent earlier in this book.[19] Even this limited use provides insights into the relationship between return and risk on a wide range of securities or groups of securities.

These three simple statistical methods were applied to objective data in Chapter 3 and in following presentation. However, another realm exists—the realm of attitudes toward risk. This realm is introduced in this section. You may recognize several terms from it such as risk averse, which TIAA-CREF uses in one of its pamphlets, and risk seeker or risk lover.

The terms standard deviation and variance are becoming increasingly widely understood in the general population and especially in the college, university, and research communities. Many hand-held calculators have special keys and procedures for preparing these two statistics, and all computer programs can produce them in a few moments after the data are entered.

The common-sense meaning of these measures of risk are easy enough to visualize even for those who are unfamiliar with them or who have not used them in a long time. Understanding these terms enhances the meanings of risk averse, risk neutral and risk taker.

To prepare a standard deviation, first calculate the arithmetic average of some series of numbers. For example, the average or arithmetic mean of 2 percent, 4 percent, 6 percent, 8

---

[18]The search for the most useful ways of dealing with financial risk continues to widen and deepen. Formal methods of dealing with financial risk started at least as early as the 1950s. Financial calculators have included simple statistical methods since the 1970s and advanced methods are now included in most software programs for financial analysis. Investment Management Division of the SEC asked for public comment in March 1995 for ways to assess risk in mutual funds. By June, they received about 1500 responses, which was far more comments than received on any previous issue on which public comment was sought. The plan of the SEC is to require mutual funds to disclose some risk-measurement on their funds. Investors seek such information and the fund companies resist the effort. Six measures of risk are published by Morningstar, one of the companies that ranks mutual funds. These six methods are: (1) the standard deviation, (2) the largest beta, (3) the highest average price/earnings ration, (4) the most concentrated in a few investments, (5) the most concentrated in one sector, and (6) the largest monthly loss in the last five years. Many other methods are in use. The beta mentioned in (2) is based on the use of standard deviations, correlations and other statistics; it shows how much this one fund (or stock) fluctuates relative to the whole stock market. (John R. Dorfman, "SEC May Extend Period for Receiving Ideas on Relaying Fund Risks to Investors," Wall Street Journal, July 5, 1995, Page C1.)

[19]See Tables 3.7 and 3.8 for these measures worked out for the eight distinct TIAA-CREF funds.

percent, 10 percent, and 12 percent is 7 percent. Other series may have the same mean, but the dispersion between the numbers may be wider or narrower. Two other series and the original one that all have the average value of 7 percent are:[20]

	Series		
X_i	I	II	III
X_1	4%	1%	2%
X_2	5	2	4
X_3	6	4	6
X_4	8	9	8
X_5	9	12	10
X_6	10	14	12
Total (Σ)	42%	42%	42%
Average ($\overline{X}$)	7.000 %	7.000 %	7.000 %
Std. Dev. (σ)	2.160	4.970	3.416
Variance (σ^2)	4.667	24.670	11.667

Obviously, the larger the dispersion of the numbers, the larger the standard deviation and the variance.

The small sigma, σ, in the formula represents the standard deviation. The radical sign says to take the square root. N represents the number of observations, X_i, stands each of the observations being considered, and $\overline{X}$ is the average of the observations. Take the differences between X_i and $\overline{X}$ and square them. Add these squared differences, take their square root and divide that result by the number of observations. The result is the standard deviation. If the standard deviation is squared, the result is the variance.

An example of the calculation using the Series I works out as follows:

---

[20]The formula for the population standard deviation is

$$\sigma = \frac{\sqrt{\sum_{i}^{N} \left(X_i - \overline{X}\right)^2}}{N}$$

This equation and a discussion of it will be found in any elementary statistics textbook.

X_i	X_i	$X_i - \overline{X}$	$(X_i - \overline{X})^2$
X_1	4	-3	9
X_2	5	-2	4
X_3	6	-1	1
X_4	8	+1	1
X_5	9	+2	4
X_6	10	+3	9
Σ	42		28
$\overline{X}$	6		

$$\frac{28}{6} = 4.6667 + X_I$$

$$\sqrt{4.6667} = 2.16025 = \sigma$$

CONCLUSIONS

This chapter presented the basics of investments. It was not embellished with numerous examples because well-informed adults can add details out of their own experience.

The underlying theme of the chapter was compound interest. Its two major variants are the amount of $1 and the present value of $1. Compound interest was termed "magical" because over a few decades the amount of $1 will grow to an astounding amount. Even though the compound interest equation itself is easy to understand, its implications are magical. Your understanding of annuities, which will be discussed in Chapter 11, will be enhanced because annuities are also a special application of compound interest. As a person who has worked with compound interest since my first year in college, the results are still startling even though the mathematics are completely understood.

The cost of living increases over the years are so large relative to their amount in the selected base year because of the processes of compound interest. The compound-interest effect in the cost of living works against the individual just as surely as it works for him when investments are made steadily over the decades. As long as the average rate earned on investments rises considerably faster than the rate at which the cost of living grows, the financial aspects of one's retirement may be quite comfortable.

Understanding the relationships between bond price changes, interest rate changes, and the remaining term to maturity on a bond are based upon a straight-forward application of compound-interest procedures. Once these procedures are demonstrated, their implications for bond prices and interest rates are quite clear. Your understanding of these procedures and their results may be used to your great advantage. Similarly, the continuing growth of common stock prices can be explained in general terms by the reinvestment process, another application of compound interest.

Two of the fundamental elements which determine common stock values are earnings and the retention of a part of those earnings for reinvestment at a positive rate of return. That part of the earnings paid out is called <u>dividends</u>. The price-to-earnings ratio and the dividend yield are used to judge the relative height of stock prices. On the basis of historical evidence including interest rates, stock prices may be seen as being overpriced, fairly priced, or underpriced. Table 8.8 presented a study that shows price-earnings ratios and dividend yields are highly correlated. Both of these elements have lower correlations with interest rates. Anyone trying to time stock market investments in terms of anticipated stock prices and interest rate changes, however, is highly likely to fail.

The quality of earnings, which refers to the ways that income and expenses are accounted for, is another vital element in assessing the present and future price of a stock. High-quality, conservative earnings tend to be associated with higher price-earnings ratios. The quality of earnings is extremely difficult even for skilled accountants to evaluate. One of the many reasons that investors not skilled in security analysis are very likely to be better off purchasing stock mutual funds is the difficulty in evaluating the quality of earnings for an individual company.

Typically, the price-earnings ratio published for a company or a stock-price index will not indicate whether the earnings are for the most recent past 12 months, the 12 months of the current calendar year, or the coming 12 months. Great care must be taken by the investor to determine what is presented if he is not to be greatly misled. Earnings for the prior year are called trailing earnings and for the coming year are called leading earnings.

Much published analysis of individual stocks and bonds, and stock and bond aggregates, is presented in terms of formal statistical analysis. The two most widely used statistical constructs, the mean and standard deviation, are used to measure the volatility of earnings, dividends, interest rates, and prices around their own average. Measures of objective risk frequently use the mean and the standard deviation. Measures of subjective risk or attitudes toward risk are measured formally in terms of risk aversion and risk seeking. Two distinctly different usages of these sets of terms were introduced. When such terms as "risk aversion," "risk seeker" or "risk lover" are used, the reader should try to discover which set of meanings is being used. These terms are often used in their respective technical meanings even in popular writings, including brochures published by TIAA-CREF.

The material presented in this chapter is the basics of investments itself; it is not merely about investment basics. These materials on compound interest, the cost of living, changes in bond prices and interest rates, quality of earnings, price-earnings ratios, dividend yields, and the reinvestment process are the very rudiments of investments. The investor's understanding of many statistical presentations of these basics is greatly enhanced if she masters the meaning of the statistical terms in which discussions are often presented.

The material presented in this chapter may be used as a permanent reference. The information and procedures presented here will not become dated. Their use is not limited to TIAA-CREF, 401(k) pension plans, and to mutual funds.

Your understanding of the earlier parts of this book and the chapters to follow will be deepened by your mastery (or review) of the Investment Basics. The material presented in this chapter and the institutional information to be presented in Chapter 9 will be of continuing worth to you.

TABLE 8.1

**MAGICAL COMPOUND INTEREST GROWTH
AT SELECTED RATES AND PERIODS**

Panel A[1]

$$\$1 = (1 + i)^n$$

Number of Years	3%	6%	9%	12%	15%
5	1.16	1.34	1.54	1.76	2.01
10	1.34	1.79	2.37	3.11	4.05
15	1.56	2.40	3.64	5.47	8.14
20	1.86	3.20	5.60	9.65	16.37
25	2.09	4.29	8.62	17.00	32.92
30	2.43	5.74	13.68	29.96	66.20
40	3.26	10.29	31.41	93.05	267.90
50	4.38	18.42	74.36	289.00	1083.70

Panel B[2]

$$\$1 \text{ PER YEAR } = \frac{(1+i)^n - 1}{i}$$

5	5.31	5.64	5.98	6.35	6.74
10	11.46	13.18	15.19	17.55	20.30
15	18.60	23.28	29.36	37.28	47.58
20	26.87	36.79	51.16	72.05	102.44
25	36.46	54.86	84.70	133.33	212.79
30	47.58	79.06	136.31	241.33	434.74
40	75.40	154.76	337.88	767.09	1779.09

[1] In words, the amount to which $1 will grow by any future year.

[2] In words, the amount to which an annuity of $1 per year will grow by any future year.

TABLE 8.2

STEALTH EFFECT OF INFLATION:
CONSUMER PRICE INDEX

	Panel A	
	Inflation Growth Rate[a]	
End of Year	3%	6%
0	100	100
10	134	179
20	186	320
30	243	429

	Panel B			
	Rise in Index in the nth Year		Increase in nth Year as a % of the Base Year Index of 100	
End of Year	At 3%	At 6%	At 3%	At 6%
10	4.0	10.7	33.3	78.3
20	5.6	19.2	86.7	320.0
30	7.3	25.7	243.0	428.0

[a]Steady rates are assumed.

TABLE 8.3

PROJECTED PRICES

Item (package)	1991	In 10 Years	In 20 Years
5% Inflation			
Car	$20,000	$32,382	$55,313
Cup of coffee	60 cents	97 cents	$1.66
10% Inflation			
Gallon of gas	$1.35	$3.18	$8.26
Monthly electric bill	$125	$294	$764
15% Inflation			
Monthly health insurance	$150	$527	$2,134
Home property tax	$1,500	$5,276	$21,347
Hospitalization	$2,500	$8,794	$35,579

SOURCE: "What the Things You'll Want Will Cost," Retirement Wealth Builder, August 1991.

TABLE 8.4

BOND VALUATION AND COMPOUND INTEREST[a,b]

End of Year	Present Value	Discount Rate		
		6%	7%	8%
1	Interest Payment	$ 66.04	$ 65.42	$ 64.82
2	Interest Payment	62.30	61.14	60.04
3	Interest Payment	58.77	57.14	55.68
4	Interest Payment	55.45	53.40	51.45
5	Interest Payment	52.31	49.91	47.64
5	Principal	747.26	712.99	680.56
	Price	$ 1,042.13	$ 1,000.00	$ 960.16

[a]Coupon rate set at 7 percent and purchased at par when initially issued. The annual interest payment is $70.

[b]In practice interest is compounded and paid semiannually. The calculation has been simplified to teach the lesson most directly.

TABLE 8.5

BOND PRICES, INTEREST RATES AND TERM TO MATURITY[a]

Term to Maturity	Market Interest Rate					
	5%	6%	7%	8%	9%	10%
1 Year	$ 101.93	$ 100.96	$ 100.00	$ 99.06	$ 98.13	$ 97.21
2 Years	103.76	101.86	100.00	98.19	96.41	94.68
3 Years	105.51	102.71	100.00	97.38	94.84	92.39
5 Years	108.75	104.27	100.00	95.94	92.09	88.42
10 Years	115.59	107.44	100.00	93.20	86.99	81.31
30 Years	130.91	113.84	100.00	88.69	79.36	71.61

[a]Assume the bond has a contractual interest rate of 7 percent.

SOURCE: Expanded Bond Value Tables. Financial Publishing Company. Boston, MA. 1970.

TABLE 8.6

STOCK PRICE GROWTH MODEL
(corporate reinvestment process)[a]

End of Year	EPS	DPS	RPS	BVPS[b]
1	$ 1.000	$ 0.600	$ 0.400	$ 6.670
2	$ 1.060	$ 0.636	$ 0.424	$ 7.090
3	$ 1.127	$ 0.676	$ 0.451	$ 7.510
4	$ 1.194	$ 0.716	$ 0.478	$ 7.460
5	$ 1.266	$ 0.759	$ 0.507	$ 8.430

[a]Rate of return on investment (BVPS) and the added investment (RPS) are both assumed to be 15 percent.

[b]With the model the stock price and BVPS are the same.

TABLE 8.7

**DJIA AND S&P 500: 1992
ESTIMATED EARNINGS**

Date of Estimate	DJIA	S&P 500
January 8, 1992	$ 205.10	$ 26.35
April 1, 1992	189.26	25.87
July 1, 1992	101.44	25.42
October 7, 1992	99.75	23.87
January 8, 1993	97.55	21.97
April 7, 1993	99.79	19.07
July 7, 1993	108.35[a]	19.09[a]

[a]Actual 1992 earnings.

SOURCE: The Outlook, Standard & Poor's, published weekly.

TABLE 8.8

**CORRELATIONS[a] AMONG STOCK, BOND AND
MONEY MARKET VARIABLES:
1967-1993**

	EP	DY	T-Bill	LT
Earning/Price Ratio[b,c]	1.000	0.852	0.580	0.676
Dividend Yields[c]	0.852	1.000	0.534	0.610
Treasury Bills[d]	0.676	0.610	1.000	0.808
Long-Term Interest Rates[e]	0.580	0.534	0.808	1.000

[a]All of these results are very highly significant.

[b]Reciprocal of the P/E ratio

[c]Standard & Poor's data

[d]90-day Treasury Bills

[e]Long-Term U.S. Treasury Bonds

TABLE 8.9

ADJUSTMENTS TO INCOME STATEMENTS

Category	Number of Occurrences	
	WSJ	AT&T
Gain from sale of assets	15	141
Tax loss carry forward	12	35
Income from discontinued operations	11	99
Fully diluted earnings	9	46
Stock splits	9	74
Reorganization and/or restructuring costs	4	12
Stock dividends	6	68
Gain from sale of investments	3	25
Effect of prior accounting changes	3	-
Loss from discontinued operations	3	-
10 categories with 1 or 2 occurrences	13	-

SOURCES: WSJ occurrence prepared by Soldofsky from various issues of the Wall Street Journal for the last week of July, 1990. AT&T occurrences gathered from analyses in Accounting Trends and Techniques, 1990.

FIGURE 8.1

CONSUMER PRICE INDEX
ANNUAL AND CUMULATIVE
1982- 1984 = 100

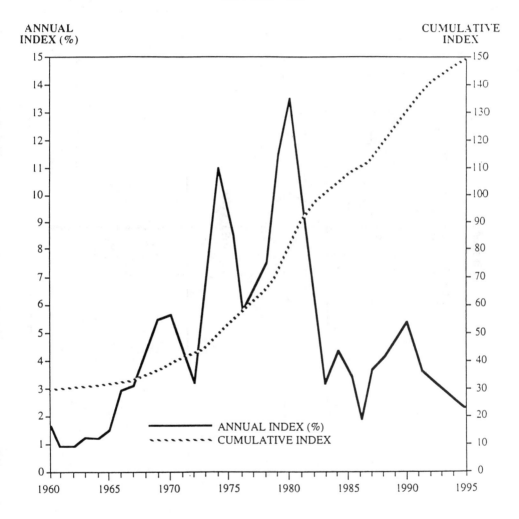

RETIRE RICHER WITH TIAA-CREF

FIGURE 8.2

SEMI-ANNUAL P/E RATIOS: 1967-1995
S&P 500 INDEX

P/E RATIO

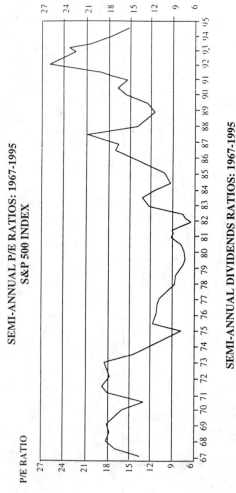

SEMI-ANNUAL DIVIDENDS RATIOS: 1967-1995
S&P 500 INDEX

DIVIDEND
YIELDS (%)

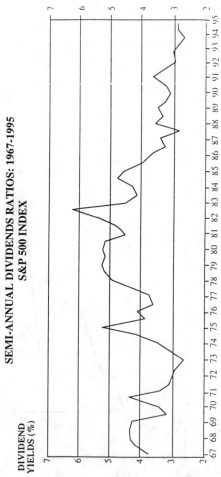

FIGURE 8.3

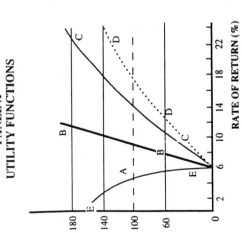

PANEL A
UTILITY FUNCTIONS

PANEL B
RISK-RETURN FUNCTION

^aUtiles fixed arbitrarily at 100 in
this case along each curve.

INVESTMENT BASICS

161

CHAPTER 9

INVESTMENT BACKGROUND

INTRODUCTION

- What are stock-price indexes?

- How can they be used to evaluate CREF-Equities and other CREF stock funds?

- How long do bull and bear stock markets last?

- How high do bull markets rise from the prior low? How far do bear markets fall from the prior high?

- When can tax-exempt municipal bonds be used advantageously?

- How much does the term to maturity affect the price-risk on bonds?

- Will I ever get my money back from TIAA-CREF?

This chapter covers several major investment background topics TIAA-CREF participants ask about in my private counseling sessions and in my seminars. If I do not raise these topics, the individuals almost always do.

STOCK-PRICE INDICES

Before discussing the use of a stock-price index to evaluate the performance of CREF-Equities or one of the newer CREF stock accounts, background on the history, construction, and uses of these indexes is very helpful. Most people know the names of the most popular indexes, but know little more about them.

The three indexes discussed and evaluated briefly are the Dow Jones Industrial Average (DJIA), the Standard & Poor's 500 Composite Index (S&P 500), and the Russell 3000 Index. Although you may know the names of several more indices, the DJIA and the S&P 500 are the best known and these two together with the Russell 3000 are the most useful for comparison with the performance of CREF's several stock accounts. Most of the other indexes have no companion earnings and dividend series. These companion series are essential for the construction of the Price/Earnings (P/E) ratio and the Dividend Yield (DY).

The primary reason for providing information on the stock-price indexes is to evaluate CREF's statement that the Russell 3000 is now the best proxy for the performance of CREF-Equities. Until 1993, CREF stated that the S&P 500 was the best proxy for CREF-Equities performance. A secondary reason is to provide some information that may be helpful if you wish to switch among the CREF-Equities and any of the other CREF funds or even to TIAA. A third reason is to present information of general interest to you as a stock investor and as a citizen concerned about the economy of your country.

DOW JONES INDUSTRIAL AVERAGE[1]

Charles H. Dow, Edward Jones, and Charles M. Bergstresser, three young financial reporters for the Kiernman News Agency started a new business in the fall of 1882. In 1883 they began publishing a stock-price average that become very popular. On June 5, 1896, they started publishing daily an average price for 12 representative individual industrial stocks.[2] Without mechanical calculators and rapidly available information, more frequent publication would have been burdensome. The initial average was just that: a simple average of 12 prices. Later they had to face the problems of what to do when a stock split or a stock dividend was declared. They probably just improvised as such events occurred and kept the procedure consistent for each type of event. Hence, the DJIA is an average, not an index.

The number of stocks in the average was increased to 20 in 1914 and to 30 in September, 1928. That increase was needed to keep the average representative as the number of industrial stocks grew. The historical chaining process has continued. In 1941 this average was computed only six times each day.

Each stock was—and is—given the weight of one in the average. Initially, the sum of the prices of the 12 stocks was added and divided by 12. The divisor was adjusted when stocks were split, paid stock dividends, and substitutions were made in order to keep the stocks representative and to maintain historical continuity. That procedure is still continued. No consideration is given to the fact that the prices and total market values of each stock (shares outstanding times the share price) differ widely. The resulting average is a simple or unweighted average.

Dow Jones & Company is still an independent, financial publisher. Its two best known publications are the Wall Street Journal and Barrons. The company went public in 1963. It used an early ticker tape with stock prices and financial information. That tape, now known as the Broad Tape, furnishes information to both the print and electronic media.[3]

STANDARD & POOR'S 500 INDEX

Standard Statistics first published a stock-market index in 1923. It was a weighted average that covered 26 industries and 223 companies. In 1926 it was re-based to 100, but it was available only on a weekly basis. In 1928 it became available on a daily basis, and it was worked backward to 1918 as its starting year. In 1941 the index was increased to 416 companies and re-based to 1935-39. Finally, in 1957 it was expanded to 500 stocks. The technology was such by that date that this weighted average could be updated and published

---

[1] Technically, the DJIA is an average, not an index, because it has no base year or period which is set at some specific number such as 100 or 10.

[2] They started publishing a railroad average in 1884. Several monthly averages of railroad stock prices were published back to 1865.

[3] In 1869 Thomas Edison developed his Universal Printer primarily to deliver stock prices instantly by telegraphic "ticker." It was an immediate success. Western Union quickly ordered several thousand.

every minute. At one time, according to company legend, 10 men were assigned 50 stocks each to prepare the S&P 500 every hour with calculators.

The Standard & Poor's Company was formed in 1941 by merging the bankrupt Poor's Publishing Company and Standard Statistics Company, which was incorporated in 1914. Both companies published corporate financial information, and provided investment advice to individuals. McGraw-Hill, the publisher of Business Week, bought Standard & Poor's in 1965. Standard & Poor's Outlook, an excellent investment advisory service, is published weekly.

On January 2, 1990, the total market value of the stocks included in the S&P 500 was $2,367.0 billion. It included 461 NYSE stocks with a value of $2,268.8 billion which was 96.6 percent of the value of NYSE stocks; 32 Over-the-Counter (OTC) stocks with a value of $69.1 billion or 2.9 percent of their total; and seven American Stock Exchange (AMEX) stocks with a value of $11.1 billion or 0.5 percent of those stocks.

Other indexes have been introduced from time to time for corporate promotional purposes. The New York Times' 25 Stock Average was started in 1911. The Value Line Index was started in 1963. The New York Stock Exchange started its present index in 1965 when it computerized its calculating systems. The Wilshire 5000 was started in the 1980s and several "mid-cap" or middle-size capitalization indexes were started in the last five years in response to public interest in the performance of stocks whose total valuation is in this range and a public willingness to pay for the additional information.

RUSSELL 3000 INDEX
The Russell 3000, a weighted average index, is published by the Frank Russell Company of Tacoma, Washington. The Frank Russell Company, which was founded in 1936, has three main divisions: Investment Strategy Consulting, Investment Management, and Data Services.

In the early 1980s, IBM, a client of the Frank Russell, asked the company to prepare a very broad market index against which the performance of stocks in their pension fund could be compared.   The result was the Russell 3000 and subparts such as the Russell 2000; companion earnings and dividend series are then prepared.[4] As word spread about its existence, other companies asked for the same information, according to Tricia M. Konus, Russell Data Services.[5]

The company now sells the information to many clients. The Russell 2000 Index, a small company index, is published daily in the Wall Street Journal. The Journal occasionally includes other comments about the index including the related prices-earnings ratio based upon a projected next 12-months earnings. These projected earnings are gathered from several different sources.

---

[4]See Kelly L. Haugton, "Russell Indexes vs. The S&P 500," Frank Russell Company, August 7, 1987. Company document provided to Soldofsky by Tricia M. Konus, Russell Data Services.

[5]Telephone conversation, July 2, 1993.

CREF CORRELATIONS WITH THE STOCK-PRICE INDEXES

CREF announced in 1993 that the Russell 3000 Index would henceforth be a better indicator of the value of a CREF-Equities unit than the S&P 500. The numbers for CREF-Equities prices, the Russell 3000 Index, the S&P 500, and the DJIA were correlated starting with March 31, 1979, the approximate date that CREF-Equities started indexing about 75 percent of its portfolio. All three indexes had correlations with the CREF-Equities unit value of above 0.99; therefore, they corresponded almost perfectly with the CREF-Equities value. The S&P correlation was 0.99825, the DJIA was second at 0.99576, and the Russell 3000 was the lowest at 0.99136. These small differences are of no practical use, but the results are curious.

BULLS, BEARS AND CRASHES

During or after seminar presentations about the relative performance of bonds, stocks and the cost of living, the most frequent question asked is: What if the stock-market crashes again? The prospect of a crash reinforces the fears that a large percentage of people have about moving onto that long, bright (dark?) ascending (descending?) retirement road.

The fear of a stock market crash prevents large numbers of people from investing in stocks in general and from investing more in stocks in their pension fund choices in particular. People from the highest paid neurosurgeons to the word-processing specialists working on this book express this fear to me. At the point of retirement this fear drives a high proportion of participants to convert part or all of their CREF to TIAA.[6] I believe this fear is a response to the lack of information about what happens to stock values after recessions and crashes, and about stock performance in the long run. The TIAA and CREF long-run performance are compared with the Consumer Price Index (CPI) in Table 5.4. The very long-run performance of stocks and bonds are compared in Tables 6.5 and 6.6.

One point needs to be reiterated before examining the record. The joint life expectancy of a couple both age 65 is just above 25 years. You can approximately adjust that figure for your own individual case. The average number of months from a stock market low to the next high has been 27.8 months since September 1929. After retirement you are likely to live through at least five such periods and might live through ten of them. Stock prices are likely to rise two-four fold during your retirement.

Table 9.1 displays the highs and lows of the stock market since September 1929, as measured by the popular Dow Jones Industrial Average of 30 stocks.[7] In addition to the dates of the highs and lows, the table displays the percentage drop from the high to the next low and the rise from that low to the subsequent high. Usually a drop of 15 percent in the average from a high is considered to define a bear market. I included the drop in the DJIA from January to

---

[6]For detailed information on this point see the TIAA-CREF Switching Before Retirement section of Chapter 11 and Table 11.10.

[7]A similar table based upon the S&P 500 would show smaller drops from high to low and correspondingly smaller rises from low to high. CREF experience has been and will be more like the S&P 500 record.

September 1957 as a bear market.[8] Table 9.2 shows the frequency distributions of these highs and lows.

The compound annual growth rate for this 64-year period since 1929 is 3.7 percent. The growth rate over the 46-year period since 1947 has been 4.6 percent.

Four points from Table 9.1 merit special comment. First, about 25 years including (World War II) passed after the start of the Great Depression before the DJIA returned to its 1929 high. Starting with 1941, each new high on the DJIA was higher than the previous high until 1968. Third, the 1971 high was down 34 points from 1968, and then the 1973 high was up 101 points. The next three highs did not exceed the 1973 high. The main reasons for this outcome were the high inflation and interest rates which were related largely to energy price increases. With the generally falling interest rates since 1979, stock prices have moved up very nicely.

The three largest bear markets in stocks in U.S. history starting with 1929 are:

49.0% from March 10, 1937 to March 31, 1938

47.8% from September 3, 1929 to November 13, 1929

45.2% from January 11, 1973 to December 6, 1974

The only one of these three remembered in history and myth is the 1929 crash.[9] Perhaps it is remembered because it lasted so long and grew so much deeper in terms of unemployment and human suffering than any other such crises. The 1973-74 decline was during the period that Watergate trials took place and President Nixon resigned, August 9, 1974. OPEC began an embargo on oil exports to the U.S. in October 1973 and did not lift the ban until March 1974. Petroleum prices increased from $3.58 a barrel at the end of 1972 to $9.07 by the end of 1974. Business activity peaked in November 1973 and contracted until the bottom of March 1975. Stock prices typically turn up before the bottom of the business cycle.

The August-to-October 1987 stock market decline of 36.1 percent was the fourth largest in percentage terms, starting with 1929, but was only 0.2 percent larger than the December 1968 to May 1970 decline.[10] Perhaps a novelist or composer will come along who will dramatize

---

[8]No official rule about what to call a "bear" market exists. I included this decline of 13.3% arbitrarily. It was the next largest decline below 15% during this 64-year period.

[9]Probably the best and most comprehensive study of this period is by Milton Friedman and Anne Schwartz, The Great Contraction, 1929-1933. National Bureau of Economic Research, Princeton, NJ: Princeton University Press, 1965.

[10]A review of the DJIA shows nine bull-and-bear cycles from 1897, when the DJIA began, to 1929. During this 32-year period, four of the bear markets had declines of more than 40 percent. One does not have as much confidence in the extent of these declines because during the first two the DJIA included only 12 stocks, and during the post World War I decline it had only 20 stocks. However, each of these periods recorded on the DJIA as a bear market covers a period of recession as reported by the arbiter of such things, the National Bureau of Economic Research, a private, nonprofit organization associated with several of the nations most prestigious universities.

the events of October 1987 when the DJIA decline 508 points in one day so that it, too, will be burned into our national memory.

Since 1929 there have been 19 bull markets; in five of these stocks prices as measured by the DJIA have more than doubled. The three that occurred since the start of World War II were:

150% from July 1984 to August 1987

104% from September 1953 to August 1957

101% from December 1941 to May 1946.

But no one extols these bull markets in song and story. Only historians like myself even seem to remark upon them.

A gentle reminder is useful to keep stock and bond price volatility in perspective. Prices of long-term bonds fluctuate through wide ranges within a year or two also. In Chapter 6 the point was made that from 1953 through 1994 annual total returns on bonds ranged from -11.3 to +25.6 percent. In Chapter 8 the point was made that a 2 percentage point rise from 6 to 8 percent in interest rates can cause a 30-year bond's price to fall over 20 percent and during a sustained inflation it could easily lose 40 percent of its value. Such gains and losses may occur quickly. In early 1993 a gain of almost 8 percent was made in two months on long-term U.S. government bonds. From mid-October 1994, the same securities lost 22 percent by the end of the year.

TAX-EXEMPT SECURITIES AND SHORT-TERM YIELDS

As the yields on savings accounts, certificates of deposit (CDs), and Treasury bills have fallen from more than 13 percent in 1982 to 9 percent in 1989, and to the 2-3 percent level in 1993, retirees and others have scrambled for higher yields. A drop in one's return from 9 percent to 3 percent results in a drop of two thirds in one's income from that source.

Prominent among the alternatives to savings accounts and CDs are both taxable U.S. government and corporate securities, and tax-exempt municipal securities with maturities of up to five years. You can hold such securities through a no-load mutual fund most easily, as will be explained. Securities with maturities beyond five years are readily available, but risks increase more sharply beyond about the five-year point. Many people have moved money from maturing CDs to stock in the quest for higher yields and some price appreciation. The risk of shifting from debt instruments to stock is very likely much greater than the risk of lengthening maturities on the debt instruments.

People inexperienced in finance may not understand the advantages of tax-exempt securities, and the very large impact of lengthening maturities beyond the 3-6 month period. This section is concerned with:

- The impact on net yield of tax-exempt securities at different income tax rates.

- The effect upon yield of increasing maturities of both taxable and tax-exempt securities from 3 months to 5 years.

- The advantages of owning mutual funds that hold taxable and tax-exempt, short-term bonds.

ORIGINS OF TAX-EXEMPT SECURITIES

Income on state and local securities is exempt from federal taxation. The law has been settled on this point since the McCulloch vs. Maryland Supreme Court case of 1824. In that case the great Chief Justice, John Marshall, ruled that the State of Maryland could not tax bank notes issued by the Second United States Bank at its Maryland branch. In 1913 Congress provided tax exemption for interest on state and local securities in order to clarify the newly adopted Income Tax Amendment to the Constitution.

This tax-exempt status has been challenged by the federal government in its search for revenue, but this challenge has not yet been successful. If it were ever successful, the cost of state and local borrowing would increase substantially, and many state taxes would have to increase to make up for this increased cost. Alternatively, many state services would have to be decreased or abandoned.

Many people believe that the alternatives to holding savings accounts or CDs that mature in one-five years are very limited. A disadvantage of a CD is that cashing it early usually results in an interest penalty. Often this penalty is the loss of the interest earned since the last payment date. On the other hand, its contractual interest rate will be paid even though the market rate drops. Partial withdrawals from CDs are not available.

Table 9.3 includes a typical maturity-rate structure up to five years on CDs, on Treasury securities, and municipal bonds. Although Treasury securities and municipals are not readily available to buy or sell in small amounts, they are conveniently available through mutual funds. The level and term structure of these rates are always changing.

In recent years the yield on tax-exempt securities has run from 70 percent to 90 percent of those on taxable securities of the same maturity. The question that you as a taxpayer and investor would like to have answered is how large must the differential be between taxable and tax-exempt securities before it is worthwhile to buy exempts.

ARITHMETIC OF TAX-EXEMPT YIELDS

As the interest on municipal bonds is tax exempt, you can accept a lower return on such a bond and have a higher after-tax return.[11] Just how that works out in your case depends upon your marginal income tax rate and the difference in the yields on the taxable and tax-exempt securities. Your marginal tax rate is the tax rate you pay in your highest income-tax bracket. Assume that you can buy into a taxable, money-market fund with a yield of 3 percent or a tax-exempt money-market fund at 2 percent. Which would be better for you?

Multiply the return on the taxable security by unity or 1 minus your marginal tax rate. This latter step will show what rate you will have after paying federal income taxes. The formula and an example are as follows:

Before-Tax Return x (1 - Income Tax Rate) = After-Tax Return

or

BT x (1-TR) = AT

---

[11] Any increase in price, however, is a capital gain and taxable as such.

.03 x (1-.30) = .021

In other words, a 3 percent before-tax return is equivalent to a 2.1 percent after-tax return. If your tax rate is higher than .30, you are better off with the tax-exempt security. If the yield on a 2.5 percent tax-exempt security and your marginal income rate is 30 percent, your before-tax equivalent rate is 3.57 percent calculated as follows:

.025 ÷ .70 = BT

.025 ÷ .70 = .0357

Table 9.4 demonstrates such equivalencies for ranges of yields and marginal income tax rates that currently appear to be reasonable.

YIELDS AND MATURITIES

Longer-term securities merit higher returns than shorter-term securities as explained in Chapter 8. The questions are how much higher a return can you earn by increasing the maturity and how much added price risk do you bear?

The answer to how much higher return you may get by extending the maturity is indicated by columns 2, 3, and 5 in Table 9.3. Before exploring that question, three important qualifications must be made. First, the steepness or flatness of yield curve as maturities lengthen must be examined. Second, this slope varies substantially over periods of months or years. The curve was quite steep in mid-July 1993, but is much flatter in mid-1995. Third, during periods when inflation is high, shorter maturities may have a higher yield than longer maturities. The last time that short-term yields were higher than long-term yields was 1982. You must keep watching or asking about the yield curve if you use a strategy of extending your maturities. Even though mid-1995 yield on the longest term Treasury bonds (30 years) is about 7.3 percent, the added return beyond the 5-year maturity, which has a yield of about 6.9 percent, is probably not worth the added price risk.

Column 4 of Table 9.3 is an index of the increase in yield on Treasury securities as a function of the lengthening of maturity as of July 23, 1993.[12] Column 6 is the corresponding index for municipal bonds. Another thing to note is whether the steepness of the yield slope increases or not as maturity lengthens. In mid-July 1993, the steepness of the slope declined as maturity lengthened. If markets were perfect and not segmented in small units, no sharp changes in rates would appear as they do in Column 8.

PRICE RISK AND MATURITY

The next step is to demonstrate the increase in price risk that is associated with the increase in maturity. The fact that price-risk increases as maturity increases was demonstrated in Chapter 8. Table 9.5 shows the prices of fixed-income securities over short periods at relevant interest rates. For example, in Panel A the coupon or contractual rate is 3 percent and the market rate ranges from 3-7 percent. The term-to-maturity ranges from three months

---

[12]This date is convenient for illustrative purposes.

to five years. As long as the coupon and market rates are the same, the price is always at par, or 100. Note that as the market interest rate rises, the price drops further and further below par. At the 1-year maturity the price will fall to $99.03 with a rise in the interest rate of 1 percentage point from 3 percent to 4 percent. The decline in price is just under 1 percent— that is, from $100.00 to $99.03. As the interest rate continues to rise, the percentage decline increases ever so slightly for successive, equal-sized rate increases. An increase of 2 or 3 percentage points in the market rate within one year would be an extremely large increase. In other words, the price risk at the 3 percent market rate is just under 2 percent for an increase in the market rate to 5 percent.

At the 5-year maturity in Panel A, the total price risk from a 2 percentage point rise from 3 to 5 percent in the market rate is almost 9 percent, which might be spread over several years. This discussion is couched in terms of interest rate increases rather than decreases for three reasons. First, short-term interest rates are currently low. They are more likely to rise rather than fall from their mid-1993 and their 1995 levels. Second, prices fall as interest rates rise. Third, the security holder usually views price decreases as unfavorable. However, if a drop in the original purchase price is experienced and a sale is made, that loss would be a capital loss and could be claimed as such on the investor's income tax. On the other hand, if rates fell from 5 percent to 4 percent, a gain would be experienced. In any case, when the security is held to maturity, the security will be paid off at par.

The decline in prices across any given row as maturity increases demonstrates the mathematical relationship between a given market rate, coupon rate, and maturity in Table 9.5. By moving to longer maturities, a gain in the market interest rate is achieved under the conditions shown in Table 9.3. When longer maturities are purchased and interest rates rise as the remaining term to maturity shortens, the typical experience may be a price decrease.

Table 9.6 compares the marginal increase in price risk with the marginal increases in return on U.S. Treasury securities as of July 23, 1993.[13] A 3 percent coupon rate is used for illustrative purposes. The price risk would be a little different for each level of coupon rate.[14]

Similarly, the marginal returns in Column 5 are the increased returns in percentage terms from increasing the term to maturity as shown in Table 9.1. Therefore, in the 1-2 year maturity row, the increase in price risk is .0094 as compared with the marginal increase in the return of .163. The marginal increase in the return by extending the maturity from 1 to 2 years is more than 17 times greater than the marginal price risk. Of course, the price risk assumes a very quick drop from 4 percent to 3 percent in the market yield. If the same

---

[13]The exact date is essential to the analysis because the term structure of rates changes every day the market is open.

[14]The Extended Bonds Tables provide coupon rates for each 1/8 percent up to 10 percent and by ¼ percent intervals for rates up to 12 percent. Column 4 shows the increase in the price rise as a percentage of the price for the next shorter row shown in the table. For example, from the 1-year to the 2-year maturity, the price drops by 93 cents or from $99.03 to $98.10. This amount, 93 cents, is .0094 of the price $99.03. It is the marginal change.

security is held to maturity, it will be paid at par. As the security approaches maturity, the market return will drop to 3 percent.

As long as the marginal increase in return is so much larger than the marginal increase in price risk, the holder can feel very safe in extending the maturity of his holdings. Both of these marginal increases are based on objective data, though attitudes toward risk are always subjective, as discussed in Chapter 8.

Panel B of Table 9.6 shows the effect of the yield falling from 5 to 4 percent. The yield shifts to 5 percent in this part of the illustration as maturity increases because the actual yield in the example was 5.26 percent.

BOND FUNDS

Relatively few people except the very wealthy buy Treasury, corporate, or municipal bonds for themselves today. Shares in a bond mutual fund are much more convenient to purchase and to sell than individual bonds. The purchase of shares or units in a bond fund probably will cost you less than individual bonds purchased through a broker. Treasury bonds, which have a maturity of 10 years or more, can be purchased for a minimum of $1,000 directly from a Federal Reserve Bank, but the process is cumbersome for most people. The individual can purchase as many $1,000 units as he wishes. Treasury notes with maturities up to 15 years can be purchased in units of $5,000.

Ten advantages for mutual bond funds are easily listed. First, you do not have to have extensive knowledge about the many and diverse characteristics of corporate and municipal securities. Second, you can buy funds that specialize in Treasuries, corporates, or municipals. Within these latter two types you can buy the quality that you prefer. Third, you can open an account for a minimum of $1,000, but many funds do have a minimum of $2,500. Further, you can add to your fund in most cases by as little as $100 per purchase. Fifth, you can withdraw as little as $500 by a check-like device to pay bills or for your own use. Sixth, you can have interest paid to you monthly if you wish, or have it reinvested. Seventh, you can very likely locate a fund that has no opening commission—front-end load—charge. These are called no-load funds.

Eighth, individual bonds are always moving toward maturity and have to be replaced when they mature. Ninth, you can switch between bond funds within the same fund family, such as Scudder or Vanguard, at no charge. Some fund families will also permit you to move into one of their stock or money market funds and back again at no added cost. Finally, and most important for present purposes, you can obtain funds with almost any maturity that you wish. Purchasing corporate or municipal bonds with shorter maturities may be a problem unless you have substantial amounts to invest. These large bond funds maintain their term of maturity relatively constant.

Only four of the best-known, no-load, mutual fund families had U.S. Treasury bond funds, corporate bond funds, and tax-exempt bond funds with maturities of less than six years at the date this material was prepared. These are as follows:

	Term to Maturity		
Fund	U.S. Treasuries	Taxable Corporate	Tax Exempt
Dreyfus	3.2 Yrs.	2.9 Yrs.	2.9 Yrs.
Federated	1.6 Yrs.	1.8 Yrs.[a]	2.1 Yrs.
T. Rowe Price	4.4 Yrs.	2.3 Yrs.	3.4 Yrs.
Vanguard	3.7 Yrs.	3.4 Yrs.	1.3 Yrs.

[a]Includes collateralized securities.

Some fund families have municipal bonds that are composed of bonds in a single state's securities so that they are exempt from both federal and state income taxes in that state. These are issued for such states as Arizona, California, Colorado, Connecticut, Florida, Hawaii, Kentucky, New Jersey, New York, North Carolina, Maryland, Massachusetts, Michigan, Minnesota, Missouri, Ohio, Oregon, Pennsylvania, and Virginia. However, most of these double tax-exempts have very long maturities and therefore, very high price risk.

WILL I GET MY MONEY BACK?

After some years of participating in a TIAA-CREF plan through their employer, individuals realize that they have built up a considerable accumulation. Many people have little experience with life insurance or annuities. Hence they often blurt out in innocence and frustration:

Will I get my money back?

I am always surprised by the question, even though I have been hearing it for 20 years. The question usually implies that the employee has been forced to pay into the pension fund against his will as a condition of getting his present job. Sometimes he means that he does not trust his employer or the insurance company to return his money at some unspecified time in the future. Table 9.7 and my comments about it are designed to put the question to rest, and they almost always do so.

First, I ask the questioners whether they are referring to their own investment. Some will say yes, but they are easily prodded into adding that the investment made by their employer on their behalf should be included as shown in the Table 9.7.

Most of these individuals indicate that just getting their money back after they retire would suit them. They typically do not understand that the money invested by their employer for them is vested immediately under the TIAA-CREF plans.

The word "vested" is often new to them in its legal meaning. The rights to something— investment in the case of the pension fund—is passed irrevocably to the individual's control, but within the limits of the conditions of the pension fund.

Second, I ask whether the questioners believe they should receive interest on the money held in the pension fund over the years that they and their employer have been investing for them. The answer is always yes, even though the questioners had not considered interest initially.

At this point I remind the questioners that if they had invested their contribution themselves, they would not have the tax-deferred advantages.

In my seminars I expose the first two rows of Table 9.7 which is projected on a screen. After my second question I expose the third row, which shows that accumulation at 9 percent interest with interest added each year in the hypothetical example.

Third, I ask if anyone knows approximately how large their annual pension benefit will be per $10,000 in their pension accumulation. I typically get blank stares or dropped jaws at this point. The correct response is just over $1000 per $10,000 invested, if the covered person is 68 and the spouse is 62 at the time the pension is started. Nine percent interest is assumed on the investment remaining in the accumulation after each payment, and the joint life expectancy is just over 25 years. Under these conditions, with full benefits to the survivor, the payments will be about $7,689 per year if interest rates remain unchanged.[15]

Fourth, I rephrase the question as follows: How long will it take you to get your money back? The answer is now quite clear and I display the last two rows in the table. Slightly over 10 years will be required to recover the investment including interest. If you and/or your spouse survive for 20 years, you will double your money.

Of course, the original question was not the best one to ask to understand the performance of a fixed-income annuity, but it is one about which large numbers of people show intense concern.

Chapters 11 and 12 elaborate on the topic of annuities.

---

[15]The annuity of about per $1,000 on TIAA accumulation based upon information received from TIAA. As I have followed this topic very little change has been observed over more than a decade.

CONCLUSIONS

Although CREF has recently suggested that the Russell 3000 Index is the best proxy for the price performance of a CREF unit, a correlation study showed that the DJIA, the S&P 500, and the Russell 3000 are all excellent proxies for the price of a CREF unit. Understanding the construction and history of stock price averages will help you monitor your CREF stock accounts.

Fear of the great stock market crashes such as those in late 1929 and in October 1987 influences many participants into reducing or eliminating their CREF holdings. Others reduce or eliminate their CREF holdings close to or at the point of retirement in the hope of gaining absolute certainty about the dollar amount of their retirement annuity. A review of the frequency and extent of stock market cycles shows that an average cycle is just over three years and that the general trend of stock prices is upward. The high on the DJIA usually increases every cycle. In several cases, the new cyclical high exceeded the previous high by 50 percent or more.

When a person retires, his life annuity for himself and his spouse is likely to continue for more than 25 years; one of the couple is likely to survive four or more market cycles. The exact price of a CREF unit the moment before or the moment after retirement is much less important than our emotional response would lead us to believe. At the time of retirement, you must keep in mind your need for gradually increasing income because of inflation.

Tax-exempt securities are a great advantage for those in the higher income-tax brackets. The break-even point at which tax-exempt securities such as municipal bonds or municipal bond funds will be useful to you is easily calculated.

When you hold fixed-income securities in addition to your investment in your pension funds, you should always be aware of the relationships between coupon interest rates, the likely change in market interest rates, and the term to maturity on your holdings. Being alert to all three variables, you can probably avoid some capital losses and achieve some capital gains by changing the maturity of your fixed-income securities as warranted by financial market conditions. However, constant attention and considerable knowledge is necessary to achieve these desirable results. These desirable changes in your securities portfolio are not without some risk, however.

Some TIAA-CREF participants are worried that they will not get back the money that they themselves have invested. The truth is that participants will receive not only their investment but also that contributed by their employer, plus interest. In terms of a simple payback, the participant's investments plus interest will be received after about 10 years of retirement. The payback period is not an adequate means of evaluating an annuity, but it may satisfy the most skeptical and least sophisticated participants.

TABLE 9.1

DJIA: HIGHS TO LOWS
1929 - 1996

Date	High	Date	Low	Change High to Low		Low to Next Notable High (%)
				#	%	
9/3/29	381	11/13/29	199[a]	182	47.8	-
9/3/29	381	3/8/32	41[a]	340	89.2	168
2/5/34	110	7/26/34	86	24	21.8	126
3/10/37	194	3/31/38	99	95	49	62
11/12/38	160	4/8/39	121	39	24.4	26
1/3/40	153	6/3/40	111	42	27.4	22
1/12/41	136	12/23/41	106	30	22/1	101
5/29/46	213	7/24/47	163	50	23.4	80
1/5/53	294	9/14/53	255	39	13.3	104
7/12/57	521	10/22/57	418	103	19.8	64
1/5/60	686	10/25/60	566	120	17.5	30
12/31/61	735	6/6/62	536	199	27.1	84
12/3/68	985	5/26/70	631	354	35.9	51
4/28/71	951	11/23/71	798	153	16	32
1/11/73	1052	12/6/74	577	475	45.2	76
9/21/76	1015	2/28/78	742	273	26.9	21
10/5/79	898	4/21/80	759	139	15.5	35
4/27/80	1024	8/12/81	777	247	24.1	66
2/6/84	1286	7/24/84	1,087	199	15.5	150
8/25/87	2722	10/19/87	1,739	983	36.1	60
10/9/89	2791	10/11/90	2,365	426	15.3	141[b]
4/3/96	5690		-[c]			

[a]An unsolved question is whether to take the bear-market low as 199 on November 13, 1929 or as 41 on March 8, 1932.

[b]This percent may turn out to be higher before the market high on this cycle is reached.

[c]From October 11, 1990 through April 1996, no decline in the DJIA was as large as 10 percent.

TABLE 9.2

BEAR AND BULL MARKETS: 1927-1995
A FREQUENCY DISTRIBUTIONS IN PERCENTAGE TERMS

Bear Markets		Bull Markets	
Decline from Prior High		Rise from Prior Low	
%	No. of Times	%	No. of Times
15.1-20.0	7[a]	20.1-30.0	4
20.1-25.0	5	30.1-40.0	2
25.1-30.0	3	40.1-50.0	-
30.1-35.0	-	50.1-60.0	3
35.1-40.0	2	60.1-70.0	3
40.1-45.0	-	70.1-80.0	1
45.1-50.0	3	80.1-90.0	2
		80.1-100.0	-
		100.1-110.0	2
		110.1-120.0	-
		120.1 & Up[b]	3

[a]One of three was 13.3%.

[b]These were 126%, 150%, and 168%.

TABLE 9.3

YIELD CURVES: 3 MONTHS TO 5 YEARS
JULY, 1993

	Certificate of	U.S. Treasury		Baa Municipal Bonds %		Baa Municipal	U.S. Treas. minus Baa
Maturity	Deposit Rates[a]	Yield (%)	Index Number of Increase[b]	Bonds %[c]	Index Number of increase[b]	Divided by U.S. Treas.	Municipal Bond Yields
COL (1)	(2)	(3)	(4)	(5)	(6)	(7)	(8)
3 Mo	2.48%	3.16%	100.00	2.84%[c]	100.00	.900	.32
6 Mo	2.85	3.36	106.3	3.02[c]	106.3	.900	.34
1 Yr	3.13	3.62	114.6	3.35	118.0	.925	.27
2 Yrs	3.77[d]	4.21	133.2	4.00	140.8	.950	.21
3 Yrs	-	4.54	143.7	4.45	156.7	.980	.09
4 Yrs	-	4.97	157.3	4.70	165.5	.945	.27
5 Yrs	4.98	5.26	166.5	4.95	174.3	.941	.31

[a]National averages of bank rates, small saver yields as of July 16, 1993

[b]Longer maturity minus 3-month return divided by 3-month return.

[c]No figure for 3-month or 6-month municipal bond yields is available from Dain Bosworth or Merrill Lynch. Probably not enough paper is available to provide such a yield. In order to have a basis for a municipal bond yield curve, I arbitrarily set the 3-month and 6-month municipal band yields at 90% of the taxable bond yields.

[d]2 1/2 Years.

TABLE 9.4

**TAXABLE AND TAX-EXEMPT
YIELD EQUIVALENTS**

Income Tax Rates	Yields On Taxable Securities								
	3.0%	3.5%	4.0%	4.5%	5.0%	5.5%	6.0%	6.5%	7.0%
	Tax-Exempt Equivalent Yields								
20%	2.40%	2.80%	3.20%	3.60%	4.00%	4.40%	4.80%	5.20%	5.60%
25%	2.25	2.63	3.00	3.38	3.75	4.12	4.50	4.88	5.25
30%	2.10	2.45	2.80	3.15	3.50	3.85	4.20	4.55	4.90
35%	1.95	2.28	2.60	2.93	3.25	3.58	3.90	4.23	4.56
40%	1.80	2.10	2.40	2.70	3.00	3.30	3.60	3.90	4.20
45%	1.65	1.93	2.20	2.48	2.75	3.03	3.30	3.58	3.85

TABLE 9.5

SHORT-TERM SECURITIES: PRICES, INTEREST RATES AND TERM TO MATURITY

Rates %		Maturity							
Coupon	Market	3 Mos	6 Mos	9 Mos	1 Yr	2 Yrs	3 Yrs	4 Yrs	5 Yrs
					Panel A				
3	7	99.00	98.07	97.12	96.20	92.65	89.34	86.25	83.37
3	6	99.25	98.54	97.83	97.13	94.42	91.87	89.47	87.20
3	5	99.50	99.02	98.54	98.07	96.24	94.49	92.83	91.25
3	4	99.75	99.51	99.26	99.03	98.10	97.20	96.34	95.51
3	3	100.00	100.00	100.00	100.00	100.00	100.00	100.00	100.00
					Panel B				
4	8	99.00	98.08	97.13	96.23	92.74	89.52	86.53	83.78
4	7	99.25	98.55	97.84	97.15	94.29	92.01	89.69	85.50
4	6	99.49	99.03	98.55	98.09	96.28	94.58	92.98	91.47
4	5	99.91	99.51	99.27	99.04	98.12	97.25	96.41	95.62
4	4	100.00	100.00	100.00	100.00	100.00	100.00	100.00	100.00
					Panel C				
5	9	98.29	98.09	97.15	96.25	92.82	89.43	86.81	84.17
5	8	99.24	98.56	97.85	97.17	94.56	91.94	89.90	87.83
5	7	99.49	99.03	98.55	98.10	96.33	94.53	93.13	91.68
5	6	99.74	99.51	99.27	99.04	98.14	97.22	96.49	95.73
5	5	100.00	100.00	100.00	100.00	100.00	100.00	100.00	100.00

SOURCE: Extended Bond Tables. Boston, MA: Financial Publishing Company, 1970.

TABLE 9.6

SHORT-TERM U.S. GOVERNMENTS:
MARGINAL INCREASES IN PRICE, RISK, AND RETURN COMPARED

Market Rates	Term to Maturity		Impact of Increasing Term Upon[a]	
			Marginal Price Risk	Marginal Return[c]
	From	To	(%)[b]	(%)
Col. (1)	(2)	(3)	(4)	(5)
PANEL A				
4%	0	3 Mo.	.00250	-
4%	3 Mo.	6 Mo.	.00251	.063
4%	6 Mo.	12 Mo.	.0048	.077
4%	1 Yr.	2 Yrs.	.0094	.163
5%	2 Yrs.	3 Yrs.	.0182	.078
5%	3 Yrs.	4 Yrs.	.0176	.095
5%	4 Yrs.	5 Yrs.	.0170	.058
PANEL B				
5%-4%[d]	2 Yrs.	3 Yrs.	.0092	.078
5%-4%[d]	3 Yrs.	4 Yrs.	.0088	.095
5%-4%[d]	4 Yrs.	5 Yrs.	.0186	.058

[a]Based on rates of Friday, July 23, 1993.

[b]Percentage of increase in rate over next shorter yield. The coupon rate is set at 3%. Based upon Table 9.5.

[c]The yield at 5 years was 5.26% as shown in Table 9.3.

[d]If market rate fell only to 4% from 5%.

TABLE 9.7

WILL I GET MY MONEY BACK FROM TIAA BEFORE I DIE?
ASSUME $10,000 CONSTANT SALARY

	Personal	Employer	Total
Annual Investment	$ 500	$ 1,000	$ 1,500
Accumulation - 20 Yrs.	$ 10,000	$ 20,000	$ 30,000
Including Interest at 9%	$ 25,580	$ 51,160	$ 76,740
Annual Annuity			
Full Benefits to Survivor[a]		$1,002 per $10,000	
Annuity on Basis of $76,740		$ 7,689	
Annuity Over 10 Yrs.		$ 76,890	
Annuity Over 20 Yrs.		$ 153,780	

[a]Assumes one spouse is 68 and the other is 62 when the 68 year old retires. Interest .
assumed constant at 9%

CHAPTER 10

TIAA AND CREF: PROCEDURES AND COMPETITORS

INTRODUCTION

- What is the vintage-year procedure for interest that applies to accumulated investments in TIAA?

- What is the money market fund procedure for interest that applies to investments in the CREF fund only?

- How does TIAA-CREF compare with its competitors in terms of investment performance, costs, and expenses?

- How does TIAA-CREF compare with its competitors in terms of benefits paid out per dollar of investment, and in the range of the settlement options available?

- What are the most important points to consider when selecting an insurance carrier?

The first two major topics discussed in this chapter are concerned with TIAA-CREF procedures that are important to your understanding of what you own and to your investment-allocation decisions. Also, these procedures will impact your retirement benefits and their fluctuations during your retirement.

The last three topics discuss TIAA-CREF's performance, cost, expenses and benefit levels and compare them with competitors who are seeking your investment dollars. Your satisfaction with TIAA-CREF and/or your decision to use one of its competitors should be based upon correct information.

The topics covered are among the most important ones to be considered in selecting an annuity company. These topics are not discussed elsewhere in this book.

VINTAGE-YEAR RATE PROCEDURES

When interest rates rose sharply in the late 1970s and into the early 1980s, TIAA and other insurance companies realized that the rates being paid on new money (that is, funds newly invested in pension plans) could not be sustained. Market interest rates were bound to fall. They realized under the procedures they were using that the continuing interest earned on money invested in 1982, for example, would have to be paid at whatever rate prevailed in 1983 and in each subsequent year.

To be more specific, if $10,000 was invested in a TIAA account in 1982, that $10,000 would continue to earn interest in 1983, 1984, 1985, and so on for many years into the future.[1] Before the end of 1982, TIAA announced the rate that it would pay on money invested in 1983. The 1982 investment was called the 1982 vintage. The rate announced on the 1982 vintage for 1983 was 12.25%. Once the vintage year rate was announced, it was maintained for the whole year. However, if market conditions change radically enough, the vintage year rate could be changed more than once. The rate for 1982 money as announced for each

---

[1] For simplicity, the interest earned on the money invested each month in 1982 during 1982 is ignored in the illustration.

subsequent year is shown in Table 10.1. The interest rates for the next five years for a 1982 vintage year investment of $10,000 were as follows:

1983	12.25%
1984	11.50%
1985	12.00%
1986	11.75%
1987	11.50%

In 1983 the participant's additional investment and interest on all of his prior investments flowed into his account. Interest at 12.25 percent rate based upon the 1982 investment of $10,000 would be credited to the account month-by-month in 1983 and earn at the designated rate for what remained of 1983. By the end of 1983, the interest based upon the 1982 vintage-year investment plus the interest on the interest for 1983 at the 12.25% rate compounded monthly would be approximately $1,300. That $1,300 would be a new investment in vintage 1983. Any funds transferred from CREF to TIAA in 1983 would be 1983 money also. In 1984, the vintage-year 1982 investment earned at the 11.50 percent rate announced for 1984. That would be another $1,150 on the original 1982 investment of $10,000. Also, in 1984 the interest on the 1982 vintage-year investment earned in 1983 -- $1,300--would earn interest in 1984 at the announced rate for 1984. Interest continues to compound on each year's new money whether from new, outside investment or from interest on interest.

When the participant retires and starts drawing benefits based upon his accumulation, his TIAA funds will be moved out of his accumulation account and into his annuity account. But the vintages will continue to be held in little packets in his annuity account as the basis of computing his pension benefits each year. His benefits will depend in part on the size of each vintage year's accumulation and the rate paid on that vintage year's balance. Starting in 1992 different rates were paid in the same calendar years for vintages originating in different years. Three different rates have been paid each year since then. These are related to the vintage year of origin.

The result is that TIAA pension benefits will very likely continue to change from year-to-year as shown earlier in Table 5.4 and as will be emphasized later in Chapter 12.

CREF'S MONEY MARKET FUND

The CREF Money Market Fund, which was started April 1, 1988, has a unique feature. Money market funds, which are generally invested securities that have 30-90 days remaining to maturity, pay interest on a daily basis. That amount is then added to the individual's investment by "buying" more units at $1.00 per unit. The price of a unit is stabilized at $1.00.

CREF's fund, which had assets of $2.8 billion on December 31, 1994, had an average maturity of 45 days on March 31, 1995. In the second quarter of 1993, CREF's money market fund changed its policy about the maturities it would hold. It now holds some Treasury notes with maturities of up to two years and non-Treasury securities of up to one year. This new policy will add to both the return and risk as discussed in the yield-to-maturity section of Chapter 10.

TIAA increases the value of a money market unit by the amount of interest earned daily. The price of a unit fluctuates with the price of the underlying securities. In 1994 the unit prices ranged from $14.2209 to $14.7954. This range of $0.5745 or 4.04 percent largely reflects price risk. The initial offering price of the money market fund was $10.000, and the increase to $14.7954 is largely the result of the re-investment of the interest. Its interest through 1994 has averaged 5.98 percent since it was opened April 1, 1988. The rate for 1994 was 4.07 percent.

TIAA AND ITS COMPETITORS

TIAA-CREF is by far the oldest and the largest insurance company serving the pension-fund needs of educational and nonprofit organizations.[2] TIAA began in 1918 and utilized a tax-deferred, salary option from the very start. This advantage was formalized in the Internal Revenue Code in 1942; the present provision, called 403(b), was reformulated in 1958.

TIAA-CREF most likely has well over 80 percent of this total market and VALIC is second. VALIC, originally the Variable Assurance Life Insurance Company, was founded in about 1955 in Washington, D.C., where it was easier to get permission to establish a variable annuity policy. In contrast, CREF ran a remarkably difficult gauntlet of insurance law and political problems in New York State in 1951 and 1952. VALIC was subsequently purchased by American General in 1968 and later moved to Houston, Texas. American General is a very successful, publicly held life insurance company. VALIC's assets are approaching $18 billion in contrast with TIAA-CREF's more than $130 billion.

The 403(b) field includes colleges and universities, research organizations such as the Institute for Cancer Research, nonprofit organizations such as the American Association of University Professors, and non-profit schools in the K-12 range such as the Cape Code Academy, as well as hospitals and churches. While TIAA dominates the college, university and academic-like research fields, VALIC dominates schools in the K-12 field. A VALIC estimate suggested that 2.4 to 3.5 million people out of an estimated 14 million eligible had 403(b) plans. VALIC believes that some 7,400 of 403(b) contracts exist in the country. TIAA-CREF has about 5,500 participating institutions.[3]

In recent years this lucrative field has attracted many of the very large mutual fund organizations such as Vanguard, Fidelity, Scudder, and Templeton. Life insurance companies such as Lincoln National Insurance, Hartford Life, and Aetna Life have entered the field. When mutual fund companies enter the 403(b) field, they must have their own life insurance company or enter into an agreement with an existing life insurance company in order to provide for annuity payments. Some of these companies provide 403(b)(7) services as mutual funds only. Under a 403(b)(7) plan, the employer can deduct contributions for a

---

[2]Parts of the earlier histories of TIAA and CREF were given in Chapter 4 and 5 respectively.

[3]Judy Greenwald, "Insurer Trouble a Wake-up Call for Non-Profits," Business Insurance, September 7, 1992, p. 16.

mutual fund on a tax-deferred basis, but the mutual fund does not itself make pensions based on life annuity plans available. Fidelity is an especially aggressive competitor. All of the major mutual funds mentioned are private companies; no information about their profitability is available.

Many universities and colleges have opened up their pension programs so that any insurance carrier that wants to compete for customers may do so on the campus. Usually such firms must pass established financial responsibility and service criteria. These firms may hold information meetings on campus and try to persuade individuals to utilize their services. After a while, the administrative task of sending money to many companies for only a few employees each can become burdensome.

How many of TIAA's 5,500 participating organizations allow its competitors to seek clients within their organizations is not known. Some of the 7,400 403(b) contracts mentioned earlier may involve double counting. None of several specialized consulting firms contacted could help me with this question or provide estimates for the total dollar value of 403(b) contracts for colleges, universities and academic research-like institutions.

LET THE BUYER BEWARE

Under these competitive conditions, <u>caveat emptor</u> or let the buyer beware is a fitting attitude. Even though the employer itself may set up standards of financial and fiduciary responsibility, hundreds of financial organizations may be able to qualify. Two firms that were offering the 403(b) plans have had serious problems. Mutual Benefit Life Insurance Company of New Jersey was on the brink of disaster in 1990 and was taken over by the State of New Jersey Insurance Department and Executive Life became bankrupt and was seized in 1991 by the California Insurance Department. These cases spent several years in state courts before decisions were made on the amounts that could be paid to their annuitants and other policy holders. The court's decisions were contested, but will probably be upheld despite large losses for the annuitants.[4]

Given the lack of knowledge of most 403(b) pension plan participants, several pieces of information should be sought before deciding whether or not to keep your present insurance carrier or to move your pension plan to another company. These characteristics fall into two separable categories. One is the past, present, and likely future performance of the

---

[4]According to a <u>New York Times</u> article, annuitants will have full access to their money after waiting seven years, but interest will accumulate at a very reduced rate. Those who demand their money back immediately will receive 55 percent of their savings (Peter Kerr, "What Customers Can Expect," <u>New York Times</u>, August 13, 1994, p. D2). According to a <u>National Underwriter: Life and Health Insurance Service</u> article, the Executive Life Insurance Company was taken over by the Aurora National Life Assurance Company. According to an Aurora spokeswoman, annuitants should not receive less than 70 percent of their former benefits. However, complaints being made to an action network for victims of this debacle say that they are receiving less than 60 percent of prior benefits (Cynthia Crosson, "ELIC Settlement Annuitants Walloped," <u>National Underwriter: Life and Health Insurance Service</u>, October 3, 1993, p. 3).

companies' various investments and its likely future performance as a provider of annuities. The other is the costs and services offered to the individual participant.

The financial performance and costs of TIAA-CREF and four of its major competitors are shown in Table 10.2. Remember that past performance is never a guarantee of future performance.

One of the most important aspects of financial performance is the announced, one-year rate as discussed in the Vintage Year Rate section. The average one-year guaranteed rate according to Morning Star, Inc., was 4.67 percent as of April 1, 1993.[5] TIAA's announced one-year rate for 1993 ranged from 7.5 percent to 8.5 percent.

The average annual contract charge in 1993 was 1.25 percent and the expenses for these variable annuity accounts average about 0.76 percent as a percent of the premiums paid. Together these charges amount to just over 2.00 percent. In addition, there may be front-end loads and/or commissions and back-end loads. One should never hesitate to ask about these charges—especially the commissions. Back-end load or surrender charges may be as high as 7 percent in the first year, but typically decline over five or seven years to zero. Some firms may charge separate fees for moving a contract from the pay-in or accumulation stage, to the pay-out or annuity stage.

One of the major guides to the future performance of a variable annuity is its own past performance. In the case of CREF, each of its four variable annuities has a record going back at least 10 years according to Morning Star. As shown in Table 10.2, only Lincoln National's variable annuities generally have 10-year performance records. Although Fidelity and Vanguard have sold mutual funds for decades, they are newcomers in the variable annuity field. The performance of their mutual funds may be used as an indicator of the likely portfolio performance of their variable annuities.

All of CREF's variable annuities have performed above the average of these instruments over the past 5 and 10 years. The performance of its competitors' variable annuities have not been nearly as good.

The availability of life annuities, which are discussed in detail in Chapter 11, is a major reason that most people use pension plans. Life annuities, however, are available only from life insurance companies. Both Lincoln National and VALIC have such companies as an integral part of their operations. Fidelity and Vanguard do not at this time. Therefore, when the participant wishes to convert her investment into an annuity these funds must be "rolled over" into an insurance company. Fidelity and Vanguard may help the participant find such an insurance company.

The importance of an insurance company's rating was discussed in Chapter 4. The fact that ratings could not be located for two of four of CREF's competitors does not necessarily show that these companies are financially weak. These companies may be too small for the rating companies to analyze or these companies may not be willing to pay the fees required by these raters.

---

[5]This rate and other data are drawn from several <u>Wall Street Journal</u> articles prepared by Ellen E. Schultz, February 9, June 15, and July 13, 1993, p. C1.

PERFORMANCE AND MARKETING COMPARISONS

This section compares the performance and marketing characteristics of TIAA-CREF and several of its major competitors. The costs, expenses, and service aspects of these companies and their pay-out policies are described and ranked to help you select among these companies and any others that are seeking your business.

SELECTING A COMPANY

Some of the major considerations in selecting a company for your 403(b) annuities are summarized in Table 10.2. This table is limited to variable annuities; fixed-income annuities are not summarized in detail, but differences among them are important also.

Four of CREF's major competitors are listed in alphabetical order in Table 10.2. CREF is clearly lowest in terms of annual costs expressed as a percentage of premiums. Neither CREF nor Vanguard have cash surrender charges. If one is truly investing to build up a fund for retirement purposes, the surrender charges are probably of little interest because few people shop around and change their insurance carrier with any frequency.

Most important is the performance record of the variable annuity funds of these five companies. Although each of these companies has been in business for decades, some do not show 10-year performance records because these particular 403(b) products have not been in existence that long. On the basis of what is available, CREF is the only company with 10-year records for each of its 403(b) funds. Each of CREF's funds have performed above the average for its type according to Morningstar's Variable Annuity Life Performance Report. Lincoln National MultiFunds are clearly second best, as shown by the summary below. TIAA-CREF and Lincoln National are both rated AAA by the Duff & Phelps rating company that Morningstar refers to for such purposes.

Surprisingly, neither Fidelity nor Vanguard offer any life-annuity options. Fidelity will hold your money, not pay interest on it, and pay it out monthly over the number of years you request; or they will help you locate (free of charge) an insurance company which provides the annuity policy you prefer. Your accumulation would be "rolled over" to that company without cost. Vanguard will make regular payments that end when your accumulation is returned to you. They have no life annuity policies.

TIAA-CREF, Lincoln National, and VALIC each seem to offer a full range of annuity policies. The Lincoln National representative said that they offer an installment policy as well as an annuity. That policy has some advantages as discussed in Chapter 11. Income is earned on their fixed-income policy as long as any investment remains in the client's account. This policy works out better than a life annuity with 10-years or 15-years certain in the event that the annuitant and/or his or her beneficiary dies before the end of the years-certain period. Under these circumstances, all of the investment plus interest would be paid out to the beneficiary or to the contingent beneficiary. That point is correct, but if the annuitant or the beneficiary live beyond the number of years-certain period, the investment is exhausted and annuity payments end, even though the annuitant and/or the beneficiary survive.[6]

---

[6]For an illustration of how a life annuity works and the amount that may be left in the account if the annuitant and/or the beneficiary dies before the end of the years-certain period, see Table 11.4 and the related discussion.

When the life annuity policies are matched in specific detail, some aspects come to the foreground in greater relief. For variable annuities, the most important factor is the total return performance of the funds. These total annual returns for the best-performing equity fund of each of the three companies with records of five years or more are:

	5-years	10-years	Ending
Lincoln National's			
Multi Fund Growth	8.44%	10.52%	6/30/93
VALIC, Separate Acct. A,			
Stock Index	11.83%	N.A.	6/30/93
CREF-Equities	13.10%	14.47%	6/30/93

As a reminder, the difference between 10 percent and 15 percent is much more than one-half because the amounts involved are growing at compounded interest rates.[7]

The differences between the traditional or fixed-income annuities are at least as remarkable as those among the variable annuities. First, to make the comparisons valid, the detailed specifications of the policies must be set forth. For the sake of this comparison, I used a popular annuity option of 20-years certain, joint or two-life option, with full benefits to the survivor.[8] Both people covered by the annuity are 65 when payments start. On the basis of these specifications, the annuity benefits per $1,000 of accumulation were as follows:

	Benefits per $1,000
Lincoln National	$4.72
VALIC	6.79
TIAA	6.56[a]

[a]Requires additional specification about
investment per year because of vintage-year procedure.

These benefits can and do change almost every year.

Another important difference must be pointed out. The Lincoln National and VALIC benefits are fixed as long as either or both of the annuitants survive. TIAA's benefits, as has been explained and shown in Table 5.2, vary from year-to-year with the performance of its portfolio.

When clients retire and start drawing upon their investment, VALIC urges clients to switch from the variable annuity account to the fixed annuity. Most people—perhaps 98 percent—did that because they did not want their benefits to fluctuate during retirement. That advice is

---

[7]See Table 6.4.

[8]The meanings of the terms are explained in Chapter 12.

in sharp contrast with TIAA-CREF's recommendations and my own as shown in Table 3.1 and 3.2, respectively.[9]

MOST IMPORTANT POINTS TO CONSIDER IN MAKING A SELECTION

Working through the many terms, conditions, and performance ratings of TIAA-CREF and its competitors is a substantial task in itself. After all of that is done, what are the most important things to consider in making a choice when you have an option? Even if you are not considering changing insurance companies, you likely want assurance that your present choice is at least satisfactory, if not the best. Even so, what may be a minor consideration in some cases could turn out to be the most important one in different circumstances.

Under most circumstances, the most important considerations are:

- The availability of a full range of life and joint-life annuity choices.

- The performance record of the variable annuity fund on which the stock-based part of your pension will be based.

- The benefits per $1,000 on the fixed-income part of your pension.

The meaning of a full range of annuity choices is discussed in Chapter 11. The past performance of a stock fund such as CREF-Equities or VALIC's Separate Account A Stock Index Fund is no guarantee or absolute assurance of what the fund's future performance will be. However, insofar as a fund is very broadly based or designed to be an index fund, the results should mirror that of the stock market in general. The performance of the fixed-income part of the insurance company's assets and its quality rating should also be reviewed. TIAA's return as an insurance company has been among the best in the nation for a long time. The difference between TIAA's fixed-income benefits per $1,000 and those of other companies is one measure of this difference. Various insurance guides such as those produced by Best & Company provide such information. Independent insurance consulting firms such as Insurance Information (Mathuen, MA), Insurance-Quote (Chandler, AZ), LifeQuote (Coral Gables, FL), or Select Quote (San Francisco) may be able to help for a fee.[10] Even so, you should make the effort to learn whether the fixed income-based pension will vary with interest rates in general as TIAA's does, or be fixed for the life of the policy as Lincoln National's and VALIC's are.

Beyond that, your decision on your investment allocation between fixed and variable income pension annuities will be based upon your acceptance of the empirical evidence and

---

[9]The benefits per $1,000 of investment under the conditions specified were obtained directly from the representatives of Lincoln National and VALIC during telephone conversations. VALIC's representative had the amount of $6.79 in a reference book. Lincoln National's representative passed my call along to their actuarial department where a second person worked out the answer of $4.72. In the case of TIAA, I provided the annuity and age characteristics for the annuity payment I was seeking. Their vintage-year scheme is so complex that their representative wrote down what I wanted and said the answer would be mailed to me. The delivery time was 16 days.

[10]These services are named in Sylvia Porter's Personal Finance Letter, June 1989.

theoretical demonstration that stocks will perform better than bonds in the long run. These positions were presented in Chapter 5. The experiences of TIAA-CREF annuitants since 1971 are presented in Chapter 12.

A second important consideration is the service provided both before and after retirement by the insurance company that you use. The elements to consider are:

- The availability of information from a person who visits your campus or place of business, or an 800 telephone number, including the training and background of such personnel. Generally, such counselors should not recommend what to do, but rather ask questions of you and sketch out the likely consequences of the alternatives considered.

- The availability of written materials explaining aspects of available alternatives.

- Retirement planning services. Usually, you should be able to ask for the consequences of different alternatives and get written answers in a reasonable period of time. For example, you might be concerned with the impact on your benefits of retiring at several alternative ages.

- Regular, written communications discussing developments in their policies and programs.

TIAA-CREF is a non-profit, mutual company which conducts research into such matters as how well retirees live and choices retirees make about where to live upon retirement. Retirees tell what tends to make for successful and unsuccessful lives after retirement. Their booklets and studies on such topics are available.

You may well want to know whether the company you select is a profit-seeking mutual fund or a profit-seeking insurance company. Some mutual funds are public companies as are many insurance companies. A mutual fund, like any other corporation, may be a closed corporation or a public corporation. A public corporation company is one whose stock may be purchased in the market. A closed corporation is one whose stock is not available to the general public. Some insurance companies are mutual companies in the sense that the policyholders are the owners and share in the profits of the company.

A third important consideration is costs such as annual fees, fund expenses, insurance expense, and surrender charges. Annual fees are the least important of these four items. If you invest in a low-earning account such as a money market fund, your fund and insurance expenses could be about as high as the income earned itself. The cash surrender charges can be so high that you had best investigate thoroughly before going with a particular organization. The surrender charge is made to help the company keep your account by penalizing you for changing. A 5 percent or 7 percent penalty on your investment in the company is substantial. Even so, there could be compelling reasons for making a change.

If you are being enticed by a persuasive, persistent salesperson, you might well ask what commission he earns on sales. If he or she will not say, try some other means of finding the answer. Find out how long he has been with the company and what his professional qualifications are in the insurance and securities businesses.

CONCLUSIONS

TIAA-CREF participants should understand TIAA's unique vintage-year procedure of adding interest earned to their investments because it will affect their total accumulation, and the stability and amount of their benefits during the annuity period. CREF's procedure of adding interest earned to its money market fund is unique. Although CREF itself does not recommend that the money market fund be used as the basis of a retirement annuity, participants should understand its operations both during the accumulation and annuity periods.

The data about investment performance, costs and expenses are vital to making comparisons with other companies that offer 403(b) pension plans. These data are often difficult to obtain and to place on the same bases so that the most meaningful comparisons can be made. Data drawn together for this chapter shows that TIAA has been superior to its competitors, but that may not continue to hold true. Settlement-options provisions are quite complex as discussed in Chapter 11. Great care must be taken in comparing these options among pension plans. The amount of benefits per dollar invested must be examined with extreme care because of its importance.

TABLE 10.1

VINTAGE-YEAR RATES: INITIAL AND LATER YEARS[a]

INITIAL YEAR RATE PAID ON FUNDS REMITTED	TOTAL RATE (%) CREDIT DURING YEAR SHOWN[b]									
	1982	1985	1988	1989	1990	1991	1992	1993	1994	1995
1982	14.00	12.00	11.25	10.75	10.00	9.25	8.00	7.50	7.15	7.15
1985		11.75	10.75	10.50	10.00	9.25	8.00	7.50	7.15	7.15
1988			9.00	9.25	9.25	9.00	8.50	8.00	7.15	7.15
1989				9.25	8.60	9.00	8.50	8.00	7.15	7.15
1990					8.50	9.00	8.50	8.00	7.15	7.15
1991						8.75	8.50	8.00	7.15	7.15
1992							7.50	7.50	7.15	7.15
1993[c]								6.82	6.88	N.A.
1994[c]									6.75	N.A.

[a]Rates are for the retirement annuities starting March 1 each year.

[b]Rates available for all years but not shown for convenience.

[c]Rates shown for 1993 and 1994 are weighted average. Starting with 1993, TIAA started to change the rates it credited more than once a year.

TIAA AND CREF:PROCEDURES AND COMPETITORS

TABLE 10.2

PROFILES OF LEADING COMPANIES OFFERING VARIABLE ANNUITIES

Topic	CREF	Fidelity Retirement Reserves	Lincoln National Multi-Funds	VALIC	Vanguard
Annual Contract Fee	None	$30	$25	$15	$25
Fund Expense	0.35%	0.24%-1.14%	0.41%-1.46%	0.16%-0.91%	0.32%-0.42%
Insurance Expense	None	1.00%	1.00%	1.00%	0.55%
Surrender Charge	None	5%[a] 1st year	7%[a] 1st year	--[b]	None
No. of Variable Annuities					
Accounts	4	8	8	8	5
5-Yr Record	4	5	6	7	0
10-Yr Record	4	0	5	1	0
No. of Accounts Performing Above Average					
5 Years	4	2	5	1	0
10 Years	4	0	4	0	0
Life Annuity Options Available	Yes	No	Yes	Yes	No
Related Insurance Company	TIAA-CREF	[c]	[d]	[e]	[f]
Insurance Company Rating	AAA	NR	AAA	NR	AA

[a]Declines 1 percent per year.

[b]Lessor of 5 percent of premium paid in last five years or 5 percent of amount withdrawn.

[c]Fidelity Investments Life Insurance Co. (No ratings located.)

[d]Lincoln National Life Insurance Co. (Rated by two rating services.)

[e]Variable Annuity Life Insurance Co. (Rated A+ to A++ by Best and AA+ to AAA by S&P.)

[f]National Home Life. (No ratings located.)

NR - Not Rated.

SOURCES: TIAA-CREF, and Morning Star Variable Annuity/Life Performance Report, July 1993.

CHAPTER 11

RETIREMENT ANNUITIES

INTRODUCTION

- Why are such a large proportion of TIAA-CREF and other pension-plan participants so uninformed about their settlement options until they are close to retirement?

- How far back into history do formal annuities go? When did formal, insurance-based annuities start in the United States?

- What are the meanings and implications of single- and joint-life annuities?

- What are the meanings and implications of guaranteed payment periods?

- How much do these several annuity options forms and payment-period options affect the benefits received?

- What are the most popular settlement options? Why?

- What is the arithmetic that underlies the life-annuity contract? What are the implications of that arithmetic for those who die soon after their annuities start, and for those who live very long lives?

- What are the differences between fixed and variable annuities?

- How do variable annuities work?

- How many retirees use TIAA and CREF Annuities?

- What changes in their allocations do participants make at retirement or just prior to retirement?

- How can additional retirement benefits be accumulated? What are lump-sum settlements?

The least understood part of retirement plans are the many options about ways you can have your retirement benefits or pension paid to you. When you convert your accumulated investment to an annuity—that is, you annuitize your accumulated investment—you must select an option on the basis of which your monthly payments will be determined. These options, which will be described, are called settlement options.

During the years you have been a TIAA-CREF participant, you may have learned the difference between the meaning of investments "marked to book" and "marked to market," the differences between fixed-income and variable-income investments, and the importance of your allocation between these two types of investment funds. However, you may not have heard about the choices you must make between a single-life annuity, a joint-life annuity and the choices you will have about the numbers of years certain (guaranteed periods) among which you must select. The meanings of and the differences among these and other parts of your settlement option are not difficult to understand when they are explained clearly and completely. The benefit levels of all available options that may be relevant in your case should be compared.

In the first retirement planning seminars I presented I was unprepared for participants' lack of knowledge and misinformation about settlement options. The consequences of the final allocation of funds between TIAA and CREF-Equities was only dimly understood or largely misunderstood. The concern that raised the greatest emotional response was how to safeguard some inheritance for a child or children. The question of what to do to provide financial protection for a disabled child led involved participants to nearly hysterical responses.

In retrospect, I should not have been so utterly unprepared for these reactions to the settlement options. I have conjectured six reasons that help explain the utter absence of information about this topic in the overwhelming majority of cases.

- The information is not part of what we hear on television, or read in newspapers, magazines, or books during our adult life.

- College courses in investments and insurance, which are only taken by a small minority, rarely - if ever - get to these topics.

- Information sent by a life insurance company may contain some information about settlement options, but we are much too busy to read it.

- The information about these settlement options is likely to be boring and difficult to read and understand.

- Little or no thought is given to the choices that will have to be made at retirement. Participants feel the choice will not be complex or important and that their employer or TIAA will tell them what is best for them and their family.

- Money has never been a high-priority topic for many participants, and they intend to keep it that way. They feel that they will always have enough income and can rely on someone else to make the settlement-option decisions for them.

The four most frequently raised questions and comments regarding settlement decisions are:

1. If I die before I start drawing benefits, who will get my money?

2. Even if I start collecting my benefits and I die within a few years, will my spouse or my children get any of my money back?

3. Can I invest my money myself and earn a higher rate of return than TIAA-CREF? My banker, broker, and lawyer tell me I can.

4. Upon retirement, why can't I get my money out of TIAA-CREF to do with as I please?

The preliminary response to the first point is that if you die before you start drawing benefits, your spouse or other named beneficiaries will be paid the amount you have in your account(s). After your death, your beneficiary should contact TIAA-CREF. Your spouse or beneficiary will be advised of the steps to take and will receive information about the options available including a lump-sum settlement. Of course, after your death you yourself will never get your accumulation back because the insurer will not know where you are, or how to send the money to you. Even with TIAA-CREF, you still can't take it with you.

Another aspect of the questions, "Will I ever get my money back," was addressed in the last section of Chapter 9, "Investment Background." The point was made there that you or your beneficiaries will not only get your money back but will also receive your employer's contribution and the income earned on both of these investments while it is in trust for you with TIAA-CREF.

The response to the second point is that your spouse and/or your children will continue to receive benefits after you die according to the option you select at the time you start receiving benefits. If you have no living relatives—or even if you do—you can designate someone else or some organization to receive benefits. Two examples are that you could have your benefits paid to your university, or to a scholarship fund in your name. In such cases you will need to work carefully with TIAA-CREF's Retirement Planning Counseling section and, perhaps, with your lawyer.

The response to the third point about higher rates of return is a little more complex. First, as was pointed out in Chapter 4, TIAA has been one of the highest-earning insurance company in the United States for many years. If you utilize a different insurance company, you may well have to pay commissions in one form or another. The TIAA and similar pension plans' tax-deferred options provide a benefit that it is almost impossible to beat as compared with plans that do not have tax-deferred options. Plans that hold forth the possibility of exceeding the return on a tax-deferred income plan from fixed-income investments are likely to be exceedingly risky. CREF's rate of return is compared with that of the stock market in general and with the best performing and largest mutual funds in Tables 5.1 and 5.3, respectively. CREF's performance has been excellent even though it has not been the best performer. Furthermore, CREF does provide for the various annuity options; mutual funds do not. CREF's combination of return performance, tax-deferred status, and variable annuities is probably the best in the nation. If you can invest in stocks or other things and consistently earn about double the market return, that may be the better approach for you. You must be confident that you can continue that return performance during your later years and that upon your death your beneficiaries can continue to do the same.

The response to the fourth point is that you can get some or all of your money out upon retirement, but there is likely to be a large income-tax consequence. A retirement transition benefit (RTB) of 10 percent of the amount annuitized can be paid to you when you annuitize your accumulated investment. The advantages and disadvantages of an RTB are discussed.

Of course, if you have an SRA you can cash it in after you are 59½ (if you comply with any other restrictions of the Internal Revenue Service) without any income-tax penalty. You may be able to withdraw from your account some or all of your regular CREF accumulation upon retirement if your employer's own regulations permit that. You must check with your employer to learn what option he is providing.

Whether such a cash withdrawal is a prudent financial option is another question. This option, which is relatively new, is not being widely used.

HISTORY OF ANNUITIES

A discussion of annuities is included in Adam Smith's 1776 <u>Wealth of Nations</u>. Adam Smith relates that the British began issuing public debt instruments with maturities beyond 90 years in the late 17th century; these were virtually perpetual debts and the interest on these debts were annuities. They were bought and sold in a market; their prices varied with interest rates.

Annuities on individual lives issued by private businesses had to wait until reliable mortality tables were prepared. One of the earliest English, scientific, mortality tables was prepared in 1693 by Edmund Halley, astronomer and mathematician.[1] Early in the 19th century, a Scottish company issued life annuities on the assumption that no one would live beyond 95 years of age. The annuity payments per pound invested were very high at the upper ages. An enterprising group went into the country looking for healthy, ninety-year-old men. These policies paid off at the rate of 33 percent for each year the insured person lived beyond age 90. Many of these older men lived well beyond 95. The investors in these policies earned a very handsome return until the insurance company went bankrupt. (The mortality rate on people at age 90 is now about 9.7 percent per year; life expectancy is 6.3 years.)

The first annuity policies in the United States were issued in the 1830s. They provided for cash payments only at death. Installment annuity policies began in the 1880s and eventually policies that continued to pay benefits to a second or contingent beneficiary were offered. In 1901 the first policy on the joint-life span of two individuals was issued. Annuity provisions—the settlement options—amongst which individuals could choose before the death of the insured continued to proliferate and became more nearly standardized.

Retirement funds for public employees and college teachers were first sought in the 1870s. The first compulsory teacher retirement funds were established in 1895 in Chicago, Detroit and Brooklyn. Columbia University's 1892 plan, the first for an American university, provided that a professor with 15 years of service at age 65 could be granted half pay at his request or that of the trustees of the college.[2]

When TIAA issued its first annuities in 1919, it used the McClintock Mortality Tables which had separate tables for men and women. They were used until 1926 when other tables were adopted. At age 65 expected life was 11.76 years for men and 13.94 years for women in the McClintock tables. The joint-life expectancy when husband and wife were both 65 was 16.08 years. Beginning in 1983 TIAA started to use tables that included its own experience. A section of that table is shown as Table 11.2. In 1990 at age 65, the life expectancies for men and women are 20 and 23 years respectively in TIAA tables. The joint-life expectancy is 26.5 years for a couple, both of whom are age 65.

Another possible reason that society has not stressed information about settlement options is the very rapid growth of life expectancy after age 65. As shown in Table 11.1, life expectancy after age 65 has grown from 12.5 years in 1935 to 19.1 years projected in 2000. That increase of 6.6 years amounts to an average increase from 1935 to 2000 of 52.8 percent.

---

[1] A. Fingland Jack, <u>An Introduction to the History of Life Insurance</u>. London: P.S. King & Son, 1912.

[2] William C. Greenough and Francis P. King, <u>Pension Plans and Public Policy</u>, New York: Columbia University Press, 1976.

Another way of viewing your own likelihood of survival is shown in Table 11.2. The likelihood table shows your chances of surviving from any given age (in 5-year steps) to any other age through 100. If you are in good health, have a happy genetic background on one side of your family, take good care of yourself, have excellent medical care and are lucky, you and/or your spouse may well live beyond your earlier dreams and remain active. Prudence dictates that you must plan for having enough income to enjoy your long, prospective retirement.

The major topics defined and discussed in the balance of this chapter are:

- Single and joint-life annuities.

- Full, two-thirds, and half benefits to the survivor of a joint-life annuity.

- Guaranteed benefits or year's certain period.

- Arithmetic of a life-annuity contract.

- Dollar impact of settlement option selected.

- Fixed-period annuity.

- Three other annuity forms (TIAA only).

- Interest payment retirement option.

- Level, graded, and minimum distribution options.

- Variable annuities (CREF only).

Other topics are SRAs, lump-sum payments, and retirement transition benefits (RTP). As a part of the discussion, the advantages and disadvantages of the various settlement options will be elaborated. The benefit levels on the many options will be compared as appropriate, and the relative usage of these many options will be given insofar as they can be obtained from TIAA-CREF.

All participants need to be reminded that TIAA-CREF is a mutual company—not a profit-seeking company. TIAA-CREF keeps its costs low as comparative data presented in Chapter 10 shows; salary levels are modest for middle- and senior-level managers.

SINGLE- AND JOINT-LIFE ANNUITIES

An annuity is a contractual stream of payments. Those payments can continue for only a few weeks, for months, for many years, or for the life of the individual or institution. The term is not usually used unless the payments are expected to continue for a number of years. These payments may be level amounts, rising amounts, declining amounts, irregular amounts, or amounts that may be interrupted for some time. Some preferred stock agreements provide, for example, that the specified annual dividends can not be paid unless the amount of the dividend is earned by the corporation. When the amount is earned, it must be paid together with any accumulated, unpaid preferred stock dividends before any dividends can be paid to the common stockholders.

SINGLE-LIFE ANNUITY

A single-life annuity is the simplest form of settlement option. Payments are made to the policyholder for the rest of his or her life based upon the amount initially placed in the annuity account and the interest earned on these funds. The amount of the payments is worked out based on the original amount in the account, the anticipated interest to be earned, and life expectancy. When a very large sample of individuals of a given age is examined, the distribution of ages at death can be predicted with very surprising accuracy. For example, see the Likelihood of Survival Table, Table 11.2. Given the pattern of deaths by age, some individuals will receive less than all of their investment plus interest as benefits, and others will receive much more than their investment plus interest under the terms of a life annuity settlement option. In advance no one can predict who will die shortly and who will live a very long life. But those who live the longest can never outlive their benefits. Table 11.3, a section of TIAA's current, merged-gender mortality table, is one of the bases on which life-annuity payments are calculated.

Under a single-life annuity, payments cease when the covered individual dies. Other settlement options include a guaranteed period or years certain clause that provides for continuing payments to a contingent beneficiary as will be illustrated and discussed.

JOINT-LIFE ANNUITY

Two topics are treated in this section. First, the meaning of joint-lives is explained and illustrated. Within this settlement option, a further clause provides choices about the benefits level for the survivor. The second topic explains guaranteed-benefits periods.

The joint-life annuity is an annuity on the lives of two people, usually a husband and wife. Payments will continue to be made as long as either of them lives. For example, in the merged-gender tables that TIAA uses, if one person is 60 and the other is 65, their expected joint-lives are 29.05 years. That means the chances are 50-50 that one of the two will be alive just over 29 years after they start receiving benefits. If the ages of a couple are 65 and 70 when they start receiving retirements, their expected joint lives are 24.50 years. When the longer lived of the two dies, benefit payments will stop.

However, if a 10-year, 15-year or 20-year guaranteed period is selected and both die before the end of the guaranteed period, benefits will continue to a secondary or contingent beneficiary.

LEVEL OF BENEFITS TO THE SURVIVOR

TIAA's joint-life settlement options provide three options for the benefit level for the survivor. After both die, a contingent beneficiary is allowed.

Under the first option, full benefits to the survivor, the benefits will remain the same regardless of which of the two annuitants dies first. This level of benefits will continue for the surviving annuitant's life.

In the second option, half benefits to the second annuitant, the second annuitant receives only half of the benefits that you, the person who purchased the annuity, receives while you are both alive. However, if the second annuitant dies first, you, the primary annuitant, will continue to receive the initial level of benefits.

In the third option, <u>two-thirds benefits to the survivor</u>, the survivor will receive only two-thirds of the original benefits level no matter which of the two joint-life annuitants dies first. If the primary annuitant is the survivor, he or she will have the benefits level reduced to two-thirds of what they had been.

If the guaranteed period has not run out at the time of the death of the longer-living beneficiary, the benefits level for that annuitant will be paid to the contingent beneficiary to the end of the guaranteed period.

A few comments are appropriate at this point. First, even though the discussion says that the payments level of the beneficiaries will not be changed at the death of one of the two joint annuitants, or that they will be fixed once the settlement-options clause have been selected, they may still be changed as the result of changes in TIAA's ability to earn and pay out interest. These changes are discussed and illustrated in Chapters 5, 10, and 12. The changes in benefits levels will not be caused by the event—death of one of the two annuitants—but they can and very likely will change at some future date because of changes in market interest rates and TIAA's ability to manage its asset portfolio. Under the joint-lives options, death may cause a change in benefits depending upon the option selected.

The second comment refers to social security benefits. In the event of the death of the primary annuitant, the spouse may elect to receive the social security benefits of the deceased as stated in Chapter 2, if the deceased's benefits were the higher of the two. In the still typical case, the husband is the primary annuitant and dies first. The surviving wife usually has been receiving a lower social security benefit than her husband, because she did not work as long or at as high a salary. Even if the wife did not work and the husband is retired and drawing social security benefits, the widow can start drawing benefits as soon as she reaches age 60 as described earlier also. The point is that the potential change in the social security benefits for the second annuitant are an appropriate consideration in selecting the level-of-benefits clause in a joint-life annuity.

Third, the second annuitant need not be the spouse. A son, daughter, grandchild, some one unrelated, a foundation, and so forth may be the secondary annuitant. In the event that the spouse is not the second annuitant, the spouse must sign a statement saying that the point is understood and agreed to willingly.

If you name a child or grandchild as the second beneficiary, a related factor to keep in mind is that your benefits will be greatly reduced because that person is so much younger and your joint-life expectancy is so much longer. For example, if you are 65 when you start drawing from your annuity and you name as beneficiary a person who is 40 years old at that time, your joint life expectancy is 44.3 years.

Occasionally a child who is disabled and/or unable to earn an adequate living is named as the second annuitant. With deaths and divorces becoming much more frequent, financial concern in a second marriage for one's own children is likely to be seen more often in selecting a settlement option. Under our changing social and economic environment, the spouse is much more likely to have built up a very adequate or handsome retirement benefit package of her or his own.

The fourth comment is a reminder that partial settlements may be used. One's total accumulation can be divided into two or more pieces for each TIAA and CREF contract. In the event that two or more annuities are used for each basic contract, the settlement options need not be the same. The settlement options used on each annuity are in no way restricted legally by what is used in your other annuities. Of course, your own planning for your likely total financial situation in retirement must be considered.

The fifth comment is that your selection of settlement options for your SRAs, if you choose to annuitize them as most people do, are independent of what you did or do for your basic TIAA and CREF contracts.

After a while the flexibility you have becomes mind-numbing and you may not want to pursue this part of the settlement options any further.

GUARANTEED PERIOD OF PAYMENT YEARS
Under a settlement option without a guaranteed payment period, benefits cease on the death of the covered person under a single-life option. Under a joint-lives policy, payments cease at the death of the last of the two to die.

TIAA's settlement options provide for guaranteed payments for 10, 15, or 20 years, or for no guaranteed period. You must choose among these four options. The benefit payments will be slightly higher if you select the shortest of these three guaranteed periods. Examples of the exact amounts to be received, depending upon the option selected, are given in Table 11.4. The longer the guarantee period, the lower the monthly or annual benefits.

Under a single-life annuity with a guaranteed period of 20 years, for the purposes of an illustration, assume that the covered person dies during the eleventh year after the benefits began. Payments will be made to the named contingent beneficiary until the end of the twentieth year. At the end of the twentieth year, payments will cease.

However, if you live beyond the end of the twentieth year, your payments will continue as long as you live, even if that is the 119 years provided for in TIAA's annuity tables. And if you should live beyond 119 years, payments will continue anyway. The contingent beneficiary will receive nothing if you live beyond 20 years.

The joint-life annuity with the guaranteed years works in just the same way. If both people die before the end of the guaranteed period the contingent beneficiary will receive benefits until the end of the guaranteed period.

DOLLAR IMPACT OF SETTLEMENT OPTION
Each of the settlement option clauses you select has a dollar impact. Rather than continue in generalities, Table 11.4 shows what that impact is in clear terms given the assumptions about the ages of the annuitant or annuitants and the interest rate. Interest rates do change and will continue to change. The data in the table were based upon a reasonable projection of an 8½ percent for interest rates in 1990. Currently one might have the anticipation that the long-term rates will be somewhat lower than they were in 1990. Lower projected interest rates will result in lower annuity benefits. However, the dollar differences between the settlement options selected will be about the same in percentage terms.

Table 11.4 shows that for a person age 68, the annual beginning-level payment annuity for a single-life annuity with no guaranteed period is $1,116 per year or $93 per month for an annuitized accumulation of $10,000. If the 10-year guaranteed period clause is selected, the benefit decreases to $1,064 or by $52 per year, which is 4.66 percent of the larger amount. You must ask yourself whether this "cost" of 4.66 percent is worthwhile when dealing with your various personal relationships or your desire to leave a sum to a foundation, charity, or so forth. If you live beyond the 10-year period, nothing will be left for any beneficiary, and you will continue to receive payments as long as you live. For the 20-year certain period on the single-life annuity, the decline in benefits when selected at age 68 is 13.26 percent. These changes in annuity benefits follow directly from TIAA's table of survivors.

To repeat, TIAA is morally and financially neutral about the selection that you make. The amounts are worked out in terms of life expectancy. The decision of whether or not to use a single-life with no guarantee or a guaranteed period of 10, 15, or 20 years has no impact on TIAA.

The joint-life section of Table 11.4 reads similarly. Two levels of benefits differences can be observed in this table. First, note the differences between the level of benefits to the survivor. However, observe that the selection of the joint-life option with two-third benefits to the survivor when the age of the primary annuitant is 68 as compared with the single-life option decreases the benefit payment by $100 or 8.96 percent per year. Next compare the no-guarantee options. One obvious reason for the decrease in benefits in the joint-life expectancy with a younger second annuitant, is the considerably longer life expectancy. With full benefits to the survivor, the annual benefits decrease another $80 ($1,016 minus $936) or 7.9 percent per year. That percentage is the "cost" of the differences as compared with two-thirds benefits to the survivor. The half benefits to the second annuitant option actually increases the benefits slightly from the two-thirds benefits to the survivor case.

The most surprising observation from the table at first glance is the very small change in benefits from the no-guaranteed period case to the 10-year guaranteed period, and only a somewhat larger decline for the 20-year guaranteed period. When you look at Table 11.3, the mortality table, the reasons are obvious. For persons at the ages of 68 and 62, the chances that both will be dead within 10 or 20 years are quite small. (A 15-year guaranteed period is available and its dollars and percentages outcomes are in line with those in the table.) These actuarial facts should have a large impact on your own, or your own and your spouse's, decision about the settlement option to choose.

ACTUAL LIFETIME ANNUITY SELECTIONS (1991 RETIREES)

The actual lifetime annuity selections of retirees in 1991 are summarized in Table 11.5. One would hope that the full implications of settlement option selections were thought through based on complete information. However, the extent to which various options were used is difficult to rationalize. First, in the case of the single-life annuity, why would 9 percent of men and 23 percent of women not utilize a guaranteed period? True, benefits decline when a guaranteed period is selected, but the decline is only about 4.7 percent for a person age 68 and less than that for a younger person. Was there no one to whom these annuitants wanted to leave some benefits in the event of their early death?

Twenty-three percent of women did not select a guarantee period. TIAA's data shows that this percentage was quite constant for four age groups: 59 and under, 60-64, 65-69, and 70 and over. One could rationalize that most of these women were married and that their husbands' benefits would be enough for him to live on comfortably. The percentage of women selecting the 10- and 15-year guaranteed periods did increase sharply as a function of age their ages when they made their choices, but those selecting the 20-year period declined sharply as a function of age from 25 percent for those 59 and under to 6 percent for those 70 and over. This last item seems somewhat inexplicable. Were there no children or grandchildren to whom they wanted to leave some money?

The joint-life annuity options selected are more in line with what one surmises from a casual knowledge of the demographics of American society. Husbands and wives both strive to protect their families. Perhaps more unmarried women are in TIAA-CREF than unmarried men. That difference could explain the higher percentage of women selecting a single-life annuity. The most surprising point within this joint-lives settlement option summary is that more people did not select a two-thirds benefit for the survivor. The living expenses of one person are somewhat less than those of two. In most cases the wife will have either lower social security benefits than her husband had or no social security benefits at all. However, she will receive her husband's higher benefits upon his death instead of her own, if she applies for it. Most people selecting the joint-life annuity option also selected the 20-year guaranteed period.

Personal reasons for the settlement option selected are complex. The point of displaying an illustration of the level annual retirement benefits data in Table 11.4, a section of a mortality table in Table 11.3, and the data on frequency distribution of settlement options actually selected in Table 11.5 is to encourage you to consider the consequences of these options more fully.

ARITHMETIC OF A LIFE-ANNUITY CONTRACT

Two alternative ways of taking your benefits from the amount that you annuitize in your account are the life annuity that has just been described and the fixed-period annuity. In the fixed-period annuity you can specify any period from 5 through 30 years. During the specified term you will get back in equal payments your initial, annuitized amount plus interest earned on the balances remaining in your account. After the end of this specified period you will receive no further payments. If you do not survive this specified period, your beneficiaries can continue to receive the same amount or an equivalent lump-sum settlement for the specified term.

The arithmetic problem is to compare the payments from these two methods and to assess two things. First, the payments on the fixed-period annuity will generally be larger than those from the life annuity because in the fixed-period annuity all of the initial investment will be paid out during the specified period. Under the life-annuity contracts for the same number of years a considerable balance will remain in your account at the end of the guaranteed period. The reason for the balance is to have exactly enough funds left to continue to pay those who live longer than the average life expectancy. You must ask yourself how important this difference is. Remember that you cannot outlive the benefits from life-annuity, but you have a very good chance of outliving the fixed-period annuity.

Second, because the fixed-annuity payments are generally larger, you can conceivably reinvest the amounts by which they exceed the payments from a life annuity with an equally long guaranteed period. If you can invest this differential amount and earn a higher rate than TIAA—considering that you are unlikely to have a tax-deferred income advantage—the fixed-period annuity may be better for you. However, you must be absolutely confident of your discipline to reinvest regularly at that equivalent or higher rate and that you will be able to invest successfully for the rest of your life and that your spouse can do that equally well if you should die.

If your likely life expectancy or the lives of both yourself and your spouse are short when you retire because of clear medical diagnoses, you may wish to get more money back sooner. Also, you may not have anyone to whom to leave an inheritance beyond the term of your fixed-period annuity.

The arithmetic of a joint-life annuity is demonstrated in Table 11.6. To be specific, a joint-life annuity with 20-year guaranteed period is selected again. The interest rate is set at 8½ percent and the husband and wife are each 65 when benefits begin. Recall from Chapter 3 that TIAA guarantees a 3 percent interest rate, but the rate it pays out depends upon what it earns.

The pension benefits in the Table 11.6 illustration were calculated as $781.01 per month or $9,372.12 per year when the amount annuitized—sometimes called the initial endowment— is $100,000. If the $100,000 is invested at 8½ percent per year, it will earn $8,500. However, after considering first-year administrative costs and the fact that the average balance in the account will be less than $100,000 the first year, the net amount earned in that year is set in the table at $8,073.86. The amount paid out over the first year, $9,372.12, is larger than the interest earned less a small administrative charge by $1,298.26. That amount deducted from the initial endowment of $100,000 leaves a principal balance remaining at the end of the first year of $98,701.74.

In the second year the net amount of interest earned is $7,963.53 and the amount paid on the annuity remains at $9,372.12. The difference, $1,408.59, is a decrease in the principal which drops to $97,293.15 by the end of the second year. Year-by-year the balance of the principal drops ever more quickly until it reaches zero toward the end of the twenty-fifth year in the illustrative case. The calculation is prepared so that the account balance drops to zero in a period of time equal to the joint-life expectation of the couple.

One meaning of the term "cash flow" can be explained at this point. The annual amount received in this example, $9,3712, is partly income (the interest earned on the declining principal of the initial endowment) and partly a repayment of the principal itself. The two elements, current interest earned and repayment of principal, are a cash flow.

Now the mechanism and meaning of the number of guaranteed years of payments or the number of years certain may be explained in more detail. At the end of the tenth year, $80,740.28 of principal is left in the account. (That assumes the interest rate paid has not changed during this ten years.) If both people die before the end of the tenth year, the benefits will continue to be paid to the contingent beneficiary at the same amount until the end of the tenth year.

If one or both of the annuitants lives on past the end of the tenth year, the balance in the account, so to speak, continues to decrease until it drops to zero just before the end of the twenty-fifth year. If both of the annuitants die before the account balance drops to zero, that amount, in effect, goes into a fund to be used to pay the benefits for those who live on beyond the end of their actuarially calculated lives. All of us know people who are living beyond age 90. The Survivors Table, Table 11.2, gave the probabilities of living from various ages starting with 65 to more advanced ages. TIAA has many annuitants over 100 years of age still on its roles. One lived to 114.

If guaranteed periods of 10 and 20 years were selected in two different cases and if the annuitants died before the end of the those guaranteed periods, the balances left in these hypothetical accounts would have been $80,704 and $37,194 respectively. The people who understand this arithmetic, and who object to the possibility of leaving such funds to the insurance company for the use of others who will live well beyond their actuarially calculated lives, should consider the fixed-period annuity.

The gradual decline in the principal shown in Table 11.6 may be likened to the decline in a home loan mortgage with a fixed rate of interest and a fixed number of years to maturity. As in the case of the home owner in the first years of the loan, most of the fixed monthly payment is for the interest on the principal. Little by little, an increasing amount of the payments goes toward the repayment of the loan itself. In the later years of the loan, most of the payment goes to repay the principal. From the lender's viewpoint, the loan is ever more rapidly being reduced to zero. As the lender recovers the principal, it will very probably be used to make other loans.

FIXED-PERIOD ANNUITY

Some aspects of the joint-lives and fixed-period annuities for both 10 and 20 years are displayed in Table 11.7. In the 10-year cases the annual fixed-period annuity is $4,387 larger each year than the joint-lives annuity. By the end of the tenth year, all of the funds in the fixed-period annuity plus interest earned will have been paid to either the annuitant himself and/or his beneficiary. Nothing is left to be paid after the end of the tenth year. The $4,387 difference annually for 10 years can be spent or invested depending upon the needs and desires of the annuitant. The joint-lives annuity is $4,387 less per year, but the two annuitants who share in this contract will continue to receive benefits no matter how long one or both live.

The $80,740 of principal left at the end of the tenth year in the joint-lives case will be reduced to zero in the twenty-fourth year. If one or both annuitants lives beyond age 85, he, she, or they will continue to receive benefits. These benefits are paid from the pooled funds, which is the essence of insurance, because most of those under identical contract forms died before the "principal" or endowment was used up. These sums unused by those who died earlier provide the continuing benefits for the survivors.

When the 20-year guaranteed period benefits under joint-lives and the 20-year fixed payment period annuity are compared, the payments are slightly larger for the guaranteed-period contract. The reason for the slightly higher payments in the joint-lives case probably is that, after the 20-year period, interest continues to be earned on the balance in the account until it reaches zero a few years later. At the end of twentieth year, some $37,000 would remain in the joint-lives account.

The shorter the fixed-period annuity, the higher will be the annual payments. For a 5-year, fixed-period annuity at the same interest rate and initial endowment, the annual payments would be $25,376.

Despite the apparent attractiveness of the fixed-period annuity, it is not widely used. In 1994 almost 15,000 new annuitants selected life annuities and only 360 chose fixed period annuities; just over 2 percent selected fixed-period annuities. My intuition is that a somewhat higher percentage of new annuitants would select a fixed-period annuity for part or all of their annuities if the differences between these two forms were more widely publicized and understood.

Three additional variations of the TIAA annuity forms need to be explored: Interest Payment Retirement Option (IPRO), Graded Retirement Benefits (GRB), and Minimum Distribution Option (MDO). Relative usage of these plans selected by 1992 retirees are as follows:

Annuity Option	Relative Use
Standard (level) Benefits	78.9%
Graded Benefits	8.4
Interest Payment Retirement Option	4.3
Minimum Distribution Option	8.4

These data are based on both the regular life annuities and the supplemental retirement annuities. The fact that one of these three options other than the standard option was used does not indicate the proportion of all 1992 retiree's benefits being paid in this form. One individual could have used two or more of these variants in 1992. In other words, these percentages probably include a little double counting. The usage of MDO and GB are increasing. In 1994 almost 18 percent of new annuitants used MDO and 14 percent elected GB for at least some part of their annuities.

THREE OTHER ANNUITY FORMS

Information received from TIAA permits the direct comparison of the regular single-life annuity with IPRO when the original endowment is $100,000, the age of the annuitant is 65, and the interest rate is 6 percent. These amounts on an annual basis are:

IPRO	$7,248
Single-life annuity	
No Guaranteed Period	9,288
10-Year Guaranteed Period	9,102
15-Year Guaranteed Period	8,724
20-Year Guaranteed Period	8,376

These amounts may differ somewhat from year to year.

INTEREST PAYMENT RETIREMENT OPTION (IPRO)

Although IPRO is an annuity in the usual sense of being a stream of payments, TIAA treats it a little differently. IPRO, which became available in 1982, pays interest on the basis of the accumulation in your TIAA account. This accumulation or principal stays in your pay-in account and is not transferred to your pay-out account. Only when your accumulation is transferred later to your pay-out account is the amount formally annuitized. CREF accounts have no payment plan comparable to IPRO.

As shown in an earlier example, this IPRO payment under the specific conditions would be 13.5 percent less than it would be with a single-life annuity with a 20-year guaranteed period. About 4.3 percent of TIAA's annuitants have elected this option to some unknown extent. Why?

The multiplicity of reasons people actually have in mind is difficult to understand. Nevertheless, in the absence of survey data or information from benefit counselor's using this option, I feel free to speculate on the reasons:

1. Misinformation and lack of knowledge about the dollar size of the other conservative options.

2. The belief that conservative financial practice requires keeping your "nest egg" intact.

3. The mistaken belief that your principal will grow while you use IPRO. (IPRO pays out all of the interest credited to the account; the principal does not grow.)

4. If you defer annuitizing your accumulation until you pass the 70½ age when you must annuitize, the end of the guaranteed period will be postponed for as many years as you use IPRO. Therefore, the chances of your dying before the end of the guaranteed period are greater, the amount that may be paid to your heirs will be larger and the final payments will come one or more years later.

5. You may postpone the annuitizing to keep your options more flexible about taking a single-life or joint-life annuity and/or the naming of a contingent beneficiary.

6. You may postpone annuitizing in order to have a higher annual benefit later. The benefit will be higher later just because you are older and that much closer to your virtual end.

What the actual motivations, and their frequency distributions are, are unknown.

GRADED RETIREMENT ANNUITIES

In 1978 a TIAA executive committee had the idea that benefits could be given the appearance of providing a hedge against inflation without the participant putting up any additional money. That idea resulted in Graded Retirement Annuities (GRA) which were implemented in 1982.

To provide rising benefits during the annuity period, a reduction of 30 to 40 percent in benefits must be taken in the first year. The money not paid out in the first year (and subsequent years) remains invested and continues to produce income.

The first part of Table 11.8 compares the first-year benefits under IPRO, the level-benefits method, and the graded benefits method. (TIAA has changed this term from "level-benefits" to "standard-benefits" in some recent publications.) The second part of Table 11.8 illustrates payments under the graduated, or graded, benefit payment method and their rise over 20 years. The payments will continue to increase at a stable rate as long as the annuity lasts. The rising payments are a pseudo-hedge against inflation because they are financed by accepting lower benefits in the early years as compared with level-benefits method.

The technique is somewhat similar to a hedge in the commodities market wherein a manufacturer protects her business or manufacturing profit from fluctuations in prices by buying in the spot (cash) markets and selling simultaneously in the future markets. At the end of a fixed period, she sells her product in the real or cash market, and covers (that is, buys) the futures she sold. The losses in one market will almost exactly match the gain in the other, and she is left with her manufacturing profits less administrative costs of the hedging operations, if several implicit assumptions work out also.

The level-payment benefit method provides the highest, first-year benefits among the three choices as shown in Table 11.8. At age 60, the first-year reduction in benefits required by the graduated-benefits payment method (GBPM), according to figures provided by TIAA, is 39.6 percent. The reduction at age 70 is 32.8 percent.

Investment in the GBPM fund continues to grow and to provide higher benefits. Annual benefits under the GBPM grow at just under 5.8 percent a year as an offset against inflation. TIAA prepares separate columns in their GBPM illustrations for its 3 percent guaranteed interest rate and expected payments at prevailing interest rates. They do not warn the participants that if interest rates decline, benefits will grow slower than their calculations show. The clever and skillful person who worked out the formula set things up so graduated benefits would rise at almost 5.8 percent forever. That rate is not far from the average annual rise in the cost of living in recent decades.

In 1992, 8.4 percent of new retirees selected GBPM. Those who selected GBPM did not necessarily place all of their accumulation in this option. Planning to put half of one's TIAA accumulation in GBPM would be high. Few people could withstand a 30- to- 40-percent decline from level annuity benefits and maintain a standard of living close to what it was pre-retirement.

Nevertheless, TIAA publications have given and continue to give the GBPM almost equal space with the level or standard benefit payment method in its discussions. One wonders why!

Since my 1992 newspaper columns on GBPM, the interest rates that TIAA pays to annuitants have fallen because of the general decline in interest rates and because of large write-offs on its bad real estate loans. The overlapping numbers given in Table 11.8 and Table 11.4 are slightly different because of slight differences in assumptions.

Also since 1991 I have counseled clients who were about 70 years old and who had most of their accumulations in TIAA. As I worked with them, the numbers showed that they would have considerably more cash flow initially in retirement than they had been using or believed that they were likely to use. What they finally did was annuitize part of their TIAA accumulation in a joint-life, level-payment annuity and annuitize the rest in a GBPM joint-life annuity. In that way they reasoned that they would have some protection against inflation. The minimum distribution option was discussed, but these clients found it too complex. It gives no continuing inflation protection. They elected to take the graded-benefits payment option rather than the minimum distribution option which is described next. The regular, level-payment annuity and graded-benefit annuity also provide the other settlement option clauses: single or joint life, and the various years certain benefit periods.

MINIMUM DISTRIBUTION OPTION

The objectives of the minimum distribution option (MDO) are to permit you to continue to build your estate on the one hand by taking lower benefit payments initially on the other hand. The program, which was started under amendments to the <u>Internal Revenue Code</u> in 1987, revises an earlier, somewhat different program which permitted distribution from a qualified pension plan to be deferred until April of the year after year in which the owners become 70½ years of age.[3] TIAA quickly added this option to its available programs. The objective was two-fold. The first objective was to prevent individual pension accounts established under advantageous provisions of the income-tax code from growing indefinitely and being used to build a larger estates for the individuals who did not need to draw upon these funds. The second was to provide the Treasury with revenue that was badly needed sooner rather than later.

A number of detailed provisions, some of which are described below, limit the applicability of the MDO, but its benefits for some TIAA-CREF participants can be described clearly by abstracting from these details.

The MDO is based on your life expectancy according to IRS actuarial tables. You may select either a single-life or a joint-life annuity as appropriate to your circumstances as in any other life-annuity case. The minimum percentage that must be paid represents your approximate chance of death in each year of life. For example, when I was 72 and my wife was some years younger, our joint-life expectancy was 22.8 years. The amount that had to be paid out was 4.38596 percent of the accumulation in this part of our MDO. (The reciprocal of 22.8 is .0438596, or 1 divided by 22.8 is .0438596.) Each year the life expectancy is recalculated.

---

[3]The first mention of 70 as the age by which withdrawals from pension plans must be started was in House Report Number 2277 in the 85th Congress, 1957-58. Tables to this report show that the ages of 70 and 72 were both considered. The "½" comes from the life insurance industry practice of using the anniversary date nearest the insured's birthday. Thus 70½ is considered the insurance age of a 70 year old person. The phrase "April 1 of the year after the year that a person turns 70½" was inserted by Public Law 98-369 in 1983. Prior to 1984 the age at which the required distribution must start to avoid income tax penalties was 70½. One could speculate that the April 1 was a matter of administrative convenience. The age of 70½ as the age by which withdrawals must be started was later used for Keogh Plans or under the Self-Employed Individuals Tax Retirement Act of 1972. (SOURCE: Letter of September 19, 1994 from Ray Schmitt, Specialist in Social Legislation, and Louisa Hierholzer, Technical Information Specialist, Education and Public Welfare Division, Congressional Research Service, Library of Congress, Washington, D.C.)

As life expectancy becomes shorter, the minimum percentage that must be paid out grows larger.[4]

One part of the funds I could put into my MDO account was my investment in my TIAA and/or CREF accounts plus earnings on these accounts after January 1, 1987. The second part of my MDO account was what I had not annuitized by age 70½ and which was earned prior to 1987. This amount, called a "grandfathered" amount, does not have to start paying out until I am 75 years old. Meantime, the earnings on the "grandfathered" amount do not have to start being distributed until I—or whomever the participant may be—am 75.[5]

Three advantages are built into the MDO. First, as long as the rate of interest earned on the accumulation (the principal) in your MDO is greater than the probability of your death at each specific calendar age, the accumulation in your MDO will continue to grow. Second, the amount earned on your MDO accumulations will continue to grow tax-deferred as long as the interest earned is greater than your annuity. Annuity payments will increase each year for a number of years. Third, at age 75 when distributions must start on the "grandfathered" amount, your annuity benefits may jump substantially depending upon the amount grandfathered. In my own case, the MDO annuity will approximately triple from the first payments at age 71 to the payment four years later at age 75. Of course, each case must be calculated on its own and depends upon the factors named: interest rates relative to probability of death, the amount initially under the MDO, and the amount grandfathered under MDO which will start being distributed at age 75.

TIAA will provide you with an illustrative schedule showing how much your accumulation is likely to grow, your single- or joint-life expectancy as the case may be according to the IRS, the projected MDO payment each year, and the likely earnings each year. The likely MDO payments will increase until you are almost age 85 and then decline swiftly as life expectancy declines. Your accumulation will rise also until some year which can be read from TIAA's individualized illustration.

The MDO permits you to switch from this option back to a life annuity at the age that you choose. I have prepared written instructions for my wife to switch back to a single-life annuity about two years after the accumulation reaches a peak. (Written instructions were prepared in the event that I am not alive at that date.)

At the death of one of the two tenants in the joint-life annuity, the life expectancy of the survivor under the one-life table will probably be shorter and the MDO payment will increase.

---

[4]A second method, called the "One-Year Less" method, is available, but does not seem nearly as attractive because it does not provide for a life annuity. See TIAA-CREF, A Practical Guide to Minimum Distribution, New York, 1992.

[5]The "grandfathered" amounts on which no distributions have to be made until age 75 appears in the Reform Act of 1986. This age has no precedent either in insurance practice or income tax law. This exception applies only to 403(b) plans such as TIAA-CREF. The amounts that may be "grandfathered" must be in the individual's annuity account before January 1, 1987. (Source: Letter from Schmitt and Hierholzer cited in footnote 3.)

The MDO option is so complicated that it is best to have the estimates prepared by TIAA's Benefits Payment Section. If the MDO is being considered, you should call TIAA at least one year before you turn age 70½. If you do not start these annuities before April 1 of the year after the year you become 70½ years of age, you will be subject to a 50 percent penalty tax on the amount that you should have received.

The MDO may not be for you if higher benefits at age 70 are more important than higher benefits later. At age 71, for example, MDO benefits will be about half or somewhat less than half of what they would be under a joint-life annuity. Initially, MDO annuity benefits may be only about 60 percent of what they would be under a single-life annuity. These percentages apply to TIAA only. MDO is available for CREF, but its performance is too variable to prepare an estimate.

VARIABLE ANNUITIES

CREF, the brilliant, path-breaking, successful innovation of TIAA and its president, William Greenough, began operations July 1, 1952.[6] It was a success from the very start. Its assets grew to $1.5 billion in twenty years and passed $60 billion in 1994 when all of the present seven accounts are included. In 1990 it offered a variable bond fund and a variable social choice fund. In 1993 it added a variable Global Equities fund and in 1994 it added a growth account and an equity index account. In 1988 it also started a money-market fund so that participants could shift funds from their equity accounts to their money market account and back again when they wished to do so. CREF balances can be moved without restriction among all of the CREF accounts or from any CREF account to TIAA as explained in Chapter 5.

The focus of this section is on CREF-Equities, as the original CREF account is now called to distinguish it from the other CREF funds that were started beginning in 1990.[7] The fact that the value of a CREF unit fluctuates with the market prices of the stocks that it holds is clear. What needs to be explained is how a variable annuity works. When you shift your CREF accumulation from a pay-in account to a pay-out account, how does CREF determine the value of a CREF unit and the number of units on which you will receive benefits each year?

The value of a CREF annuity unit is kept separate from the value of an accumulation unit. The July 1952 price of the annuity unit was $10.00 and on April 1, 1995, it was $123.94. It has grown at the compound rate of 10.8 percent since inception and at a somewhat higher rate over the last 10 years.

---

[6]For a very brief discussion of the public policy problems that had to be surmounted before CREF could start operations, the advantages and disadvantages of a variable annuity as contrasted with the traditional fixed-income annuity, and portfolio policy decisions as CREF has evolved, see Chapter 5, Section 2, CREF.

[7]For convenience, CREF-Equities will be referred to as CREF in this explanation of how a variable annuity works. CREF-Equities has 88.4 percent of all CREF assets, CREF-Money Markets price fluctuates very little and CREF-marketable Bonds cannot be annuitized as of June 1995.

The exact operation of a variable annuity is not widely understood. Not one person who has attended my seminars or who received individual counseling had ever seen the calculations demonstrated. The example given as Table 11.9 is realistic, but may not exactly reproduce CREF's own results.

A number of assumptions are necessary to build the example. First, assume that a participant retired in March 1986, and at the end of that month he had $134,700 in his CREF accumulation account. Assume that the price of a CREF annuity unit on March 31 was $67.35. At that price the $134,700 accumulation purchased 2,000 annuity units. The participant selected a joint-life annuity. He was 67 at the time and his wife was a little younger so that their joint-life expectancy worked out to exactly 25.0 years. He and his wife will receive as annuity the value of 80 annuity units per year (2,000 ÷ 25). At one time Greenough considered calling this form a fixed-unit annuity because the benefits were based upon a fixed number of annuity units and a variable price per unit. Term "fixed-unit annuity" may have been clearer than the term finally used, "variable annuity." It is a variable annuity because the price of an annuity unit changes.

CREF's variable benefits are revalued only once a year for convenience. The date chosen for revaluing the benefits was May 1 based upon the price of a unit on March 31 of that year. In the first year of the annuity only, the participant is guaranteed a 4 percent return. Hence, in computing the benefits 1.04 percent of the March 31 price of the annuity unit is used. In the example, the price was $67.35 on March 31 and 1.04 percent of that price was $70.044. The pension benefit was then 80 annuity units times $70.044 or $5,603.52.

After the first year, the variable annuity fluctuates with the price of the annuity unit. The increases and decreases in the value of the CREF annuity unit in percentage terms are shown in the lower section of Table 11.9. The benefits, which are changed on May 1 of each year, are shown also.

In the first year of CREF benefits, the annuitant will find that his CREF benefits will be about 30 to 40 percent below what the same number of dollars would have purchased in terms of a TIAA annuity. The difference is based upon the higher interest rate assumption over the life of his TIAA annuity. CREF guarantees 4 percent in the first year only. After that the CREF annuity fluctuates with the price of the unit itself. As the average return on CREF has been higher than the average return on TIAA's fixed-income securities, the CREF benefits turn out to be higher than TIAA's after a lag of about 4-8 years starting with 1980 as shown in Table 12.1. TIAA and CREF benefits were compared in Table 5.4 together with the cost of living. CREF performance was compared with that of the best-known market price indices in Table 5.2 and with that of the largest and best-performing mutual funds in Table 5.3. In Chapter 12 additional TIAA-CREF annuity and cost of living comparisons are made.

TIAA-CREF SWITCHING BEFORE RETIREMENT

One of the more wrenching, soul-searching, risk-attitude revealing decisions that participants must make as they approach retirement is their decision about their balance between TIAA and CREF-Equities or the other, newer CREF accounts. Only those who own no CREF-Equities and are extremely secure in their belief that stocks are too risky to keep as a part of the basis for their retirement income do not ruminate about their TIAA-CREF Equities balance decision. This decision may well turn out to be one of the most important ones TIAA participants must make.

Two underlying fears motivate the decisions of most participants who switch all or part of their accumulations from CREF-Equities to TIAA a few years prior to retirement or at the point of retirement itself. One is the fear of inflation and the other is the fear that a stock-market crash "would wipe me out" just after retirement.

The fear of inflation is a legitimate one and the answer to inflation protection is far from clear for most people. The fear of inflation may be addressed in five different ways. CREF retirement benefits have very clearly and strongly outpaced inflation. This outcome was demonstrated in Table 5.4 from 1982 through 1994. While the cost of living increased 54 percent during that period, CREF benefits increased more than 250 percent. During this same thirteen years, TIAA benefits decreased 13 percent as interest rates fell. Table 6.6 showed that stock returns have been about 50 percent higher than bond yields going all of the way back to 1871. Figures 12.1 and 12.2 and Table 12.1 make this same point about the better performance of CREF as compared with that of TIAA. TIAA benefits have not kept up with increases in the cost of living.

True, the CREF benefits do move down as well as up. The downward revision may be as much as 20 percent or more in some individual years and twice since CREF began in 1952, it moved downward in two successive years. The last time that occurred was 1973 and 1974. Yet, over a reasonably long time horizon, the upward revisions have far exceeded the downward revisions. Tables 9.1 and 9.2 summarized the history of the bull and bear stock markets since 1927. The long trend of stock prices is upward because of the reinvestment process as demonstrated in Table 8.6.

What remains true is that during periods when inflation is rising—for example, from 4 to 6 percent or from 6 to 9 percent—stock prices are most likely to fall. Such periods of rising inflation will undoubtedly be experienced again in the United States, but no one can tell how high the inflation rate may rise or how long each episode may last. Past history may be the best guide to the future path of inflationary periods.

Maintaining your TIAA-CREF-Equities within the ranges suggested by TIAA-CREF, and Soldofsky in Tables 3.1 and 3.2 is recommended. When making your final investment allocation decisions these ranges and the prudent, broad framework guidelines discussed in Chapter 1 should be revisited. Before reviewing the extent to which individuals have switched out of CREF to TIAA, the reasons individuals tell me that they have switched or are considering switching all or part of their accumulations from CREF-Equities to TIAA are summarized and answered as follows:

1. Initial-year benefits per dollar of accumulation are about 30-40 cents higher per dollar invested for TIAA than they are for CREF. (This observation is correct. Experience shows that CREF benefits may take about 4 to 8 years to overcome this initial difference.)

2. Fear of large drops in CREF benefits during retirement. (The benefit history reviewed shows the likely extent of such fluctuations, and that TIAA benefits fluctuate also although the smaller range.)

3. The observation that the stock market was "too" high at the date of retirement and had to fall sooner or later. (A review of the history of stock market cycles and stock-price indexes levels is the appropriate response to this fear.)

4. Life experiences, advice of family and friends, and recommendations of authority figures.

5. Direct recommendations of their employer's staff-benefit personnel. (One must review their background, training, and experience before accepting such judgment that will affect your financial well being for the rest of your life and that of your spouse.)

6. The belief that TIAA benefits will be a fixed amount for the rest of your life and that of your spouse.

Other possible ways of protecting your income from inflation, in addition to keeping the recommended allocation range for CREF-Equities are mentioned, but not elaborated. These are working longer, working part-time for your present or another employer, working part-time for another employer, consulting or writing. Each year that you continue to work after about age 60 will add about 10 percent per year to your retirement benefits. The reasons are that more will be paid into your retirement plan, the accumulation in the retirement plan will continue to increase tax deferred, and your accumulation will have fewer years to support you after you retire.

Surveys of retirees by TIAA-CREF and other organizations report that most retirees regret that they did not provide enough inflation protection for themselves during retirement. What they believed to be good financial planning prior to retirement turned out not to be so. The longer one is retired, the more likely he is to discover that his planning was inadequate if income is mostly in the form of fixed-income benefits such as TIAA.

THE CREF TO TIAA REALLOCATIONS
TIAA-CREF had 245,000 retirees at the beginning of 1993. Table 11.10 shows the number and percentages receiving various combinations of TIAA and CREF in retirement. Some 47 percent of the retirees were receiving TIAA benefits only and about 1 percent were receiving CREF benefits only. Nothing can be said about the proportions of TIAA and CREF income for those receiving income from both sources. One thing that is known is that CREF benefits per account are almost 20 percent larger than they are from TIAA.

The first four items in Panel B (items a, b, c and d), Table 11.10 show that a very substantial proportion of retirees switched from some or all of the CREF funds to TIAA at or within five years of retirement. Of those who expected to receive TIAA benefits only in retirement, 39 percent switched all of their CREF allocations to TIAA. Of this 39 percent, about three-fourths made this switch to TIAA within five years of their retirement. The extent of switching from CREF to TIAA just prior to retirement, other earlier transfers, and transfers by participants on the brink of retirement cannot be summarized systematically, but is extensive.[8]

The record of changes in TIAA and CREF benefits, and the comparisons of these changes with the cost of living were reexamined earlier. Clearly, the changes in TIAA and CREF benefits over the coming decades will not exactly replicate past changes. However, based upon theory and empirical data, I do believe that the CREF benefits will perform much better than TIAA benefits over all, but not necessarily each year.

RETIREMENT TRANSITION PAYMENTS AND LUMP-SUM PAYMENTS

Retirement Transition Payments (RTPs) were started in 1972 under pressure from participants. These payments were set at a maximum of 10 percent of the amount annuitized. The reason given for the 10 percent maximum was that no more was permitted under New York State's insurance laws. The purpose was to provide more cash upon retirement for those who wanted or needed it for such things as moving expenses, home improvements, or travel expenses. No question is asked about the purpose of the RTP when application is made. The RTP could come close to doubling the first year's cash flow from your annuity benefits.

Several precautions need to be stressed. First, if you take a 10 percent RTP, your retirement benefits in all subsequent years will be 10 percent less. Second, your first-year cash flow from retirement benefits alone may well be much larger than you had expected relative to what your net spendable income was just prior to retirement. An approach to estimating these first-year retirement benefits compared with net spendable income while working is an important part of the material presented in Chapter 12. Third, the RTP is 10 percent of what you annuitize, not 10 percent of your total accumulation. Hence, if your accumulations amount to $1,000,000, for example, and you annuitize on $600,000 initially, your 10 percent RTP will be $60,000. Of course, when you annuitize the remaining $400,000, you can elect another $40,000 RTP.

About one out of five retirees elects to utilize the RTP according to William C. Greenough.[9] He also notes that many retirees did not take the full 10 percent that they could draw.

Lump-sum payments can be drawn from your SRA at any time you are beyond 59½ years of age without penalty. TIAA reports that almost 20 percent have SRA accounts. SRA

---

[8]One of my TIAA-CREF contacts went far beyond what I could have reasonably expected in drawing together the bits of scattered information included in Table 11.10. TIAA-CREF does not collect this information systematically, but it is in their records and available to their researchers and public relations staff. The administrative time in gathering the data must have been considerable. I would not have urged my contact to pursue this information unless I believed in its importance for participants who are struggling with their final accumulation allocation decisions at or close to the point of retirement.

[9]William C. Greenough, It's My Retirement Money - Take Good Care Of It, The TIAA-CREF Story, Homewood, IL: Irwin, 1990.

accounts were started in 1972. Before then additional investments up to the 20 percent of your salary could be made in your regular account.

In 1990 TIAA-CREF permitted more generous lump-sum withdrawals from regular CREF with permission of the employer.

CONCLUSIONS

Most people give little or no thought to settlement options until they are close to retirement. Discussions of the many forms that retirement annuities options may take are rarely found in books and articles. The use of annuities goes back to the eighteenth century; Adam Smith discussed some annuity forms at length in his 1776 The Wealth of Nations. The use of annuities for teachers in the U.S. began in the late nineteenth century, and TIAA has been issuing them more than 75 years.

Single-life and joint-life annuities are very widely used by insurance companies in the United States. Payments to annuitants are calculated accurately because of very extensive mortality tables that have been accumulated. However, fixed-annuity benefits do change with the changing level of interest rates and the portfolio performance of each insurance company.

When the participant retires, she has several choices. She must decide whether she wants a policy with a guaranteed life period or not. If she selects a guaranteed life period, she must select one of the four guaranteed periods offered. She must also select among three forms of the benefit streams, if she selects a joint-life annuity. The form that she chooses depends upon such things as her present wealth, health, and the independent income that the joint tenant—usually her spouse—has.

Benefit payments on a single-life annuity with no guarantee period cease upon the death of the annuitant. Benefit payments on a joint-life annuity cease on the death of the second to die if a guarantee period was not selected. Payments on both of these contracts will continue as long as the individual(s) live. Joint-life contracts also have years certain or guaranteed payment periods; if the insured individual(s) die before the end of the guaranteed period, payments will continue to the secondary beneficiary until the end of the period selected.

The single-life annuity with no guaranteed period provides the largest benefit per dollar of the amount annuitized. These benefits decline the longer the actuarial life expectancy of the annuitant and the longer the guaranteed period. Data were provided showing the frequency with which the various settlement options were selected by men and by women. These frequencies provide no guidance for individual decisions, which should be made on the basis of each individual's circumstances.

Fixed-period annuities are made available, but are little used. They are just barely mentioned in TIAA-CREF information. However, in some special circumstances such as a short expected life (lives) after retirement and having no heirs, they may meet an individual's needs admirably. As the arithmetic of annuities showed, the death of the individual(s) before the end of the guaranteed period leaves a large percentage of the original endowment in the account. These remaining amounts go toward continuing the payments of those individuals who live longer than the average. The insurance company itself does not gain from these early deaths. However, the individual who knows about how long she has to live because of a disease such as cancer or AIDS, may wish to use the fixed-period annuity to receive considerably larger amounts of cash during her remaining lifetime.

The arithmetic of annuity payments, which is easy to understand, shows how the balance of the remaining endowment diminishes at an increasing rate over time. This arithmetic is the key to understanding why some people prefer a fixed-period annuity and why insurance companies can contract or continue to make payments to life annuitants as long as they live.

Fixed-income annuities are based upon fixed-income securities such as bonds and mortgages. Payments under these "fixed-income" annuities do change from year to year with changing market interest rates and the portfolio performance of the insurance carrier. Variable annuity payments change each year. The amount they pay depends largely upon the performance of the stocks in which the insurance company invests. The number of annuity units to which the individual is entitled depends upon his original endowment and his individual- or joint-life expectancy. His annual payment, except in the first year, is the product of the fixed number of annuity units he has times the market price of a unit. CREF's variable annuity will make a first-year payment which is 30-40 percent less than that of its TIAA income annuity based on the same starting endowment. Experience shows that the annual payments on the CREF-Equities variable annuity may take 4-8 years or more to grow to what the amount of the TIAA annuity based upon the same endowment.

Other payment forms such as the interest on principal only, graded benefits, minimum-distribution options, retirement-transition payments and lump-sum settlements were described. These forms are not widely used, but may be very advantageous in your special circumstances. They should be considered before you make your final and irrevocable decisions on the annuity form you select.

Many TIAA-CREF participants rebalance their TIAA-CREF allocations at the point of retirement or within a few years before that date. Both TIAA-CREF and Soldofsky recommend that substantial proportions of CREF be kept during retirement as detailed in Chapters 1 and 3. The data and theory for these recommendations were briefly summarized in this chapter based upon what was presented in more detail earlier. The number and extent to which participants have switched part or all of their funds from CREF to TIAA were presented as far as they are known. The consequences of such shifts are very likely to be unfavorable as viewed from a 5-10 year or longer perspective. Although the topic of this chapter is the explanation of the retirement annuity options themselves, the long-run effects of imprudent reallocation decisions could turn out to have a much larger financial impact upon retirement benefits than the selection of alternative annuity options and strategies.

TABLE 11.1

LIFE EXPECTANCY AT AGE 65

Year Born	Further Life	% Increase Since 1935
1935	12.5[a] years	-
1950	13.9	11.2
1965	14.6	16.8
1980	16.4	31.2
2000	19.1	52.8

[a]Means that if you survive to age 65 your chances are 50-50 to live to 77.5 years of age.

SOURCES: Historical Statistics of the United States, Part 1. Washington, D.C., U.S. Government Printing Office, 1975.

Statistical Abstract of the United States, 1990. Washington, D.C., U.S. Government Printing Office, 1990.

TABLE 11.2

LIKELIHOOD OF SURVIVAL: AGE 65 AND UP (%)

Panel A - Women

From				To			
Age	70	75	80	85	90	95	100
65	95.6	88.8	77.9	61.3	39.7	18.9	6.2
70	-	92.9	81.5	64.1	41.5	19.8	16.8
75	-	-	87.7	69.0	44.7	21.3	12.2
80	-	-	-	78.7	51.0	24.3	8.0
85	-	-	-	-	64.8	30.8	10.1
90	-	-	-	-	-	47.6	15.6
95	-	-	-	-	-	-	32.8

Panel B - Men

From				To			
Age	70	75	80	85	90	95	100
65	92.3	80.8	64.8	45.2	25.5	10.9	3.1
70	-	87.5	70.2	49.0	27.6	11.8	3.4
75	-	-	80.2	55.9	31.6	13.5	3.8
80	-	-	-	70.0	39.4	16.8	4.8
85	-	-	-	-	56.4	24.1	6.8
90	-	-	-	-	-	42.8	12.2
95	-	-	-	-	-	-	28.4

SOURCE: TIAA-CREF 1983 Mortality Table.

TABLE 11.3

MERGED GENDER MORTALITY TABLE

Age	Death Rate Per 1000	Life Expectancy (Years)	Age	Death Rate Per 1000	Life Expectancy (Years)
65	7.955	22.35	80	35.309	11.34
66	8.736	21.53	81	39.172	10.74
67	9.622	20.71	82	43.458	10.15
68	10.612	19.91	83	48.205	9.59
69	11.706	19.12	84	53.457	9.05
70	12.906	18.34	85	59.250	8.54
71	14.222	17.57	86	65.615	8.04
72	15.677	16.82	87	72.560	7.57
73	17.295	16.08	88	80.100	7.13
74	19.099	15.35	89	88.254	6.70
75	21.113	14.64	90	97.039	6.30
76	23.366	13.94	91	106.450	5.93
77	25.884	13.27	92	111.436	5.57
78	28.695	12.61	93	127.012	5.24
79	31.828	11.96	94	138.067	4.93
			95[a]	149.565	4.64

[a]The table continues up to 118 years of age.

SOURCE: TIAA-CREF 1983 Table A. Merged Gender Modification 1

TABLE 11.4

LEVEL ANNUAL RETIREMENT CASH FLOW
From a $10,000 Annuity (1990)

Settlement Option	Cash Flow	Cost Relative To Single Life $	%
Single Life - No guaranteed period	$1,116	--	--
10-year guaranteed period	1,064	52	4.66
20-year guaranteed period	968	148	13.26
Joint-Life (Survivor)			
Two-thirds benefit to survivor			
No guaranteed period	1,016	100	8.96
10-Year guaranteed period	1,014	102	9.14
20-Year guaranteed period	1,002	114	11.22
Full benefit to survivor			
No guaranteed period	936	180	16.13
10-Year guaranteed period	934	182	16.31
20-Year guaranteed period	918	198	17.74
Half benefit to second annuitant			
No guaranteed period	1,018	98	8.78
10-year guaranteed period	1,017	99	8.87
20-year guaranteed period	1,007	109	9.78

Note: Assume the insured's age is 68, the spouse's age is 62, and the interest rate is 8 1 percent.

TABLE 11.5

LIFETIME ANNUITY SELECTIONS
(1991 - ALL Ages)

Settlement Option	Participants (%)	
	Male	Female
Single-Life		
No guarantee period	9	23
10-Year guaranteed period	7	20
15-Year guaranteed period	3	9
20-Year guaranteed period	6	14
Joint-Life[a]		
Two-thirds benefit to survivor	15	5
Full benefit to survivor	55	24
Half benefit to second annuitant	5	5

[a]20-year guaranteed period usually selected by those using the joint-life option.

SOURCE: Comparing TIAA-CREF Income Options, New York, TIAA-CREF, 1992, p.13.

TABLE 11.6

ARITHMETIC OF A LIFE ANNUITY[a]

Payment Year	Principal at Start of Year	Interest Earned on Remaining Principal	Annual Payments of $9372.12 Less Interest	Principal Remaining at End of Year
1	$100,000.00	$8073.86	$1298.26	$98701.74
2	98701.74	7963.53	1408.59	97293.15
3	97293.15	7843.80	1528.32	95764.83
5	94106.58	7572.92	1799.20	92307.30
9	85939.08	6878.69	2493.43	83445.65
10	83445.65	6666.75	2705.37	80740.28
15	67415.31	5304.19	4067.93	65347.38
20	43311.26	3255.33	6116.79	37194.47
24	15543.97	895.10	8477.02	7066.95
25	7066.95	201.00	7810.10	0.00

[a]Payments: $9,372.12 annually. Assumptions: Life expectancy 24 years, 10 months; guaranteed period 10 years; full benefits to each annuitant; age of annuitants 65; monthly payments; interest rate 8.5 percent.

TABLE 11.7

COMPARISON OF JOINT-LIVES AND FIXED-PERIOD ANNUITIES

Type of Annuity	Period 10 Years[a]	20 Years[a]
(1) Joint Lives	$11,180[b]	$11,047[b]
(2) Fixed-Period	15,567	10,517
(3) Annual Difference (2 - 1)	$ 4,387	$ 480
(4) Balance of Endowment at End of Period[c]:		
Joint-Life Annuity	$80,740	$ 37,195
Fixed-Period Annuity	$ 0	$ 0

[a]Refers to guaranteed period or fixed-period annuity as appropriate.

[b]Includes some TIAA administrative charges.

[c]As an explanation of the higher joint-lives annuity I suggest that more money is invested longer.

TABLE 11.8

IPRO, LEVEL ANNUITY, GRADED RETIREMENT BENEFITS COMPARED[a]

Annuity - First Year	Age 60	Age 65	Age 70
IPRO	$9,564	$9,564	$9,564
Level Benefits	10,824	11,257	12,024
Graded Benefits	6,528	N.A.	8,076

Graded Benefits Started at Specific Age	
Age 60	Age 70
1st year	$6,528	$8,076
2nd year	6,900	8,544
3rd year	7,296	9,036
4th year	7,728	9,552
5th year	8,172	10,104
6th year	8,640	10,692
7th year	9,132	11,304
8th year	9,660	11,964
9th year	10,224	12,648
10th year	10,812	13,380
11th year	11,436	14,148
12th year	12,096	14,964
13th year	12,792	15,828
14th year	13,536	16,740
15th year	14,316	17,712
16th year	15,132	18,732
17th year	16,008	19,812
18th year	16,932	20,952
19th year	17,916	22,164
20th year	18,948	23,448

[a]Table assumes interest is earned and paid out at a constant rate, $100.000 is the initial accumulation, one-life annuity, and 10-year's certain. For graded benefits payments continued to grow as long as the individual lives. 1991 Data.

TABLE 11.9

CREF's VARIABLE ANNUITY VALUATION PROCESS: SIMPLIFIED ILLUSTRATION

Assumptions:

1. $134,700 transferred to CREF annuity on March 31, 1986.

2.   CREF Annuity Unit Value: $67.35.

3.   Number of Annuity Units Purchased: 2,000.

4.   Assume 25-year, joint-life expectancy[a].

5.   Annuitant receives value of 80 CREF units each year.

6.   First year only annuitant receives 4% guarantee regardless of actual performance.

First Year (Starting May 1, 1986)

CREF Units	CREF Annuity Unit Value	First-Year Guaranteed Return + 4% of	Annual Annuity
80	x {$67.35	$67.35)} =	$5,603.52

Second and Subsequent Years

Year Starting May 1	Retirement Year	CREF Units	% Change in CREF Unit Value	Revised Annuity[b]
1987	2	80	+23.03	$6,894
1988	3	80	-11.20	6,122
1989	4	80	+12.07	6,861
1990	5	80	+11.76	7,668
1991	6	80	+ 7.90	8,273
1992	7	80	+ 6.08	8,836

[a]Assumption convenient and realistic for two people in their middle or late 60s.

[b]Prior year's annuity revised by change in CREF.

TABLE 11.10

TIAA-CREF ALLOCATIONS OF RETIREES (1993)

Number of Accounts in:	Panel A Receiving Number	Annuities %
Total Accounts	245,000	100
TIAA	242,000	99
CREF	130,000	53
TIAA & CREF	127,000[a]	52
TIAA only	115,000[b]	47
CREF only (100% CREF)	3,500	1

Panel B

Transfers Just Prior to Retirement

[a]Some but not all transferred funds, from CREF to TIAA prior to retirement.

[b]About 20% of those who had CREF funds transferred them to TIAA.

Other Earlier Transfers[*]

[c]57% of those receiving TIAA benefits only had some CREF accumulations at an earlier date.

[d]39% who expected to receive TIAA only held some CREF funds earlier.

Near Retirees[+]

55% of near retirees who switched some CREF to TIAA did so within five years of retirement.

74% of these who switched from CREF to TIAA did so within the past five years.

33% of near retirees receiving CREF transferred some of their funds to TIAA or among CREF accounts before retiring. (Presumably the latter are a very small percentage.)

[*]Data based upon a representative sample of retirees and participants nearing retirement. Data provided by letter from TIAA-CREF.

[+]Not retired at date of sample survey.

CHAPTER 12

RETIREMENT INCOME AND CASH FLOW

INTRODUCTION

This chapter builds on all that has gone before, but it can also stand on its own strengths. Your depth of understanding and willingness to accept and utilize what is presented in this chapter will be enhanced by your understanding of TIAA's products in particular and the relative performance of broad classes of securities in general.

The six major questions presented in this chapter are:

- Why do so many participants shift some or all of their pension-fund accumulations from CREF-Equities near their retirement age?

- How well has that strategy worked for them?

- How well have TIAA and CREF benefits performed since 1970 on an absolute and relative basis?

- How well have TIAA and CREF benefits performed compared with the cost of living?

- What are the limitations of the projections in my Annual TIAA-CREF Benefits Reports?

- How can I best go about comparing my pre-retirement cash flow with my post-retirement cash flow?

Long before you annuitize some or all of your TIAA and CREF accumulations, you probably have given much thought to this topic and have sought advice from whomever you could. Transferring funds from your accumulation accounts to your annuity accounts reflects both a happy decision and a very uneasy decision. The decision is a happy one for most participants because it confirms that the decision to retire fully or to part-time work has been made. The decision is an uneasy and emotionally disturbing one because you cannot be certain about what your real annuity benefits will be five, 10, or 20 years into the future. (Real benefits are your dollar benefits adjusted for changes in the cost of living.)[1]

Many people start worrying seriously about their final funds allocation between their TIAA and CREF accounts five or more years before their initially planned retirement date. Table 11.10 described the extent to which participants shifted CREF-Equities to TIAA just before retirement and within five years of retirement.

You may have found very little information about how TIAA and CREF performed for retirees either in company-published materials, or from friends and retired colleagues. Even if you know people who retired on TIAA-CREF pensions some years ago, you may be very reluctant to ask them about how well they are doing financially.

---

[1] See The Cost of Living Section in Chapter 7 for a detailed discussion on this point.

Three things seem to explain the motivations for shifting funds from CREF to TIAA at the point of retirement or a few years before retirement. Individuals shift from CREF because they believe the stock market is "too high," "too volatile," or "too likely to collapse" just after they retire. They are attracted to TIAA because they believe it will give them a stable or fixed income in retirement. Rarely do I hear participants say that they will keep their CREF because it will give them the best chance to have a part of their retirement benefits grow faster than the cost of living. No one I have talked to who was planning to retire soon was familiar with TIAA-CREF's suggested funds allocation guidelines as reproduced in Table 3.1. Some of those who are shown the guidelines that suggest up to 40 percent of their accumulation be in CREF up to retirement are quite surprised. TIAA-CREF is careful not to recommend a TIAA-CREF allocation to carry into retirement, but some TIAA-CREF publications do provide data on past CREF performance for retirees.

In Chapter 7, Investment Basics, the reasons for the long-run growth of common stock prices as measured by the well-known averages were discussed and demonstrated in Table 7.6. In Chapter 9, Investment Background, the history of stock market volatility was reviewed. The data shows that stock-market cycles from high to low, and back again have lasted on average about 3½ years. During your retired lifetime, which may be as long as 25 years, you may live through 6 or 7 such cycles. That the mythical, feared, market collapse is most unlikely to be timed exactly with the date of your retirement. Besides, over your remaining lifetime, the stock market prices will cycle ever upward and provide you with your best chance of exceeding the cost of living with the CREF part of your retirement benefits. In Chapter 3 the absolute and relative measurements of the risk in TIAA or CREF funds were concluded with a presentation of attitudes toward risk.

The event that has come as the greatest surprise to retirees is the decline in TIAA benefits that started for 1987 and later retirees, and continued for both new and earlier retirees through 1994. Participants who started to receive TIAA benefits in 1987 have had them shrink by almost 15 percent through 1994. TIAA benefits held steady in 1995 and 1996. They may well drop again at the beginning of 1997. The obvious reason for these declines is the drop in market interest rates as discussed in Chapter 3 and elsewhere.

PERFORMANCE OF TIAA AND CREF ANNUITIES SINCE 1970

The data in Table 12.1 presents TIAA and CREF annuity benefits in a way that permits exact comparisons from year to year from any year in which these benefits were started to the latest available year.[2] Five standardized assumptions were used to maintain uniformity and parallel computations from year to year: $100,000 annuitized initially, a joint-life annuity, 20-years certain, full benefits to the surviving spouse, and ages of the annuitant are 62 and 65 in the

---

[2]The data in this table were specially prepared by TIAA-CREF for Soldofsky. These data were originally prepared for the years 1970 through 1983, and they have been updated annually. The TIAA benefits are changed annually on January 2 and the CREF benefits are changed on May 1. After the request for the updated information is sent in, the figures are not usually received until July or August. An interesting sidelight is that the TIAA and CREF updates have been prepared separately by these two organizations.

first year that benefits are received.[3] In Table 12.1 data for years 1970, 1975, 1980 and 1985 only are presented and then starting with 1985 data for each year through 1995 are presented. The reason for omitting some early years is to simplify and shorten the table, while showing enough information so that you can be confident the starting date was not selected to distort that data to favor either TIAA or CREF.

As you look across the first row (1970) showing the monthly benefit payments separately on TIAA and CREF, note that payments on TIAA started at $635 per month in 1970 and rose to $787 in 1980, peaked at $916 in 1982, and stayed at that level until 1989. The obvious reason for this rise in benefits through 1989 and their subsequent decline was the rise in interest rates and their later decline, which is still ongoing. The CREF benefits started at $479 in 1970, which was almost 25 percent less than the TIAA benefits based upon the same-sized investment, $100,000.

The reasons for the initial year difference are in the assumptions. One difference is that TIAA assumed at that time a 7 percent return for the life of the TIAA annuity, but guaranteed 4 percent for CREF in the first year only. After the first year, CREF benefits fluctuate in accordance with the market return on the CREF-Equities portfolio. In most years the initial CREF benefits were about 40 percent to 45 percent below the TIAA benefits. Second, TIAA computes the participant's annuity based on its vintage-year technique as explained in Chapter 10. The changes in the average price of a CREF unit also helps explain these initial year differences. The reasons for CREF's variable benefits were explained in the Variable Annuity Section of Chapter 11.

The stock market did not fair well during the 1970s because of rising interest rates. From the 1970 starting year as shown in Table 12.1, CREF benefits did not exceed TIAA benefits until 1986. For those people who started their annuities in 1975, CREF benefits exceeded those of TIAA by 1983. For those who started to receive their annuities in 1980, CREF benefits exceeded TIAA benefits in 1985, or in the sixth year benefits were received. You can examine the rest of the Table 12.1 from this same point of view.

Another way to view the data is to ask how much would have been received per month if all funds had been annuitized in TIAA? In 1970 a 100 percent TIAA annuity would have brought in $1,270 per month. That amount was first exceeded by a 50-50 portfolio in 1981.

A third way to trace the history of the TIAA benefits for earlier retirees is to follow first-year benefits in each starting year. In 1970 the initial TIAA benefit was $635, it rose to $773 in 1975, to $828 in 1980, peaked at $993 in 1985, and has since dropped back to $647 in 1995.

A fourth useful way of looking at the benefits is to scan each row and to observe how few declines in the TIAA-CREF total occur. A large part of the reason to have a 50-50 portfolio at retirement is to stabilize total retirement benefits. As you look across the rows at the simulated experience of participants retiring in each individual year, you may be struck by the

---

[3]Each of the settlement option clauses were discussed in Table 11.5. Chapter 11 illustrates the dollar impact of these various assumptions. Even though the settlement options that you select are different from those utilized in Table 12.1, the percentage changes will be almost the same over the past years.

gradual drift upward in the total benefits. The most important reason for keeping CREF-Equities into retirement is to help offset inflation.

PERFORMANCE OF TIAA, CREF, AND THE COST OF LIVING

The performance of TIAA and CREF benefits as compared with the cost of living are reported in Table 12.2. The data starting with 1970 as a base year are shown for every fifth year. The data are scaled in each row to a base of 100 so that you can read how TIAA and CREF performed relative to each other and to the cost of living from each starting point. The TIAA and CREF data used are those presented in Table 12.1.

The data in Table 12.2 tell a terrible, but true tale for retirees who opted to place most or all of their retirement benefits in TIAA. The 1970 retirees found that their real income from TIAA was cut in half by 1980 and their CREF income fell even further. From 1980 up to 1995, these retirees—if they survived (as most of them probably did)--have had their TIAA benefits fall further below the cost of living. Their CREF benefits have increased very sharply for them since 1975, but the 50-50 combination of the two has not caught up to the increase in the cost of living since 1970.

Those who retired in 1975 have done considerably better financially. By 1980 their real income in terms of TIAA benefits was down about one-third, while their real CREF benefits were down only about 20%. By 1985 their CREF benefits had outrun the cost of living while real TIAA benefits were down almost 40 percent, while real CREF benefits were up about 10 percent. By 1995 real TIAA benefits were down more than half while CREF benefits had grown almost twice as much as the cost of living. A 50-50 combination of TIAA and CREF would have exceeded the cost of living by just over 20 percent by 1995.

The stories for 1980, 1985 and 1990 retirees are similar. For 1980 retirees the cruel reality is that TIAA benefits started dropping in 1990 and stand now only slightly above their 1980 level. Meanwhile, the cost of living continues to rise. The real TIAA benefits for 1980 retirees are down almost 40 percent, while real CREF benefits are up 250 percent. The outcomes for 1985 and 1990 follow the same pattern, but not enough time has passed for such dramatic differences for TIAA and CREF retirement benefits to emerge.

The general trends exhibited over the last 25 years will continue, but the exact numbers cannot be foretold. But surely, as pointed out many times, over a period of 5-10 years or more the superiority of retirement benefits from equity securities over fixed-income securities will show itself.

Another very useful way of viewing the performance of TIAA and CREF is to compare each of them with the cost of living (CPI) on a chart. Figures 12.1 and 12.2 are two such charts, which incorporate several useful features. First, they are prepared on a ratio or semi-logarithmic scale. On such a scale the vertical distance between 100 and 1,000 is exactly the same as the distance between 1,000 and 10,000. A constant rate of growth is represented by a straight line. Second, the TIAA and CREF monthly benefits used are the ones given in Table 12.1. Third, the CPI is scaled to 100 for the initial-year value of TIAA so that you can easily and quickly compare changes in TIAA benefits with those of the CPI. The CREF values grow much faster than the TIAA benefits or the CPI over all, but not necessarily every year. Fourth, the periods 1987 through 1995 and 1980 through 1995 have been used to form periods that are long enough to be useful to demonstrate the differences in changes in TIAA and CREF benefits, and at the same time reflect very relevant experience. By relevant experience is meant the experiences of older friends who retired with TIAA-CREF benefits; experiences that are so recent you can empathize with them and believe that experience could easily be replicated during your own retirement years. Fifth, a small insert in the bottom of each chart compares the actual changes in TIAA, CREF, and the CPI over the period represented. A final line of the insert shows what TIAA and CREF would have had to have been to exactly keep up with the CPI.

In Figure 12.1, TIAA and CREF monthly benefits start at $828 and $462, respectively. These amounts are based upon an initially annuitized amount of $100,000 in each account, and the other assumptions given in Table 12.1. The CREF benefits start at 46 percent less than the TIAA benefits partly because of the initial year 4 percent assumption described earlier. Remember also that those utilizing CREF for many years before retirement will have much higher total accumulations than those utilizing TIAA only.

A substantial percentage—perhaps 10 percent or more—of participants attending my seminars have told me and others present that they have always had a 50-50 allocation between TIAA and CREF-Equities. When asked how much higher their CREF accumulation was than their TIAA accumulation, the answers were invariably in the 40-60 percent range or even a little higher.

Two points are clear from this experience. First, those who used substantial amounts of CREF during the 20-30 years prior to their retirement will have much higher benefits than those using TIAA only. Second, by using a 50 percent CREF allocation strategy for those many years prior to retirement despite the first-year differential between TIAA and CREF benefits, their total benefits level in that first year probably will be as high or higher than they would have had with a TIAA strategy alone. By carrying their CREF percentage into retirement, they have a much better chance of keeping their benefits rising with inflation. Even if they switch a part of their CREF accumulation to TIAA just before they start receiving benefits, they are far ahead of those who never used CREF. Remember though, that if your CREF accumulation has grown very large relative to TIAA, you may wish to transfer some funds to TIAA or use one of the strategies discussed in Chapter 11. Before making your final allocation decisions within the narrow, TIAA-CREF framework, you should review your total portfolio balance against the broad allocations framework discussed in Chapter 1 and shown as Table 1.1. A further step is to compare your likely cash flow from working one more year with your likely cash flow from your total retirement benefits for being retired in the same calendar year. For example, you may be considering 1997. Work out your likely cash flow as described assuming you continue to work. Also work out your likely cash flow if you are retired in 1997. Compare the likely cash flows for 1997 on these two bases. (Working out these estimates on the assumption that you are either retired or working for the whole year provides a simpler and clearer result.)

CASH FLOWS: WORKING AND RETIRED COMPARED
A major problem in the year or years immediately prior to retirement is estimating the cash flow you will have on which to live. Many people make large errors in these estimates; usually they underestimate their retirement cash flow. These underestimates may be as much as 25 to 50 percent.

Such large underestimates of retirement cash flow can have at least three serious consequences. First, if likely retirement cash flow is viewed as being much too low, the individual may continue to work another year or more even though he may have clear and strong reasons for retiring. Second, more money than needed may be drawn in regular benefits from the individual's TIAA-CREF accounts than required to support his way of life. Consequently, he may seek to reinvest some or all of that excess cash flow. The rates on reinvestment are most likely to be less than that earned by TIAA or CREF, particularly because of its income tax shelter. The long run returns on TIAA and CREF relative to TIAA's competitors were discussed in Chapter 5. Third, he may shift funds unnecessarily from CREF to TIAA in the search for more current cash flow when the more prudent thing would have been to leave more or all of his accumulation in CREF as a pseudo-hedge against continuing inflation as discussed in Chapter 8. Your plans for the first few years of retirement may well depend upon your estimates of your cash flow for those years.

The three primary things that are most likely to be overlooked when making preliminary post-retirement, cash-flow estimates are the end of your personal, monthly investments in TIAA-CREF upon retirement, the end of your before-tax payments into social security, and the receipt of social security benefits. The primary, regular additional outlay that you may have to consider is a premium for Medigap insurance, an insurance policy to help pay costs to fill the gap between Medicare coverage and your health insurance coverage before retirement. If you are under 65 and not yet qualified for Medicare, your insurance outlay may be much larger. You should check with your employer and elsewhere, if necessary, to get firm estimates of what the outlay for such insurance may be.

The term cash flow has been used in earlier chapters and is used in this chapter because it means something quite different from income as the term is used in business accounting or in accounting for federal income taxes. In Chapter 11 one meaning of cash flow was defined by demonstrating that a part of your TIAA and/or CREF annuity is a return of your original investment and that of your employer, and the rest of it is a return of income earned on those investments. In a similar sense, a part of your social security benefits are partly a return of your payments into the system and partly income on those payments, but the system is more complex than that as discussed in Chapter 2. A considerable part of your social security benefits are subject to federal income taxes even though they are not income in a strict, business accounting sense.[4] Similarly, the money received from the sale of a house or the

---

[4]That part of the payments into your social security account paid by your employer have never been subject to income taxes. That half of these payments you made into social security were included as part of your income and were subject to income taxes. Now you must pay some income taxes on that part of the social payments that were never subjected to income taxes.

cashing of a certificate of deposit is largely not income. The recovery of the original payment for a house is a return of capital (in one sense of that word) and the rest of it is very likely a capital gain for income tax purposes. Tables 12.3 and 12.4 show benefit payments that are mixtures of various cash streams whether income or not. One must go through the routine set out in these tables to compare cash flow before-and-after retirement or to compare what one's cash flow would be for the coming year if he or she worked or retired that year. Other paradigms or routines may result in the same bottom line, but my format is very useful.

Two steps are involved in these tables. The first is to summarize your TIAA and CREF investments, and the second is to estimate your working and retirement cash flows.

Several preliminary, preparatory steps are necessary. First you should contact your local social security office and have them prepare an estimate of your social security benefits for the date at which you are planning to retire. This office will also prepare estimated benefits for several alternative dates if you wish. You should probably ask TIAA-CREF to prepare estimates of what your benefits are likely to be for one or more different starting retirement dates.[5] In addition, they will prepare estimates for more than one combination of TIAA-CREF allocations. You may wish to know what your retirement benefits will be with the current accumulations in each account, or what they would be if you shifted some of your CREF funds to your TIAA account just before you annuitize them. One convenient way to get estimates is to request that TIAA-CREF prepare a separate example of what the change in benefits would be if you shifted $10,000 of CREF to TIAA. With such numbers you can explore the initial-year dollar impact of switching different amounts from CREF to TIAA.

In addition, TIAA-CREF will prepare the whole menu of benefits for you based upon single and joint-life annuities. If you want estimates for the fixed-period annuities, you must request these also. Separate requests must be made for your SRA benefits, for IPRO benefits, and for the minimum distribution option, if appropriate. If you wish to utilize partial settlements, that can be done easily by calculating some percentage of the total benefits for TIAA and CREF shown in the forms prepared for you.

Even though separate requests must be made for estimates of your regular TIAA and CREF benefits and for your SRA benefits, that can all be done with one telephone call. As much as five weeks may pass between your initial request and the receipt of your estimates.

Single persons and couples filing jointly whose adjusted gross incomes are $25,000 or less, or $32,000 or less, respectively, are not subject to federal income tax on OASI payments they receive. For single filers with income of $25,001 to $34,000, 50 percent of the social security benefits are subject to federal income taxes. For these persons with adjusted gross income above $34,001, 85 percent of the additional benefits are taxable. For couples filing jointly those thresholds are $32,001 and $44,001, respectively. IRS guides for filing 1995 income taxes and other income-tax guides will include worksheets to facilitate these calculations.

[5]Also check with your staff benefits person about what accumulated vacation, sick leave and other benefits you may receive upon retirement. Such benefits may be available as a lump sum or be received regularly over a period of several months.

ANNUAL BENEFIT REPORT

The personalized Annual Benefit Report that you receive after the first of each year has so many assumptions built into it that it must be used with great caution. The more years you have until your projected retirement date, the less accurate and useful this report is. Five reasons for this declining accuracy are suggested. First, observe that both your TIAA and CREF-Equities benefit estimates assume a 6 percent return until your proposed retirement date, as shown in the Report. Although the 6 percent is only about one-fifth below the TIAA contractual return for the first half of 1995, the CREF performance may be well above or below 6 percent from now to your retirement.[6] The longer that period, the more likely the return CREF-Equities is to be above 6 percent.

The actual performances of TIAA and CREF from 1952-1994 are given in Table 6.3, and bond and stock performances since 1871 are given in Table 6.6. The projected TIAA benefits depend upon the current and future announced vintage year rate of your TIAA investments as described and illustrated in the first section of Chapter 10. As pointed out earlier in this chapter, one thing that was very unexpected by retirees was that these vintage year rates themselves would be reduced and actual TIAA benefits would fall as shown in Table 12.1. Some TIAA benefits started falling in 1988 after retirees had been receiving benefits only a year or two. Some TIAA benefits have been cut as much as 14.5 percent.

Second, CREF benefits are based upon a 4 percent return in the first year only, even though CREF benefits in all probability will average more than twice that rate. Third, the benefit estimates assume that you will continue investing at the same amount per year in your accounts until you retire. In fact, most participants are looking for considerable salary increases and proportionate increases in their annual TIAA-CREF investments. You may start an SRA and further increase your retirement benefits if you have not already done so. Fourth, look closely at the retirement date that TIAA-CREF has recorded for you. If you now have a different most likely date for starting your annuity, call TIAA, ask them to change your records, and ask for a new estimate of your retirement annuities.

Fifth, the importance of a 4 percent assumption in your first year of CREF benefits only cannot be stressed too much. As commented upon earlier, your first year's CREF benefit is most likely to be in the range of 35 percent to 45 percent below that of TIAA benefits for the same number of dollars invested. Perhaps the best way to observe the impact of that effect is to look back at Table 12.1, and to read and compare the benefit outcomes in each row.

The importance of the assumptions in your Annual Benefit Report are best illustrated by a detailed example, such as the one given in Table 12.3. In this example, the TIAA and CREF accumulations are set at $200,000 each in order to emphasize the importance of the underlying assumptions in the estimated benefits. In working toward your TIAA-CREF benefits, you need to summarize your projected accumulations first and then prepare a similar worksheet on which to estimate your benefits.[7]

---

[6]In this section, CREF refers to CREF-Equities only in order to simplify the discussion.

[7]Worksheets are provided at the end of this book for your convenience.

Three points need to be made about the $200,000 used in the example. First, $200,000 in each of two accounts is reasonable for a person who has been a TIAA-CREF participant for more than 20 years and has an ending annual salary of about $50,000, the amount used in the Table 12.4. Second, if a participant had invested the same amount each month in TIAA and CREF, the final accumulation would have in fact been about 40 percent or more higher for CREF. However, for the sake of emphasizing the impact of the assumptions upon the benefit estimates, using the same accumulation in these accounts contributes to clarity. Third, no investment in SRAs is assumed for the sake of simplicity again.

Part B of Table 12.3 abstracts from information shown in TIAA/CREF's Annual Benefit Reports in order to present the most essential elements for this demonstration. The estimated retirement benefits for TIAA and CREF shown are consistent with the assumptions about the settlement options used in Table 12.1 and elsewhere. Under these assumptions, TIAA and CREF benefits worked out to $18,200 and $12,192 annually, respectively, for early 1993. The estimated CREF benefits are $6,008 or 33.0% less than those for TIAA. The question is, "Why?" Paraphrasing a cliché popular among politicians, the answer is in the assumptions.

As pointed out earlier and stated under 4 at the bottom of the table, TIAA benefits reflect the vintage year in which investments were made, and CREF assumes a 4 percent return for the first year of the benefits only. Although each year the rate earned by each TIAA account is different, based upon the vintage year rates for 1992 displayed in Table 10.1, the average rate of return is about 8 percent. That rate is assumed to continue for the life of the annuity in the Annual Benefits Report even though Table 10.1 shows clearly that those rates have been reduced very sharply since 1982. (The effect of reducing the vintage year rates is reflected in the actual reductions in TIAA benefits as shown in Table 12.1.) CREF benefits are properly and reasonably set for the first year of the benefits. CREF is understandably unwilling to project what its future total annual returns on CREF may be over any specified period of years.

Another observation made previously based upon real information in Table 12.1 is that CREF benefits generally have grown to be equal to or larger than TIAA benefits within 4-8 years since 1975. For those who retired between 1970 and 1975, that period was over 10 years.

In the illustration in Table 12.3, if the participant had shifted all of her CREF funds to TIAA just before retirement, she would increase her pension benefits in the first year of her retirement. The increase would amount to $6,008 in the first year or 19.8 percent more than the $30,392 total. A worksheet, W.1, that you can copy is provided at the end of the book. You may want to use it to prepare your own annuity estimates for various combinations of TIAA and CREF.

The first-year cash flows are readily prepared from the information in Part A at the top of the table. The ratios near the middle of the page are called cash-flow ratios because they reflect both the return on your accumulation and the return of part of that accumulation itself. The TIAA cash-flow ratio varies by small amounts from year to year as suggested by the changes in first-year benefits in Table 12.1. The CREF first-year, cash-flow ratio is considerably more variable. However the changes implied in the future years' cash-flow ratio are the key to understanding the risks and rewards of your variable annuity.

The cash-flow ratios for TIAA and CREF may be used to explore the impact on your prospective benefits from each of these accumulations by simulating different TIAA-CREF allocations just before retiring. For example, the cash-flow ratios in this case are .0910 and .0606 as shown in Table 12.3. Perhaps you want to know that the prospective benefits would be if TIAA accumulations were increased to $300,000 or 75% and CREF was reduced to $100,000 or 25% of the total of $400,000. The calculations are as follows:

	Accumulation	Ratio	Annuity
TIAA	$300,000	.09100	$27,300
CREF	100,000	.06096	6,096
			$33,396

The projected annuities would increase from a total of $30,392 to $33,396 or by $3,004, which is 9.9 percent. The question that must be considered very seriously in cases like this one is whether an immediate 9.9 percent increase in the first retirement year's annuity is worth reducing this part of your pseudo-hedge against inflation?

The analysis of your projected Modified Cash Flows in retirement as compared with your Modified Cash Flow while working, which is demonstrated next, should be completed, considered, and thoroughly understood before making a decision at retirement to shift any or all of your CREF-Equities or other CREF accounts to TIAA.

In this chapter an annuity based on CREF-Bonds is not considered because at this date CREF-Bond accumulations cannot be annuitized. Furthermore, as discussed in Chapter 3, CREF-Bonds are inferior to TIAA in terms of both return and risk. CREF-Money Market accounts can be annuitized, but as discussed in Chapter 3 also, the return on money market instruments is very likely to be low relative to the other choices for annuities. Circumstances could change if a rising, continuing inflation is in the future as you see it. Annuitizing CREF-Global Equities is a viable option, but, as demonstrated in Chapter 3, the volatility of a variable annuity based upon this option is very likely to be markedly higher than an annuity based upon CREF-Equities.

WORKING AND RETIRED CASH FLOWS FOR THE SAME YEAR
One way of determining the immediate financial effect of retirement upon yourself and your family is to simulate your cash flow for the next full year depending upon whether you are working, or retired and receiving your TIAA-CREF benefits.

Earlier the point was made that retiring and starting your pension benefits are separate decisions. You can postpone utilizing all or part of your accumulations until April 1 of the year after the year you become 70½.[8] You can start receiving the social security benefits to which you are entitled after you retire, even though you do not start receiving your TIAA-CREF benefits.

A full calendar year is used for convenience in these cash-flow simulations. Trying to trace more exactly the financial impact of retiring in any particular month of a year is awkward.

---

[8]See Chapter 11, footnote 3 for a discussion of the legislative history of this age.

That can be done, but little or no advantage for this more detailed procedure can be suggested. What you probably want to know is how your cash flows compare on a monthly or annual basis. Once you have prepared the annual cash flows, you can divide them by 12 to find the monthly cash flow. An implicit assumption is that by the time you are ready to retire you have some cash resources that you can utilize if your benefits do not start the day after you receive your last paycheck. With a little attention, your pension benefits can start virtually the day after your last paycheck is received, if you want that to happen. You only have to contact your social security office and TIAA and CREF far enough in advance to have that done. Probably three to four months is enough lead time to prevent a lapse in income, but it may be not long enough to do some of the planning.

Tables 12.4 and 12.5 show useful routines for comparing your projected cash flows assuming either that you are working the next full year or that you are retired and start receiving all of the pension benefits which you have earned. One can make the same type of projected comparison for the second or third year into the future, but those projections will be increasingly less accurate the further into the future you set them. Some of the obvious things that can happen between the present date and a date several years into the future are sharp changes in your salary, changes in benefits because of changes in the TIAA returns, changes in the market value of CREF units, changes in social security benefits, and changes in income taxes as they apply to either your salary and/or to your benefits.

One way of understanding Tables 12.4 and 12.5 is to read down them line-by-line and to understand the purpose of each line. Note the instructions to the arithmetic for adding and subtracting the dollar estimates on each line to arrive at the bottom-line estimates.

A brief summary of the three most important differences between the working and retired columns in Table 12.4 is helpful. First, in the working case, the current budget-line salary is used. After you retire, no salary is received. Of course, partial retirement or some salary from work might be earned. After retirement social security benefits and TIAA-CREF benefits are considered a salary replacement. Second, the tax-deferred salary option obviously disappears when no further salary is paid by your employer. Line 5 is necessary because it represents a deduction from your taxable income and a corresponding investment in your pension plan. Third, you will no longer have FICA taxes (line 14) deducted from your salary. All of the years you have been working, FICA has been a tax or cash deduction from the income you have been earning. The net amount of your paycheck is a special type of cash flow because of items such as FICA and the adjustment for your tax-deferred salary option. The elimination of the FICA tax on your retirement cash flow removes this drag upon your useable income or modified cash flow.

The key to your first-year retirement cash flow as compared with your working cash flow is the difference between the total of your TIAA-CREF benefits plus social security benefits and your budget-line salary. Generally, commentators in this specialized analytical field believe that a person is doing very well if his immediate retirement benefits are about two-thirds of his working income. The details about income-tax and other differentials are typically avoided.

In the illustrative cases (which are quite typical of faculty and administrators when the total payment to TIAA-CREF amounts to 15 percent of salary), new TIAA-CREF retirees receive amounts far above their working cash flow. I also assume that these new retirees are 65 or older and have worked under TIAA-CREF for at least 20 years. For those individuals who have voluntarily invested up to the 20 percent of salary limit, the retirement cash-flow percentage is quite handsome as compared with their working cash flow.

Tables 12.4 and 12.5 differ primarily in the amount of the salary and the underlying accumulations which result in the different projected in TIAA-CREF benefit levels. In Table 12.4 the salary level is $50,000 and in Table 12.5 it is $100,000. Other differences follow from the salary differences. Social security benefits will differ because in the $50,000 case the social security tax (FICA) and the social security benefit (OASI) are below the approximate 1994 coverage level of $60,000.[9] Taxable salary for OASI only above the $60,000 level, which now moves upward each year with the increase in the cost of living index, does not increase social security benefits. Presumably, the $50,000 person has had a salary below the maximum social security level most of his working life and the other person has been well above the maximum most of her working life. The differences in other income at the two salary levels are based upon summary data provided in a little known document published annually by the Internal Revenue Service. The publication dates of these data are always at least five years behind the tax year for which the data are summarized. Income taxes and other amounts are clearly related to the income difference as well.

LINE BY LINE CALCULATION OF CASH FLOWS

Included in this line-by-line discussion is relevant commentary. On line 1, Table 12.4, the Working column in Table 12.4, the gross or budget-line salary is entered. The assumption is made that the participant is using the available tax-deferred salary option. If his personal investment in the TIAA-CREF plan is 5 percent or $2,500, that amount is entered on line 5 and will be deducted in computing gross income. The limit on tax-deferred personal investments is $9,500 per year even though that may be less than the allowable 20 percent for the tax-deferred salary option as discussed elsewhere. Personal contributions, if any, to SRAs should be included on line 5. One objective of these two lines is to enter the amounts required on the income-tax computation and another is to enter the amounts which will reflect the wage and salary cash income of the participant.

Note that health insurance outlays are not included on these forms because the individual is likely to be paying for health insurance while working and will likely have to purchase some form of health insurance coverage after retirement. If the total health insurance outlay is expected to increase upon retirement, that increase should be deducted from line 17 to improve the accuracy of the simulation.

The information for line 2 of Table 12.4 can most easily be gathered from last year's income-tax return. If you have reason to believe that for the year being simulated—probably next year—other income will be higher or lower than the present year, enter the most likely amount. In the prepared simulations the assumption was made that interest and dividends would be the same whether the participant continues to work for his present employer or not. In some cases the participant may take a part-time position almost immediately, or continue or expand some other income-earning activity.

---

[9]The social security tax is 6.2 percent to the $60,000 ceiling, but medical tax of 1.45 percent was uncapped starting in 1994.

Line 3 is for your projected TIAA-CREF pension. This information is found in your Annual Benefits Report. However, remember the critique of the limitations of this Report. Before entering the numbers from your Report, consider what modifications you want to ask TIAA-CREF to provide for you that they may be willing and able to accomplish. For example, they will provide projections for various planned retirement dates, but are unlikely to build in your anticipated salary increases. They will not use different assumptions for interest rates before or after retirement. They will complete retirement benefit estimates for you with different TIAA-CREF allocations.

If your retirement is some years into the future, you can probably prepare a useful estimate of what your accumulations are going to be by adding to the accumulation shown in your latest Report the amount of the current year's investment, the interest on that total investment and prepare a new total. You can continue that process for some years into the future and use your cash-flow ratio to estimate a useful number for your estimated retirement benefits. The Working Longer section of Chapter 7 suggests another way of estimating retirement benefits even further into the future.

Line 4, Social Security benefits information, can be obtained through your local social security office or by mail based upon a form your local or regional office sends to you.

Line 6, Gross Income, is the sum of the information in the appropriate columns on the first four lines. In the Working column, deduct the Tax-Deferred Salary Option, Line 5, because that item by definition is deferred from your taxable income.

The objective of the next three lines is roughly to duplicate the information that will be included in the coming year's Taxable Gross Income. Now that a part of social security benefits is taxable, an additional line, Line 7, must be included. If your projected gross income excluding OASI income is more than $32,000 in 1994 for a couple filing jointly, some number will have to be placed on line 7 under the Retired columns.[10]

As Gross Income in both the 50-50 case and the 100% TIAA case is above $44,000, 85 percent of those social security benefits are taxable. This amount calculated according to the information in footnote 4 above $44,000 is $2,910. The nontaxable part of social security benefits,$2,910 ($19,400 - $16,490) is placed on line 7 and will be deducted in calculating the Gross Taxable Income (line 10).

---

[10]The thresholds for income taxes on social security benefits are as follows starting in 1994.

Filing Status	Maximum % Subject to Federal Income Taxes	
Single Tax Payer		
$25,001-$34,000	50%	
Above $34,000		85%
Married Couple Filing Jointly		
$32,001-$44,000	50%	
Above $44,000		85%

Line 8, Itemized Deductions, is estimated at $6,000 whether the participant is working or retired. The assumption is that she will make no notable changes in her expenditure pattern in the first year of retirement especially with her cash flows staying much the same. The presumption is that this family does itemize its deductions, which is very likely if they own their own home, pay property taxes, state income taxes, give liberally to charities, and still have some interest to pay on their home mortgage. The estimate is confirmed by IRS studies of personal income tax reports.

Line 9, Exemptions, were $2,450 per person in 1994. The amount has increased approximately with the cost of living increase in recent years. The assumption is that this couple has no dependents. Conceivably, a dependent parent could be living with them, but a dependent child is unlikely given their ages.

Line 10, Taxable Gross Income, is calculated readily by adding lines 7, 8, and 9 and deducting that total from the amount on line 6, Gross Income.

Line 11, Federal Income Taxes, is calculated on the basis of the 1994 income tax rates. The federal income tax rates was 15 percent on the first $38,000 of taxable income, 28 percent on taxable income from $38,001 to $91,850, and 31 percent for taxable income from $91,850 to $140,000. The federal income taxes in the three columns are different because the Gross Taxable Incomes are different.

Line 12, State Income Taxes, will be different in each state because of peculiarities of state law and differences in income tax rates. Some cities levy income taxes in addition to state and federal income taxes. You might calculate your state income taxes directly using instructions prepared by your state's revenue service or you might do it the easy way. I have my clients look up their federal and state income tax payments from their latest tax reports and calculate their state income taxes as a percentage of their federal taxes. Unless something very radical has happened to the income tax codes, that percentage will be an excellent proxy to use in preparing the projected 1994 (or whatever the next relevant year turns out to be) state income taxes. Just multiply the 1994 federal income tax estimate by the percentage relationship of your state to federal taxes and insert those numbers on line 12.

Line 13, Net After-Tax Income, is an interesting concept even though it is not necessary in preparing your Modified Cash Flow. It represents what is left of your income after deducting your federal and state income taxes from your Taxable Gross Income. When you use itemized deductions, as has been assumed, your property taxes are included. A case could be made for deducting FICA, which you cannot avoid, in calculating your Net After-Tax Income, but that step is not taken. Your Exemptions are added back to the total because they do not represent any direct cash outlays; they are merely a concession on the part of the government that you may keep a part of your own income. Similarly, the Nontaxable amount of OASI payments must be added because they are part of your net income.

In preparing the Cash-Flow Analysis section, Line 14, FICA or the Federal Insurance Contributions Act is a mandatory deduction of 7.65 percent from your salary up to a maximum of $60,600 in 1994. The social security tax is 6.2 per up to $60,600 in 1994. The 1.45 percent for hospital insurance applies to all wages and salaries. In earlier years, the social security and hospital insurance had the same maximum amount.

Line 15, Adjusted Gross Income, is calculated easily by deducting from line 6, Gross Income, the three taxes, Federal and State Income taxes plus FICA, lines 11, 12, and 14.

Line 16 is the same as line 8. All of the expenses on this line are presumed to report actual cash outlays for qualified deductions permitted by the income-tax regulations.

Line 17, which is Line 15, Adjusted Gross Income, less the qualified deductions, is a Modified Cash Flow. Of course, not all or even most of your daily living expenses including travel, entertainment, and medical expenses are included. Capital outlays such as home repairs, replacement of appliances, automobiles, and so on are not included, as I am using the term. The term is what it is in this format.

Table 12.5 is identical in concept with Table 12.4, but the salary level is doubled to $100,000. The first and most notable difference of this doubling of the salary and using reasonable assumptions for all of the other items is that the Modified Cash Flow in the $100,000 case (with the 50-50 allocation) is 62.7 percent of the salary and in the $50,000 case it is 80.0% of the salary. Four explanations for this lower percentage in the lower salary level case are noted. First, in the $50,000 case the social security benefits are not at the ceiling level and a small amount of social insurance impact as described in Chapter 2 favors the lower income. In the $100,000 case, social security benefits are relatively less because these benefits are based on a ceiling salary of $60,600 currently. This ceiling has been rising since the individual was first covered. Second, dividend and interest income in the $100,000 case is more than double what it is in the $50,000 case. Third, more of the federal and state income taxes are at the higher marginal income tax rates. Fourth and finally, FICA tax is not double in the $100,000 case what it was in the $50,000 case because of the FICA coverage ceiling on the social security portion of the tax.

USING MODIFIED CASH FLOWS
The concept of Modified Cash Flow as it is used is wonderfully helpful in comparing your Working and Retired Cash Flows. This "bottom line" will facilitate making important decisions about a possible transfer of funds from CREF to TIAA at the point of retirement and will help you decide what you can and cannot afford at the start of your retirement.

In the present, realistic case profiled in Table 12.4, a transfer of funds from the $200,000 in CREF to TIAA is unnecessary to maintain a modified cash flow at the pre-retirement level. Even with the present 50-50 TIAA-CREF allocation, cash flow is likely to be 15-20 percent higher than it was in the prior full year. With a 100 percent TIAA allocation, cash flow could be 30 percent higher.

This projected Retired Modified Cash Flow is above the amount it would be from working, which is also presumably about the same as the amount in the prior year (1993 in the illustration). This result raises the question of whether or not all of the TIAA-CREF accumulations should be annuitized upon retirement. Obviously, annuitizing about 15-20 percent of your accumulation could be delayed up to the time you are almost 70½ plus as described earlier. The advantage of delaying annuitizing is that the remaining accumulation, the part not annuitized, will continue to grow on a tax-deferred basis at the rates that TIAA-CREF will be able to earn. You can annuitize this $30,000-$40,000 at any time you wish up to the age it must be annuitized to avoid the 50 percent tax penalty. If you are approaching the tax-penalty age and still do not need the added income for whatever personal and financial reasons exist at that time, you can postpone receiving part of the cash flow still longer by using the minimum distribution option as discussed in Chapter 11.

If an individual is in a financial position similar to that illustrated in Table 12.4 and has SRAs in addition to the regular TIAA-CREF accounts, the analysis poses the same question about whether to annuitize the SRAs immediately or not. For most people in this position, the answer will be to postpone. An advantage of the SRAs in these circumstances is that they can be "cashed" or annuitized whenever you desire or need to do so. You can "cash" SRAs partially or fully and obtain a lump sum that you may use for any (legal) purpose whatsoever.

One minor caution is in order. If you are making your allocation decisions shortly before the March 31 date on which the CREF annuity unit is revalued, your CREF annuity may be either somewhat higher or lower than you anticipated.

CONCLUSIONS

TIAA-CREF participants who shift all or part of their pension funds from CREF-Equities to TIAA at the point of retirement or shortly before retirement do so mostly out of misplaced fear and short-sightedness. They would be well advised to keep their debt-equity allocations within the guidelines recommended in this book by the author and by TIAA-CREF itself. TIAA-CREF participants at the edge of retirement are not the only ones who exhibit such poor judgment. Participants of other 403(b) plans and the even greater numbers of individuals who have corporate 401(k) pension plans behave similarly.

Table 12.1 shows that retirees who took all their benefits based on TIAA's fixed-income portfolio, discovered this allocation did not work out well for them in the long run even though it was advantageous for the first several years of retirement. Those who started with 50-50 allocation of their investment accumulations between TIAA and CREF have had very few, if any, years in which their total benefits from these two sources declined. Starting about 1983 the performance of CREF's equity-based benefits was little short of sensational through 1993. Of course, this same very rapid increase in equity prices is not likely to repeat itself soon. Another period like the unwinding of the inflation of the late 1970s and early 1980s that depresses equity prices is not likely for another decade or more.

As shown in Table 12.2, TIAA benefits have been falling further and further behind the cost of living. From 1970 to 1980, a period of rising inflation and rising interest rates, real TIAA-benefits fell by almost half. To be fair, CREF benefits fell even further during the decades of the 1970s. Real benefits are the actual benefits received adjusted by the cost of living. Benefits from CREF, whose performance reflects the total stock market, have generally increased more rapidly than the cost of living. The extent of the risk of year-to-year fluctuations in CREF benefits were discussed in several earlier chapters.

Real income—real pension benefits—from a 50-50, debt-equity allocation has been highly successful strategy for the past 25 years and more. A higher allocation of funds to equities at retirement is not recommended because that strategy increases the year-to-year fluctuations in benefits.[11] Social Security benefits are an element of stability to a retiree's real income because they are structured to keep up with the cost of living. However, the higher one's pension benefits, the lower the proportion of OASI benefits to the total benefits. The OASI benefits have a maximum level based upon the percentage of the contributions paid on salary and the ceiling on the amount of salary covered.

The projected TIAA and CREF benefits shown in your individualized Annual Benefits Reports have a number of serious limitations based upon the underlying assumptions built into the estimated benefits. The more years you are away from your likely retirement, the less

---

[11]Henry Kaufman, the popular and prescient economist, who is sometimes called Dr. Doom, foresees increasing volatility in the bond and stock markets because of the globalization of American-style financial markets, and the changing world-wide infrastructure of unregulated credit creation outside of the banking system and the control of the central banks. Henry Kaufman, "Structural Changes in the Financial Markets: Economic and Policy Significance," Economic Review, Federal Reserve Bank of Kansas City, Second Quarter 1994, pp. 5-15.

useful are these estimates. TIAA benefits estimates are probably understated somewhat as experience and analysis shows. CREF benefits are quite accurate for the first year because of the way the variable annuity works. After the first-year CREF benefits fluctuate with the stock market. Their trend will be upward but year-to-year fluctuations may be wide. These same limitations will be found in all other 403(b) and 401(k) pension projections to a greater or lesser degree for similar reasons.

CREF's first-year benefits per dollar of investment annuitized are likely to be as much as 40 percent below TIAA's, but you must keep in mind that your CREF accumulation at the date of retirement will be much higher than it would have been if the same amount had been regularly invested in TIAA rather than CREF for two decades or more.

A procedure for comparing first-year TIAA and CREF benefits per dollar of benefits received was demonstrated. The benefits that should be used are those provided in your Annual Benefits Report despite their several limitations. TIAA will provide you with update estimates and build in alternative retirement dates and allocation assumptions. This procedure is useful in helping you estimate what the impact would be on your benefits of shifting a part of your CREF accumulation to TIAA just before you retire.

A second procedure demonstrated in Chapter 12 illustrates how to estimate what your retirement cash flow from all sources will be in the projected retirement year. It also illustrates how to compare that cash flow with what it would be if you were retired that year rather than working. These results are highly useful for several decisions. They will help you determine whether you need to work longer or not to increase your retirement income. Second, they will help in the decisions about shifting part or all of your CREF-Equities to TIAA prior to retirement. Third, they will help you decide whether you can postpone taking a part of your benefits and let the rest of your accumulation continue to grow tax-deferred until a later date. Your benefits on your entire accumulation must be started by April of the year after the year you become 70½ years of age or a severe income tax penalty will be imposed upon you. However, using the minimum distribution option device will enable you to postpone receiving part of your benefits a few years longer if that strategy is appropriate for you.

Almost everything that has been written about how to retire richer by using your TIAA-CREF, 403(b) pension plan is true also for those using a corporate 401(k) plan. The details and operations of the investment vehicles used in a 401(k) plan may be somewhat different from those used by TIAA-CREF. Basically, all of these 401(k) plans provide investment options among fixed-income and equity securities. The performance history of the available 401(k) investment allocation options will provide strong clues to their likely future investment performance together with descriptions of the investment policies of each option. These performances can be rated on the same type of risk-reward scales used for TIAA and CREF, and the fixed income and equity markets.

All of the Investment Basics and Investment Background analysis and information provided in Chapters 8 and 9 is equally applicable to choices about investment allocation selection within 401(k) plans. The need to be circumspect in selecting and using in-house and hired financial planners applies equally to 401(k) plans. The problems of health and health insurance planning after retirement are no different whether one spends her working years in the public or private economy. The characteristics, advantages, and limitations of settlement options are well covered on Chapter 11. Given the hundreds of insurance companies that provide settlement option plans, you are likely to find some novel plans not covered by the discussions in Chapter 11, but it provides an excellent basis for your own analysis. It should provide a basis for asking further, insightful questions. If further information is needed, an independent, very experienced specialist should be sought. That person may be an insurance consultant, a specialized accountant, lawyer, or banker. Your settlement option selections and investment allocations are too important to your continuing standard of living to be treated casually.

I assume that you, my dear reader, would prefer to retire richer and stay richer for the rest of your life, when that can be done by better decisions. Your better decisions will help you and your loved ones live without having an unfavorable financial effect upon anyone. Retiring richer is not a zero sum game.

TABLE 12.1

TIAA-CREF BENEFITS MATRIX: 1970-1995

Assume $100,000 Accumulation Transformed to an Annuity Account
Annuity to Start After Annual Recalculation (5/1 each year)[a]
20-Years Certain, Full Benefits for Surviving Spouse
(Husband, 65, Wife 62)
(Monthly Benefits)

YEAR BENEFITS START		Annuity Income Year													
		1970	1975	1980	1985	1986	1987	1988	1989	1990	1991	1992	1993	1994	1995
1970	TIAA	635	757	787	916	916	916	916	916	898	898	881	838	830	830
	CREF	479	362	435	824	1116	1372	1219	1366	1526	1647	1747	1913	1943	2053
	TOTAL	1114	1119	1222	1740	2032	2288	2135	2282	2424	2545	2628	2751	2773	2883
1975	TIAA		773	818	970	972	972	972	972	949	949	928	874	864	864
	CREF		581	699	1323	1792	2205	1958	2194	2452	2646	2807	3073	3120	3298
	TOTAL		1354	1517	2293	2764	3177	2930	3166	3401	3595	3735	3947	3984	4162
1980	TIAA			828	998	1000	1000	1000	1000	966	966	941	878	866	866
	CREF			462	875	1185	1457	1294	1450	1621	1749	1855	2031	2063	2179
	TOTAL			1290	1873	2185	2457	2294	2450	2587	2715	2796	2909	2929	3045
1985	TIAA				993	993	993	993	993	963	963	935	865	852	852
	CREF				533	722	882	789	888	988	1066	1131	1238	1257	1329
	TOTAL				1526	1715	1875	1782	1881	1951	2029	2066	2103	2109	2181
1986	TIAA					991	991	991	991	961	961	932	861	848	848
	CREF					574	706	627	702	785	847	899	984	999	1056
						1565	1697	1618	1693	1746	1808	1831	1845	1847	1904

	1987	1988	1989	1990	1991	1992	1993	1994	1995
1987									
TIAA	991	991	973	946	943	915	847	833	833
CREF	599	532	594	665	719	762	835	847	896
TOTAL	1590	1523	1567	1611	1662	1677	1682	1680	1729
1988									
TIAA		954	941	930	924	897	833	819	819
CREF		523	586	655	706	749	820	833	880
TOTAL		1477	1527	1585	1630	1646	1653	1652	1699
1989									
TIAA			941	919	896	886	824	810	810
CREF			523	585	531	669	733	744	786
TOTAL			1464	1504	1427	1555	1557	1554	1596
1990									
TIAA				904	896	874	814	800	800
CREF				475	513	544	595	604	639
TOTAL				1379	1409	1418	1409	1404	1439
1991									
TIAA					873	835	802	789	789
CREF					559	593	649	659	697
TOTAL					1432	1428	1451	1448	1486
1992									
TIAA						835	790	779	779
CREF						475	520	528	558
TOTAL						1310	1310	1307	1337
1993									
TIAA							758	760	760
CREF							508	516	545
TOTAL							1266	1276	1305
1994									
TIAA								712	716
CREF								470	497
TOTAL								1182	1213
1995									
TIAA									646
CREF									517
TOTAL									1163

ᵃAssume participant retired January 1 of year indicated.

RETIREMENT INCOME AND CASH FLOW

TABLE 12.2

PERFORMANCE OF TIAA, CREF AND THE COST OF LIVING: 1970 - 95
(Base Year Adjusted to 100)

Base Year	Item	1970	1975	1980	1985	1990	1995
1970	TIAA	100.0	119.2	123.7	144.3	141.4	130.7
1970	CREF	100.0	75.6	90.8	172.0	254.5	428.6
1970	C/L[a]	100.0	188.7	212.4	277.3	336.9	385.8
1975	TIAA	--	100.0	105.8	125.5	122.8	111.8
1975	CREF	--	100.0	120.3	227.7	422.0	567.6
1975	C/L[a]	--	100.0	153.1	200.0	242.9	278.3
1980	TIAA	--	--	100.0	120.5	116.7	104.6
1980	CREF	--	--	100.0	189.3	350.9	471.6
1980	C/L[a]	--	--	100.0	130.6	158.6	181.7
1985	TIAA	--	--	--	100.0	97.0	85.8
1985	CREF	--	--	--	100.0	185.4	240.3
1985	C/L[a]	--	--	--	100.0	121.5	139.1
1990	TIAA	--	--	--	--	100.0	88.5
1990	CREF	--	--	--	--	100.0	136.0
1990	C/L[a]	--	--	--	--	100.0	114.5

[a]Cost of Living as measured by the Consumer Price Index.

TABLE 12.3

COMPARING TIAA AND CREF-EQUITIES RETIREMENT BENEFITS AND ASSUMPTIONS[a]

Part A

Total Accumulation	For Year Ending December 31		
	Regular Acct.	SRA	Total
TIAA	$200,000	--	$200,000
CREF Equities	200,000	--	200,000
CREF Money Market	--	--	--
Total	$400,000		$400,000

Illustration of your first year's annuity income, assuming a 6% rate of return until retirement.

If current premiums continue, first year's estimated income			
	Regular Acct.	SRA	Total
TIAA			
Standard Benefit method	$ 18,200.0	--	$ 18,200.0
CREF-Equities	$ 12,192.0[b]	--	$ 12,192.0[b]
Total estimated benefits	$ 30,392.0	--	$ 30,392.0

Part B

Cash-Flow Ratios (First Year Only)			
	TIAA Total	CREF Total	Total
1. Accumulations	$200,000	$200,000	$400,000
2. Promised Annuity	18,200	12,192	30,392
3. 2 Divided By 1	.0910	.06096	--
Estimated 100% TIAA Annuity			
Total Accumulation	$400,000	--	$400,000
Times TIAA Cash-Flow Ratio	.0910	--	--
Estimated 100% TIAA Annuity	$36,400	--	$36,400
4. Rate of Return			
Assumptions	TIAA		
Until Retirement	6%	6%	
During Retirement	--[a]	4%[b]	

[a]Depends upon vintage year. See Ch. 10. Rate reduced to 7%, July 1, 1993.

[b]First year of retirement only. After that the rate depends upon the actual total rate of return. The variable annuity will fluctuate almost exactly with the total annual rate of return.

TABLE 12.4

WORKING AND RETIRED CASH FLOWS AT AGE 68
WHOLE YEAR: 1994

Item	Working	Retired 50% TIAA 50% CREF	100% TIAA
1. Gross Salary	$50,000	$ --	$ --
2. Other Income: Interest	2,000	2,000	2,000
Dividends	1,000	1,000	1,000
Other	--	--	--
3. TIAA-CREF. Pension $400,000 Accumulation	--	30,392	36,400
4. OASI (Social Security) Husband $14,311			
Wife[a] $ 5,089	--	19,400	19,400
5. Tax-Deferred-Salary-Investment[b]	-2,500	--	--
6. Gross Income	$50,500	52,792	58,800
Income Tax Computations			
7. Nontaxable Part of OASI Receipts above $44,001[c] (Married Filing Jointly)	$ --	$ 2,910	$ 2,910
8. Itemized Deductions (Excluding income taxes)	6,000	6,000	6,000
9. Exemptions [$2,400 per person-estimate]	4,900	4,900	4,900
10. Taxable Gross Income [6 - (7 + 8 + 9)]	39,600	38,982	44,990
11. Federal Income Taxes	6,148	5,975	7,657
12. State Income Taxes	1,844	1,792	2,297
13. Net After-Tax Income [10 - (11 + 12) + 9 + 7]	$36,508	$39,025	$42,846
Cash-Flow Analysis			
14. FICA Tax Payments[d] (7.65% to $60,000)	$3,634	$ --	$ --
15. Adjusted Gross Income [6 - (11 + 12 + 14)]	38,874	45,024	48,846
16. Itemized Deductions (-)	-6,000	-6,000	-6,000
17. Modified Cash Flow	$32,874	$39,024	$42,846

[a]1994 basis; wife six years younger.

[b]Could be as much as $9,500.

[c]For married couple filing jointly on gross income 50% above $32,001 and 85% above $44,001 of OASI are subject to Federal Income Taxes. For single taxpayers the amounts are $25,001 and $34,000.

[d]FICA is the Federal Insurance Contributions Act.

TABLE 12.5

WORKING AND RETIRED CASH FLOWS AT AGE 68
WHOLE YEAR: 1994

Item	Working	Retired 50% TIAA 50% CREF	Retired 100% TIAA
1. Gross Salary	$100,000	$ --	$ --
2. Other Income: Interest	3,000	3,000	3,000
Dividends	4,000	4,000	4,000
Other	--	--	--
3. TIAA-CREF. Pension $800,000 Accumulatio	--	60,784	72,800
4. OASI (Social Security) Husband $17,573[a]			
Wife $10,829	--	28,402	28,402
5. Tax-Deferred-Salary Option[b]	-5,000	--	--
6. Gross Income	$102,000	96,186	108,202
Income Tax Computations			
7. Nontaxable Part of OASI Receipts above $44,000[c]	$ --	$ 2,910	4,260
8. Itemized Deductions (Excluding income taxes)	15,000	15,000	15,000
9. Exemptions [$2,400 per person-estimate]	4,900	4,900	4,900
10. Taxable Gross Income [6 - (7 + 8 + 9)]	82,100	71,386	84,042
11. Federal Income Taxes	18,020	15,048	18,592
12. State Income Taxes	5,406	4,514	5,578
13. Net After-Tax Income [10 - (11 + 12) + 9 + 7]	$58,674	$60,984	$79,772
Cash-Flow Analysis			
14. FICA Tax Payments[d]	$5,035	$ --	$ --
15. Adjusted Gross Income [6 - (11 + 12 + 14)]	73,539	75,624	84,032
16. Itemized Deductions (-)	-15,000	-15,000	-15,000
17. Modified Cash Flow	$58,539	$60,624	$69,032

[a]1994 basis; wife six years younger.

[b]Could be as much as $9,500.

[c]For married couple filing jointly on gross income above $44,000 85% of OASI are subject to Federal Income Taxes. For single taxpayers the amount is $34,000.

[d]FICA is the Federal Insurance Contributions Act. The social security tax was 6.2 to $60,600 and the Medicare tax which is uncapped is 1.45 percent. The Medicare tax applies to only $95,000, because of the $5,000 tax-deferred salary option.

FIGURE 12.1

**TIAA, CREF AND CPI
1980-1995**

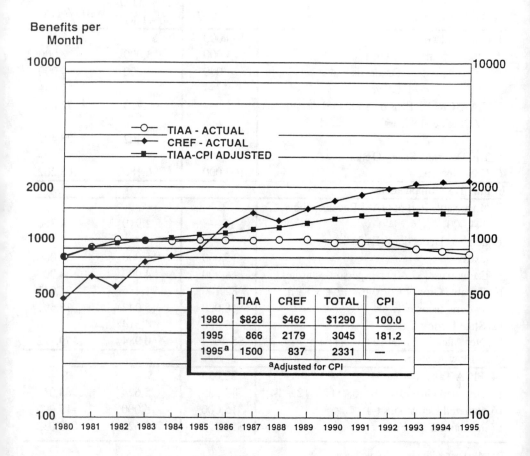

	TIAA	CREF	TOTAL	CPI
1980	$828	$462	$1290	100.0
1995	866	2179	3045	181.2
1995[a]	1500	837	2331	—

[a]Adjusted for CPI

FIGURE 12.2
TIAA, CREF AND CPI*
1987-1995

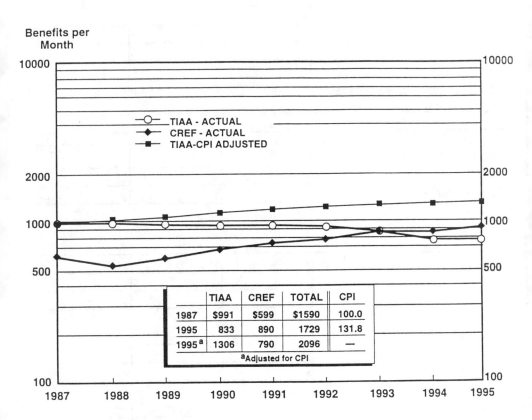

Benefits per Month

	TIAA	CREF	TOTAL	CPI
1987	$991	$599	$1590	100.0
1995	833	890	1729	131.8
1995 [a]	1306	790	2096	—

[a]Adjusted for CPI

*See Table 12.2 for assumptions.

WORKSHEET #1

**COMPARING TIAA AND CREF-EQUITIES RETIREMENT
BENEFITS AND ASSUMPTIONS[a]**

Part A			
Total Accumulation	For Year Ending December 31		
	Regular Acct.	SRA	Total
TIAA	$	$	$
CREF Equities			
CREF Money Market			
Total Accumulation	$	$	$

Illustration of your first year's annuit income, assuming a 6% rate of return until retirement

If current premiums continue, first year's estimated income

	Regular Acct.	SRA	Total
TIAA			
Standard Benifit method	$	$	$
CREF-Equities	$	$	$
Total estimated benefits	$	$	$

Part B			
Cash-Flow Ratios (First Year Only)			
	TIAA Total	CREF Total	Total
1. Accumulations	$	$	$
2. Promised Annuity			
3. 2 Divided By 1	$	$	$
Estimated 100% TIAA Annuity			
Total Accumulation	$	$	$
Times TIAA Cash-Flow Ratio			
Estimated 100% TIAA Annuity	$	$	$

4. Rate of Return

Assumptions	TIAA	CREF	
Until Retirement	6%	6%	
During Retirement	--[a]	4%[b]	

[a]Depends on vintage year. See Ch. 10. Rate reduced to 7%, July 1, 1993.

[b]First year of retirement only. After that the rate depends upon the actual total return. The variable annuity will fluctuate almost exactly with the total annual rate of return.

WORKSHEET #2

**WORKING AND RETIRED CASH FLOWS AT AGE 68
WHOLE YEAR: 1994**

Item	Working	Retired 50% TIAA 50% CREF	100% TIAA
1. Gross Salary	$	$	$
2. Other Income: Interest			
Dividends			
Other			
3. TIAA-CREF. Pension $400,000 Accumulation			
4. OASI (Social Security) Husband $14,311			
Wife[a] $ 5,089			
5. Tax-Deferred-Salary-Investment[b]			
6. Gross Income	$	$	$
Income Tax Computations			
7. Nontaxable Part of OASI Receipts above $44,001[c] (Married Filing Jointly)	$	$	$
8. Itemized Deductions (Excluding income taxes)			
9. Exemptions [$2,400 per person-estimate]			
10. Taxable Gross Income [6 - (7 + 8 + 9)]			
11. Federal Income Taxes			
12. State Income Taxes			
13. Net After-Tax Income [10 - (11 + 12) + 9 + 7]	$	$	$
Cash-Flow Analysis			
14. FICA Tax Payments[d] (7.65% to $60,000)	$	$	$
15. Adjusted Gross Income [6 - (11 + 12 + 14)]			
16. Itemized Deductions (-)			
17. Modified Cash Flow	$	$	$

[a]1994 basis; wife six years younger.

[b]Could be as much as $9,500.

[c]For married couple filing jointly on gross income 50% above $32,001 and 85% above $44,001 of OASI are subject to Federal Income Taxes. For single taxpayers the amounts are $25,001 and $34,000.

[d]FICA is the Federal Insurance Contributions Act.

SELECTED REFERENCES

Bamford, Janet, et al. The Consumer Reports Money Book. Younkers, NY: Consumer Reports, 1992.

Belth, Joseph. A Consumer Handbook on Insurance (2nd ed.). Bloomington, IN: University of Indiana Press, 1985.

Berger, Lisa. Feathering Your Nest: The Retirement Planning Primer (The IDS Financial Library), New York, NY: Workman Publishing, 1993.

Bogle, John. Bogle on Mutual Funds: New Perspectives for the Intelligent Investors. New York, NY: Irwin Professional Publishing, 1993.

Brill, Jack A. and Alan Reder, Investing from the Heart. New York, NY: Crown Trade Paperbacks, [Social Investing], 1993.

Budish, Armond. Avoiding the Medicaid Trap (2nd ed.). New York, NY: Henry Holt, 1995.

Cleary, David and Virginia Cleary. Retire Smart. New York, NY: Allworth Press, 1993.

Dolan, Ken and Dario Dolan. Straight Talk on Money. New York, NY: Simon & Schuster, 1993.

Downes, John and Jordon Elliot Goodman. Barrons Finance and Investment Handbook (3rd ed.). New York, NY: Hauppauge, 1990.

Dunnan, Nancy. Dun & Bradstreet Guide to Your Investments. New York, NY: Harper Perennial, 1993.

Garber, Amy Hollands (Ed.). The Vanguard Retirement Investment Guide. Burr Ridge, IL: Irwin Professional Publishers, 1995.

Herzfeld, Thomas J. and Robert F. Grach. High-Return, Low Risk Investment (2nd ed.). New York, NY: McGraw-Hill, 1993.

Lasser, J. K. Lasser's Retirement Planning Handbook 1989-90. Englewood Cliff, NJ: Prentice Hall, 1988.

Malkiel, Burton G. A Random Walk Down Wall Street (5th ed.). New York, NY: W.W. Norton & Company, 1990.

Miller, Alan J. Standard & Poor's 401(k) Planning Guide. New York: McGraw-Hill, 1995.

Pivar, William H. Real Estate Investing from A to Z. Chicago, IL: Probus Books, 1993.

Porter, Sylvia. Sylvia Porter's Planning Your Retirement. Englewood Cliff, NJ: Prentice Hall, 1991.

Price Waterhouse. The Price Waterhouse Personal Financial Advisor. Chicago, IL: Irwin Publishers, 1995.

Quinn, Jane Bryant. Making the Most of Your Money. New York, NY: Simon & Schuster, 1991.

Savage, Terry. New Money Strategies for the 90s. New York, NY: Harper Business, 1994.

Siegel, Jeremy J. <u>Stocks for the Long Run</u>. Burr Ridge, IL: Irwin, 1994.

Shane, Darlene V. <u>Financial Planning After 50</u> (United Seniors Health Cooperative). New York, NY: Harper & Row, 1989.

Tobias, Andrew. <u>Managing Your Money</u> (3rd ed.). New York, NY: Brady Computer Books, Prentice Hall, 1992.

Van Caspel, Venita. <u>Money Dynamics in the 1990s</u>. New York, NY: Simon & Schuster, 1988.

Wall, Ginta. Our Money, Our Selves: Money Management For Each Stage of A Woman's Life. Younkers, NY: Consumer Reports, 1993.

Weinstein, Grace. <u>Lifetime Money Management</u> (2nd ed.). Detroit, MI: Gale Research, Inc., 1993.

White, Shelby. <u>What Every Woman Should Know About Her Husband's Money</u> (Turtle Bay Books). New York, NY: Random House, 1993.

BIBLIOGRAPHY

Barsky, Neil and Susan Pulliam, "Hidden Risks—Life Insurers Loans on Real Estate Cause Ever-Rising Worries," Wall Street Journal, January 31, 1992. p. A1.

Belth, Joseph M., A Consumer Handbook, 2nd ed. Bloomington, IN: University of Indiana Press, 1985.

Bernstein, Peter L., Capital Ideas. New York: Free Press, 1992.

Black, Pam, "The Right Time for Market Timers?" Business Week, July 12, 1993, pp. 152-153.

Burton, Lee and Robert J. Brennan, "New Medical-Benefits Accounting Rule Shown Wounding Profits, Hurting Shares", Wall Street Journal, April 22, 1992, p.C1.

Business Week, "How Reliable Is the Consumer Price Index," April 29, 1991, pp. 70-71.

Carleton, Jim, "Downtown Vacancy Rate Hits a Six-Year High," Wall Street Journal, April 20, 1993. p. A. 2.

Clements, Jonathan, "Market Timing Is a Poor Substitute for a Long-Term Investment Plan," Wall Street Journal, January 17, 1995.

Crosson, Cynthia, "ELIC Settlement Annuitants Walloped," National Underwriter: Life and Health Insurance Service, October 25, 1993, p. 3.[1]

Davis, Richard G., "Inflation: Measurement, and Policy Issues," Quarterly Review, Federal Reserve Bank of New York, Summer, 1991, pp. 13-24.

Donnelly, B., "Profit Quality Erodes Making Them Less Reliable," Wall Street Journal, Oct. 18, 1990, p. C1.

Dorfman, John R., "SEC May Extend Period for Receiving Idea for Relaying Fund Risks to Investors," Wall Street Journal, p. C1, July 5, 1995.

Ehrenfeld, Temma, "Time to Time the Market," Newsweek, September 6, 1993, pp. 56-57.

Financial Compound Interest and Annuity Tables, 2nd ed. Boston, MA: Financial Publishing Company, 1960.

Friedman, Milton and Anne Schwartz, The Great Contraction, 1929-1933. Princeton, NJ: National Bureau of Economic Research, Princeton University Press, 1965.

Graham, John and Campbell Harvey, "Market Timing Ability, and Volatility Implied in Investment Newsletters' Asset Allocation Recommendations," NBER Working Paper No. 4890, National Bureau of Economic Research, Cambridge, MA, March 1995.

Greenbook - 1992: An Overview of Entitlement Programs. Committee on Ways and Means, U.S. House of Representatives, Washington, DC, 1992.

---

[1] Executive Life Insurance Company (ELIC)

Greenough, William C., A New Approach to Retirement Income. New York: TIAA, December 1951.

Greenough, William C., It's My Retirement Money-Take Good Care of It, The TIAA-CREF Story, Homewood, IL: Irwin. 1990.

Greenough, William C. and Francis P. King, Pension Plans and Public Policy. New York: Columbia University Press, 1976.

Greenwald, "Insurer Trouble a Wake-up Call for Non-Profits," Business Insurance, September 7, 1992, p. 16.

Haugton, Kelly L., "Russell Indexes vs. the S&P 500," Frank Russell Company, August 7, 1987. (Company document provided by Tricia M. Konu, Russell Data Services.)

Insurance Forum, "Special Ratings Issue, September/October 1992.

Jack, Fingland A., An Introduction to the History of Life Insurance. London: P.S. King & Son, 1912.

Jerski, Laura and Frederick Rose, "Executive Life Bailout Springs a Leak," Wall Street Journal, April 2, 1993. pp. A5.

Kaufman, Henry, "Structural Changes in the Financial Markets: Economic and Policy Significance," Economic Review, Federal Reserve Bank of Kansas City, Second Quarter 1994, pp. 5-15.

Lester, Robert M., Forty Years of Carnegie Giving. New York: Charles Scribner's Sons, 1941.

Lipin, Steven, "Chase Writes Down $200,000,000 Chunk of Bad Assets, Plans Big Stock Sale," Wall Street Journal, April 26, 1993. p. A2.

McFarlane, Dale D. and Ira Horowitz, "Risk and the Business Decision," Business Horizons, Summer, 1969, pp. 88-95.

Porter, Sylvia, Personal Finance Letter, June 1989.

Schmitt, Ray and Louisa Hierholzer, Information Specialists, Congressional Research Service, Library of Congress. Letter dated September 28, 1994.

Schultz, Ellen P. E., "Passing the Buck," July 7, 1992, p. C1.

Schultz, Ellen E., "Choosing the Wrong Variable Annuity Can Be Costly," Wall Street Journal, February 9, 1993, p. C1.

Schultz, Ellen E., "Variable Annuity Buyers Warned to Check the Underlying Funds," Wall Street Journal, July 13, 1993, p. C1.

Shobet, Jack and Richard Rikert (eds.) Accounting Trends and Techniques. New York: American Institute of Certified Public Accountants, 1990. (Published annually.)

Soldofsky, Robert M., Common Stock Investing 1900-2000. Ann Arbor, MI: University of Michigan Press, 1971.

Soldofsky, Robert M., "On Determining the Optimal Retirement Age," Academe, July-August, 1986, pp. 17-23.

Soldofsky, Robert M., Performance of Long-Term Marketable Securities: Risk-Return, Ranking and Timing - 1961-1984. Financial Analysts Research Foundation, University of Virginia, Charlottesville, 1986.

Soldofsky, Robert M., and Garnet Olive, Financial Management. Cincinnati, OH: Southwestern Publishing Company, 1974.

Stanger's Investment Advisor, July 1992, p. 12.

Stanger's Investment Advisor, May 1995, p. 30.

Statistical Abstract of the United States, Washington, DC, Government Printing Office, 1994.

Steinmetz, Greg, "Equitable Feels Pressures of a Newly Public Concern," Wall Street Journal, September 23, 1992. p. B3.

Swalm, Ralph O., "Utility Theory - 'Insights' Into Risk Taking," Harvard Business Review N-D 1966 pp. 123-136.

TIAA-CREF The CREF Global Equities Account, New York: TIAA-CREF, 1992, pp. 13-15.

TIAA-CREF, A Practical Guide to Minimum Distribution, New York: 1992.

Van Horne, James C., Capital Market Rates and Flows, 3rd ed. Englewood Cliffs, NJ: Prentice Hall, 1990.

Vogel, Thomas T., "Lingering Pain," Wall Street Journal, p. A1, December 30, 1994, p. C1.

Wagner, Jerry, Steve Shellans, and Richard Paul, "Market Timing Works Where It Matters Most....In the Real World," Journal of Portfolio Management, Summer 1992, pp. 96-97.

INDEX